FROMMER'S

1983-84 GUIDE TO ORLANDO, DISNEY WORLD & EPCOT

by Marylyn Springer

Published by Frommer/Pasmantier Publishers
A Simon & Schuster Division of
Gulf & Western Corporation
1230 Avenue of the Americas
New York, New York 10020

ISBN 0-671-46918-5

Manufactured in the United States of America

*Although every effort was made to ensure the accuracy
of price information appearing in this book,
it should by kept in mind that prices
can and do fluctuate in the course of time.*

CONTENTS

MAPS

For DAS, a dreamer of dreamers and the architect of a magic kingdom

---

Inflation Alert

It is hardly a secret that inflation continues to batter the United States as it does everywhere else. The author of this book has spent laborious hours attempting to ensure the accuracy of prices appearing in this guide. As we go to press, we believe we have obtained the most reliable data possible. Nonetheless, in the lifetime of this edition—particularly its second year (1984)—the wise traveler will add 15% to 20% to the prices quoted throughout these pages.

Chapter I

Introducing Orlando, Disney World, & EPCOT

WHO WOULD EVER have figured that here in the land of the brave and the free a meek little creature beloved by few, loathed by many, would one day become a national hero?

But that's just what happened when the childlike mind of creative cartoonist Walt Disney dreamed up a better mousetrap that was eventually to capture the child in all of us.

Dredge back into your memory and up will pop that M-i-cccccc, k-e-yyyyyy, M-o-u-s-e refrain that many of us sang along with little curly-haired Annette Funicello and her all-American cohorts in Mouse ears who enlisted us all in the Mickey Mouse Club.

Children all over America, then all over the world, joined that bunch of mouse-lovers, got a set of those plastic ears, and sat down in front of the television set to laugh and sing with Annette as Disney's crazy characters cavorted across the stage.

Little Annette and her playmates grew up, but many a Mouseketeer remained a child at heart, memories of those mouse-, duck- and rabbit- filled Saturday mornings still strong in their hearts—and still capable of creating a little mistiness in even the most jaded eye.

Those magical moments and memories of childhood live on in even the most sophisticated of us, making Mickey an ageless creature, one whose dragging tail and big ears can turn us in seconds from reality-facing adults to squealing children, eyes aglow with excitement, hearts full of the wonder only imagination can create.

But no one—not you, not even your toddler—loves Mickey more than Orlando's entrepreneurs. For them the Mouse that roared his way through Central Florida turned boondock into boom town. For them Mickey is a phenomenon whose image has acquired icon-status here in Central Florida. You see those big ears, that red suit, and those yellow gloves everywhere: smack in the middle of a high-powered executive's desk lamp, holding a telephone in a banker's office, or peeking beneath the monogrammed cuff of a Harvard grad's Ivy League, button-down Oxford cloth.

It was Mickey who turned this collection of cow pastures into a city and turned many of the meek into millionaires. These good ol' boys and girls aren't forgetting it: "I have a little shrine in my bedroom," swears one now-prosperous hotelier. "Every morning I get up, pull the little drapes in the shrine open . . . and kiss Mickey's feet."

Yes, indeed, a little mouse changed the face of this land forever and cynical realist that you are, he will worm his way into your heart mere minutes after you arrive here. Fight it as you will, sooner or later that smug smirk will disappear, your eyes will begin to glow, and you will clap and cheer as gleefully as all the other "youngsters" around you, your overlay of sophistication swept away by the wide-eyed eternal child that lives within each of us.

Now Disney "imagineers" have gone and done it again, sinking millions of dollars into a new creative effort called Environmental Prototype Community of Tomorrow (EPCOT). Planning on this multimillion project began years ago, when the cartoonist decided he wanted Disney World to keep growing and changing. Since it was no secret that the mass of the population was growing from baby boom to young adulthood, clever Disney World planners set out to create something that would appeal to the adult in all us children.

To do that they combined the magic of life-size animated figures with the latest technology available from some of the nation's largest corporations. They came up with a look into the future as inspiring and scientific as it is entertaining.

Here in this brand-new Disney "world," laser beams and liquid neon create volcanic eruptions and steamy swamps. Solar energy moves you around, and oddball agricultural advances make your garden grow in places plants have never before sprouted.

At EPCOT you peek far beneath the earth into a tumultuous subterranean world where oil bubbles and burns. You trace mankind's history from scratchings on cave walls to millisecond satellite communications, from the invention of the wheel to the creation of moon-bound rockets.

Your imagination soars, stimulated by the weird and wonderful images only Disney's huge staff of imaginations could create. You get a look at the ways in which past can become future, and future can become a spectacle we never imagined in our wildest dreams.

At yet another new "world," Disney creators introduce you to the world around you *now*. You see the Eiffel Tower and the Doge's Palace, hear the atonal harmonies of Japan and China, taste the teas of the United Kingdom, and yodel with an Alpine maid. Here in World Showcase you visit the Great Wall of China on a screen that wraps around you in a massive circle created by nine cameras that were transported to parts of China never before filmed for a western audience. You go on a shopping spree in Mexico, plummet over Niagara Falls, ride in the Calgary Stampede, and streak over the Brittany coast.

It's all there waiting for you, the magic of a child's small world and the wonders of an adult's rapidly expanding horizons. Strange new worlds and old familiar ones are touched by that starstruck Disney magic that turns mundane into mysterious, humdrum into heady.

But Disney World is not all there is to this sandy central strip of Florida.

Adorable as is that Mouse, he has plenty of competition. So much, in fact, that the Orlando Chamber of Commerce, which once suggested you could see it all hereabouts in three days, now says you'll need a week, better yet two, to make the most of the magic.

Legion is the competition here for your attention and, let's face it, for your tourist dollar. Sweet Shamu, the world's heftiest ballet star, pirouettes his four tons gracefully on an enormous tail and plants gentle, if somewhat damp, kisses on willing cheeks at Sea World. Daring aerial performers swing from the flying trapezes and lion tamers cuddle their toothy friends at Circus World. Champion waterskiers fly through the sky and form human skiing pyramids in the shimmering waters of Cypress Gardens.

But all is not tourist here. Orlando was, after all, just a sleepy little village where life moved slowly most days and hardly at all on others. Amid the plastic and the neon that accompanied Disney World here, you can still find sun-dappled streets where huge trees drip Spanish moss, and the azure waters of Orlando's dozens of lakes sparkle. Take time to explore, via the Chamber of Commerce's self-guided auto tour, for instance, and you'll turn up gem after gem: a rambling old Tudor-style home beside a sand-trimmed lake; verdant rolling hills lined with verandahed Old Florida homes, kept primped and painted; serene small parks and impressive large ones filled with strange and beautiful tropical exotica.

Roam the byways around Orlando, and discover glamorous small towns like Winter Park, which calls itself, justifiably, Little Europe, or New England-village lookalike Mount Dora, dotted with lakes, rocky bluffs, and citrus trees.

It's all here, as it has been since Orlando got its name from hero-soldier Orlando Reeves, who was killed by an Indian arrow after he saved the tiny village with his warnings of the impending raid. It's all here, just as it has been since an enclave of 85 pioneers settled here in 1875, but these days you have to spend a little time searching for the real Orlando. When you find it, in all its pristine antique elegance, you'll discover an intriguing side of this city of many faces, a region of Florida lovingly endowed by nature, built by man, and made famous by a mouse—a magic kingdom indeed.

The Reason Why

You will come to Orlando not for that sun, sand, and salt spray that attracts 36 million visitors a year to the Sunshine State, but because you want to see what all the Central Florida hoopla is about—and you won't be disappointed.

Here the sun rarely sets on a good time, the smiles are genuine, and the welcome warm. It's a section of the state untouched by the sophistication of neighboring cities farther south on this peninsula, one of those places in the nation where people are just a little more innocent, a little more trusting, a little less cynical.

Soft southern drawls are common here, but they mix easily with the clipped consonants of northern arrivals and the distinctive accents of west and midwest.

Things move a little more slowly in Central Florida, and you're expected to demonstrate the patience and good manners exhibited by those who have learned to live with the procrastination that often prevails here.

Roll with the tide a little. Throw off some of the I-want-it-now aggressiveness that gets things done in big cities. Lean into this quiet village-turned-metropolis, and it will repay your patience with the warmest of welcomes, the most loyal of friendships, and a gentle goodwill that's often missing in more cosmopolitan climes.

Climate

You don't come here for sand and sea, but you can still rest assured the temperatures are in the usual balmy Florida ranges. It will always be warmer here than in any more northern city from which you may hail. Because Orlando is smack in the center of the state, however, it benefits less from cooling—and warming—breezes generated over the ocean; so this city is often a few degrees colder in winter and warmer in summer than other places in the state. A sweater or shawl should cover most of the winter weather, however, with perhaps a jacket for some extra-cold days in January and February.

You can expect cool (cold is considered a four-letter word in Florida) temperatures from mid-December through March, with temperatures rarely dropping below the 50s and ever-warmer temperatures from there on, up to record-breaking 90s to 95s in the hottest days of summer. Things begin to cool down again about early October, when an Indian summer, just a little warmer than you find in New England, brings cooling relief.

In summer, the fewer clothes the better, with this exception: Keep in mind that your winter-white body is not prepared for the burning Florida sun. Don't head off for a day at Disney World or one of the other attractions dressed in the bare minimum. You will, in a word, fry. Instead, layer a few things on and take them off if you're too warm, but keep them handy to slip back on when the sun starts to burn.

SUNTANS AND SUNBURNS: If it's sun you want, that's what Central Florida will give you—it has plenty to spare. What Central Florida cannot yet provide is a cure for sunburn. Hoteliers and doctors, if need be, will hold your hand, commiserate, bring you an aspirin, and smear some aloe plant jelly on your back, but that's cold comfort when you're on fire.

No matter how innocent those rays of sunshine may look zipping through the window, no matter how many clouds seem to be between you and the sun, Ole Sol is attacking your epidermis. Skin that has spent months, perhaps years, swaddled in clothes and far from the warming rays is no match for that golden glow. Suntan oils can help, but recall what happens when you apply heat to a frying pan full of oil, and you'll get some idea of how your unsuspecting cells are being sautéed.

Sunscreening lotions are very effective products, and combined with a sensible sunning schedule and a few protective pieces of clothing—like broad-brimmed hats, sunglasses, and cover-ups—will earn you a nice tan, sans that tattletale trail of peeled skin. A tanning schedule that works for many goes something like this: Stay out of the sun between 11 a.m. and 2 p.m., at least for the first few days. During other hours, get only ten minutes of sun the first day, 15 the second, then 25, 35, 50, 75, and on the seventh day 105 minutes.

HURRICANES, RAIN, AND TROPICAL STORMS: Storms make dramatic headlines, so you have no doubt heard about Florida's headliner clashes with the forces of nature. No doubt about it, hurricanes are frightening, even to those who have sat out many a roaring wind, but—and this is the important part for visitors— they are *never* a surprise.

Thanks to a hardworking weather service and some pilots with strong stomachs and iron nerve, Floridians now know far in advance when a storm is brewing. Pilots fly into the eye of the storm and keep tabs on its progress, reporting to Floridians who plot it on weather charts the way other Americans do crossword puzzles. Everyone begins to batten down long before a storm nears land.

What's more, because it's an inland city, Orlando gets the brunt of far fewer storms. If one does reach this far into the state, it's usually wound down to a bad-tempered rainstorm by the time it gets here.

Most important to you, as a visitor to the state, is that you will have plenty of time to leave the area, or the state, if a big wind is about to blow. But even if you stay, strict building codes have forced builders to create structures as impervious as possible to wind and rain damage. Besides, emergency crews with lots of practice are always on hand to help you weather the storm. Officially, the season for these storms is June to November, but summer storms are rare—most occur between August and November.

In Florida, rain is not much like rain anywhere else in the nation. This state is part of the tropics, so rainstorms here are likely to be awesome sights for newcomers. It rarely rains in boring gentle drizzles or all-day downpours here. Instead, the sun suddenly begins to drop behind huge black clouds, the sky rumbles and roars, lightning begins to flash, and from the sky pours a violent lashing rainstorm, the intensity of which will awe and perhaps terrify you. Down it comes with ear-splitting, eye-blinding intensity, then, poof, it's gone as quickly as it came. Sun returns, blazing down on the waters, shattering droplets into a cataclysm of rainbows, spreading nature's art gallery across the sky.

You needn't fear one of these downpours, just get out of it into someplace dry and protected—and don't forget all that advice you've heard on staying safe in a thunderstorm. You also needn't leave wherever you are just because it's started to rain. In most cases those drops will disappear very soon, or slacken to a fine mist that may dampen your shirt but won't sop your spirits. Floridians are used to this kind of rain, and all attractions are well prepared with plenty of raincoats for sale and lots of interesting places for you to seek shelter until the sun returns.

Just so you'll know: June, July, August, September, and October get the most rain—about six or seven inches a month usually—November through May about half that.

Finally, Orlando is one of the few places in the state that experiences early morning fogs. Most longtime Florida dwellers have forgotten what a fog looks like and how to cope with it, so traffic tends to jam when the gray rolls into town. Once again, however, that indomitable sunshine generally sweeps away the soup by mid-morning, so don't bother to change your plans if you can't see the building next door at 6 a.m. some morning. All will be well. Soon.

Visitor Information

Central Florida has ten very busy years of experience in answering the questions and the needs of visiting travelers, so you'll find plenty of places in the state and in this region ready, able, and more than willing to answer your questions.

GENERAL FLORIDA TOURIST INFORMATION: Start at the top, the **Florida Division of Tourism**, Visitor Inquiry Section, 126 Van Buren St., Tallahassee, FL 32301 (tel. 904/487-1462), where Floridians with all the answers—and all the brochures—can tell you everything you ever wanted to know, and perhaps far more, about the Sunshine State and this popular Central Florida region. Mention any specific interest you might have,

GETTING AROUND FLORIDA
(Driving Times and Distances)

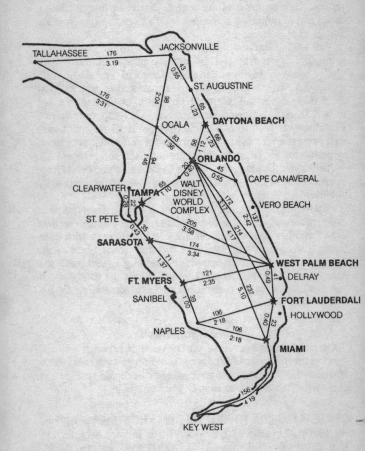

Map courtesy of Alamo Rent A Car

and they'll respond with lots of information on how and where to do what you want to do. Florida also has a fine publication, *Florida Vacation Guide,* which costs just $1 and is crammed with information on all regions of the state.

If you're an outdoor type, the **Florida Department of Natural Resources,** Division of Recreation and Parks, Room 613, Commonwealth Blvd., Tallahassee, FL 32303 (tel. 904/488-7326), has files and files of information on state parks and what each has to offer.

Fishing and hunting fans love Central Florida, which abounds with game and with great freshwater fishing holes. You can get all the details on where to find the whoppers from the **Florida Game and Freshwater Fish Commission,** Bryant Bldg., Tallahassee, FL 32304 (tel. 904/488-2975), which will tell you all you need to know, stopping just short of guaranteeing you a fish or venison dinner.

One Central Florida county has so many lakes it's called Lake County. At the **Lake County Chamber of Commerce,** 601 N. Shore Dr., Eustis, FL 32726 (tel 904/357-3434), you can get a rundown on fish camps and guides.

If hunting is your game, call this toll-free number to find out what season is when: 800/282-8002. They also have fishing information here.

If you're interested in camping, the **Florida Campground Association,** P.O.Box 13355, Tallahassee, FL 32308 (tel. 904/893-4690) has a long list of private campground owners in Florida and descriptions of camp facilities. Another camping and parks information resource is the **National Parks Service,** U.S. Department of the Interior, Washington, DC 20025, which has general information on national parks in Florida.

Hikers can find out what trails make interesting hikes from the **Florida Trail Association,** P.O. Box 13708, Gainesville, FL 32604 (tel. 904/378-8823).

Travel agents are very well-informed people who have a wealth of information at their fingertips and computers. They'll be happy to help you plan a trip to the state.

If you're a frequent flier, the travel agent's Bible, **Official Airline Guides,** 2000 Clearwater Dr., Oak Brook, IL 60625 (tel.800/323-3537), publishes a *Pocket Flight Guide* that's crammed with information on airlines flying to the area and around the state.

CENTRAL FLORIDA TOURIST INFORMATION: Take your questions—and your troubles if need be—to the **Orlando Chamber of Commerce,** 75 E. Ivanhoe Blvd., Orlando, FL 32802 (tel. 305/425-1234), where dozens of smiling and well-informed Orlandoites are on hand to help.

In the tiny cow capital, Kissimmee, you find the **Kissimmee Chamber of Commerce** on East Monument Ave., Kissimmee, FL 32741 (tel. 305/847-3174), and the **Kissimmee/St. Cloud Convention and Visitor's Bureau** on East U.S. 192, Kissimmee, FL 32741 (tel. 305/847-5000, or toll free 800/327-9159, or in Florida 800/432-9199), both as fiercely loyal to their small town as they are down-home friendly in their welcome.

In **Winter Park** write or call the Chamber at 150 N. New York Ave., Winter Park, FL 32790 (305/644-8281) and in **Mount Dora** at Alexander St. and 3rd Ave., Mt. Dora, FL 32757 (tel. 904/383-2165).

WALT DISNEY WORLD AND EPCOT INFORMATION: A huge staff is on hand at **Walt Disney World** to answer your questions. Call them at 305/824-4321.

For World Key Information which can tell you most anything you need to know about Disney World in general but is specifically designed to answer **EPCOT** questions, call 305/827-7414.

To make **reservations** at hotels on Disney World property, call 305/824-8000 (best time to call is after 5 p.m. when things slow down a bit), or write to **Walt Disney Travel Co.,** P.O. Box 22094, Lake Buena Vista, FL 32830. Ask for a copy of the *Walt Disney World Vacation Guide* which explains all the hotels and facilities in the World. Walt Disney Travel Co. also has a number of money-saving package tours which include admission to Disney World, hotel, and often transportation. They'll be happy to outline them for you.

USEFUL INFORMATION: For **police or medical emergency** anywhere in the area, dial 911. . . . For **minor medical problems** Family Emergency Center, 6001 Vineland Rd., one block west of Kirkman Road (tel. 351-6682), is open 9 a.m. to 9 p.m. daily and accepts Master and Visa Cards for payment. . . . For medical help 24 hours and a **medical referral service,** call the Florida Medical Referral Service operated by the state. Toll-free number is 800/432-4440. Some doctors listed by the service will even make "house" calls at your hotel or motel. . . . To find out what **weather** to expect, call 851-7510 in Orlando, 846-3121 in Kissimmee. . . . Get a **babysitter** from Tuck In Tots (tel. 859-8928), or check with your hotel's Guest Services desk. . . . **Pet emergencies** can be handled at Veterinary Emergency Clinic, 882 Jackson Ave., Winter Park, FL (tel. 644-4449). . . . **International House of Pancakes,** 6005 International Dr. (tel. 351-0031), is near Disney World on International Drive and is open 24 hours. . . . A quick **cleaner** is Orchid One Hour Cleaners, 5901 S. Orange Blossom Trail (tel. 851-0262). . . . **Western Union** is at 847-4838 in Orlando, 847-4838 in Kissimmee. . . . Your films can be developed overnight at **Champagne Color Camera,** 1917 N. Orange Ave. (tel. 894-3362), and at many hotel guest-services desks. . . . Get **out-of-town newspapers** at Orange Avenue News, 59 N. Orange Ave. (tel. 422-0954). . . . If you don't mind admitting your age, you can save a bundle of money in **Orlando's Senior Season,** from September to mid-December, when dozens of attractions and hotels offer discounts up to 50% to anyone 55 and up. The Chamber of Commerce can give you exact details on Senior Season. . . . Want a lasting memory of your WDW trip? Have your visit **videotaped** at any of the area's attractions. Holiday Video Recording Service will do the job for $95 for two hours, $35 each additional hour. Call them at 305/628-6550 in Orlando, 305/933-2515 in Kissimmee. They're available 24 hours a day.

Tips on Food and Lodging

Traveling happy as opposed to hectic is often just a matter of a little planning, so here are a few tips for making your Central Florida sojourn as trouble-free as possible.

HOTELS AND MOTELS: Every part of the state has a high season in Florida, and Orlando has its prime time, when hotels and motels are packed and everything else keeps pace.

In Central Florida that time is Christmas, when the thundering hordes come pouring into the magic of Disney World, Sea World, and the rest, to see what imagination can create for Christmas. Sure, you can take your chances, but driving from hotel to motel to guest house looking for a room is a pretty silly way to spend your vacation. You can avoid that fate with the simplest of remedies: Reserve ahead. That goes for other holiday periods too—Easter, Thanksgiving, Washington's Birthday, and the busiest summer months of June, July, and August, when youngsters are out of school and lots of other people are planning the same summer sojourn you are.

There are dozens of moderately priced hotels and motels in

Central Florida and many representatives of major national chains like Howard Johnson's, Holiday Inn, and Days' Inn. Here are the toll-free numbers for the major chain operations in moderate price brackets so you can call yourself and check them out. (Motel 6 and Day's Inn toll-free numbers vary by state. Check with toll-free information—800/555-1212—for the area from which you're calling.)

Best Western (tel. 800/528-1234); **Econo-Lodge** (tel. 800/446-6900; in Virginia 800/582-5882); **Holiday Inn** (tel. 800/238-8000); **Howard Johnson's** (tel. 800/255-3050); **Quality Inns** (tel. 800/228-5151); **Ramada Inns** (tel. 800/228-2828); **Red Carpet Inns** (tel. 800/323-4444); **Rodeway Inns** (tel. 800/228-2000); **Scottish Inns** (tel. 800/643-8960); **TraveLodge** (tel. 800/255-3050).

A few words on saving money on Florida hotel rooms: Small motels on U.S. 192, Orange Blossom Trail, and Colonial Drive are cheaper (sometimes 50% or more) than hotels at or in Disney World. There's no doubt about it: Hotels on Disney World property are expensive, but their cost needs to be balanced against transportation expenses elsewhere, particularly if you're flying in and renting a car. Since all transportation is free inside Disney World, you might come out spending less by renting a room there, when you consider the cost of a car rental, gasoline, and the like. You may also *not* come out cheaper, but think about it.

A boon for budget-watching families is the area's no-charge-for-children policy. Only the smallest motels charge for children (usually kids under 18, but check age cut-offs to be sure), and then it's often only a nominal charge, nothing likely to break the bank account. That no-charge edict assumes you and the youngsters are sharing a room, however, which requires a considerable amount of camaraderie. Families who'd like to stretch out a bit without kicking someone's shoes under the bed might consider villa accommodations—I've named some in Disney World and some outside—which offer many amenities and plenty of parental privacy.

As everywhere, motels and hotels closest to Disney World tend to be the most expensive, with prices dropping as you go farther afield (major sports resorts are an exception to that, however), and naturally those with fewer amenities (like restaurants and game rooms) are less expensive.

Prices I've quoted are for a room for two, and almost always include two children up to 18 years old in the price. Those prices, at least at most motels and hotels, do change seasonally with highest rates charged at the most popular visiting times—holidays and summer—dropping in January, after Easter until mid-June, and from about the first week in September to Thanksgiving.

RESTAURANTS: Nothing changes faster in Florida than restaurants that go into and out of business faster than you can whip cream. I've tried to recommend restaurants here that have been around long enough to be considered winners in the war of the whisks, but I'm offering no guarantees on prices or continued existence.

One happy note, however. Restaurants in Orlando tend to be less expensive than their counterparts elsewhere in the state. Even posh, elegant restaurants considered expensive by Orlando standards are unlikely to top $25 a person for dinner. Many, many more—hundreds in fact—offer fine fare at moderate prices with entrées right in the $10 to $15 bracket and many times at budget rates under $10.

What's more, Florida is home of the early-bird special, so if you're one of those people who likes getting out to dinner before 6 p.m., you can often find complete dinners in the $5 to $8 range, particularly in less busy seasons.

I've tried to indicate here what I think you'll pay per person for dinner entrées, which in Florida usually include salad, vegetable, meat, bread, butter, and often coffee. If you like a bottle of wine or a martini or two before, and something chocolatey after, your bill will naturally rise accordingly.

Central Florida restaurants are much more casual than their counterparts in almost any other section of the state. Here a tie is reserved for only the most spectacular dining spots, and you'll see many men without them even *there*. For men, a jacket in hand, not necessarily on shoulders, is good insurance and will do just fine, even in peak seasons.

At most moderately priced restaurants in the area, you'll feel overdressed in anything more than a golf shirt. T-shirts, cut-off blue jeans, sandals, and scruffy-looking things are *outré* most anywhere these days, need I say?

For women, dresses or good-looking pants outfits go anywhere, designer jeans almost anywhere. A warm blazer or shawl is worth its weight in summer, when some restaurants turn air

conditioners down to Arctic temperatures, as well as in winter,
when nature adds a little of her own air conditioning.

Local Foods

Florida has some interesting culinary treats you may not have
encountered before, and you'll find most of them right here in
Central Florida.

So much seafood comes from the waters on either coast that
it's hard to know where to start, but you might try pompano, a
delicate, flaky white fish much loved by gourmets and often
cooked in paper. Stone crabs are a special Florida treat, and it's
nice to know no one has to kill anything to get them. Stone crab
fishermen on the state's west coast capture the crabs, break off
one large claw, and throw the crabs back into the deep, where
they grow another claw to replace the missing pincer. Stone
crabs are best during their harvest season from mid-October to
mid-May. After that they'll come from the freezer. Eat them
cold with drawn butter or steamed.

Florida lobsters, which appear on what seems to be every
single menu in the state, are nothing like their Maine brothers.
Instead they're much smaller and much cheaper, although their
flavor is comparable. (I expect plenty of argument on that state-
ment.)

Apalachicola oysters are a Florida specialty, grown up there
in the curve of the Panhandle. They're as different from their
Bon Secour Alabama brothers as they are from any other oysters, so try them and become an oyster connoisseur. Rock
shrimp, sometimes called "langostinos," are something like
shrimp-size lobsters. Clams and scallops are abundant—there
are two kinds of scallops, bay and deep sea, the former much
tinier and sweeter.

Fresh hearts of palms occasionally show up on Orlando
menus. A delicacy far superior to the canned variety, they're cut
from the heart of the cabbage palm with a technique learned
from the Seminoles. Once you try them, you'll be spoiled for the
canned variety forever.

From the many nationalities that have merged on this land
(Bahamians, Cubans, Indians, Spanish, English, French),
Floridians have acquired a taste for crusty Cuban bread; steaming conch chowder (made from the creature that lives inside
those shells you "listen" to); paella, a rice, seafood, and vegetable
combination; piccadillo, a mix of ground meat, olives, and raisins

in a spicy sauce; pilau, a spicy stew found in the St. Augustine area; and Creole foods.

You'll find those and many, many foreign flavors in Orlando, plus some of the best home-cooking of any section of the state—fried chicken, corn, fresh vegetables right off the farms of neighboring Zellwood, and strawberry shortcake piled with massive berries from the fields of nearby Plant City.

Citrus

There's something breathtakingly beautiful about the citrus groves that blanket the rolling hills of this central section of the state. Orange and gold fruit add a pointillist's touch to mile after mile of emerald green stretching from horizon to horizon.

In cold snaps those old tires you see piled up in the fields are odoriferously burned to heat the air and keep frost from the delicate fruit. Huge sprinklers serve much the same function by keeping the ground wet and warm to ward off frost.

At groves throughout Florida, you can get out in the field and pick your own oranges, grapefruit, lemons, and limes right off the tree (then recover from your labors with a free glass of fresh-off-the-tree orange juice!). Send some home to friends here or abroad, and if you're taking fruit home by plane, be sure to put your name or some identifying ribbon on it, since everyone else on the plane is likely to have some too. You can't take the fruit into Canada or abroad personally, but you can ship it there.

If you'd like to see frozen orange juice in the making, visit the Minute Maid plant at Auburndale, 11 miles east of Lakeland on U.S. 92, from November through mid-April for free tours.

You'll find citrus of some kind or another here every month of the year. Here's a look at some of the different kinds you can try:

Navel oranges—best from November to January; recognizable by their tiny "navels" and smooth skin, usually almost seedless and easily peeled.

Valencia oranges—March to July, juicy and aromatic.

Temple oranges—January to March, a favorite eating orange with a lightly pitted skin.

Murcott oranges—February to April, almost red inside.

Hamlin oranges—October to December; seedless, thick-skinned, a juice orange.

Pineapple oranges—December to February, very juicy and very sweet.

Tangelos—December to March; a cross between tangerines and oranges, with an easy-peel skin.

Tangerines—December to February, the zipper-skin fruit.

Duncan grapefruit—October to May; a thick, pale-yellow skin, very juicy and seedy.

Seedless grapefruit—November to June, smooth yellow skin, few seeds.

Pink seedless grapefruit—October to May, rose-colored interior.

Other interesting fruits are the tiny pucker-inducing kumquats, often used in jellies; Persian limes (the big green ones); Key limes (the little yellow ones imported here from Key West); and Ponderosa lemons, often nearly as big as a large orange.

You can even try citrus wine! It's made at Florida Vineyard and Fruit Gardens at Orange Lake, between Gainesville and Ocala, and sold in most liquor and some grocery stores as well as at roadside Stuckey's stores along the Florida Turnpike.

Citrus candies and jellies, goat's milk fudge, and coconut patties are favorites in Florida, too. You can buy coconuts (which are brown and slosh when you shake them if they're ripe) already hulled in grocery stores.

Food festivals are favorite entertainment in Florida and range from the corn festival in nearby Zellwood each May to the Strawberry Festival in Plant City in February.

Chapter II

GETTING TO AND AROUND ORLANDO AND DISNEY WORLD

ONCE UPON A TIME, getting to and around Orlando was only a little less difficult than a cross-country trek by mule train. Roads had all the "toos" of a driver's worst nightmares: too few, too narrow, too crowded, too bad.

But no more. Now there are few, if any, areas in the state as accessible as Central Florida, which has a road system much envied by more populous areas of the Sunshine State.

That same once-upon-a-time-ugh also applies to Orlando's airport, once little more than a cleared cow pasture, but today a full-fledged jetport. In 1982, in fact, Orlando proudly opened a sleek new terminal building, 48 gates, and runways long enough to welcome no less an aircraft than that airborne record-breaker, the supersonic Concorde.

Rest assured that beloved Mouse does not miss an opportunity even here: Orlando airport arrivals can stroll right off the plane and over to a Disney information desk where tickets, information, maps, and even a set of Mouse ears are available!

Those arriving by train can step to the platform at Kissimmee, the official Walt Disney World Amtrak stop, and from there it's only minutes to the Kingdom by car, bus, taxi, or hotel jitney.

Finally, for those arriving by car—and that's far and away the way most people get here—four- or six-lane highways streak into and through the area from every direction.

In fact, getting here can be fun. Billboards along roadways entice you to area attractions so colorfully, amusingly, and informatively, you'll begin to be caught up in the excitement of this giggly slice of the Sunshine State long before you step onto the macadam of Main Street U.S.A.

Getting There from Anywhere

BY AIR: Florida's own airline, Air Florida, flies in here from nearly every major city in the state and is joined on the Disney-bound route by American, Delta, Eastern, Northwest Orient, Northeastern, Ozark, Pan Am, Piedmont Republic, TWA, United, USAir, and Air South. More are expected to join those shortly as the glamour and hoopla of EPCOT lure throngs of visitors here. All of those airlines touch down at Orlando International Jetport, a sleek, modern facility still small enough to be simple to negotiate.

The new $300-million airport sports attractive boutiques, even a unisex barber/beauty shop. An intriguing collection of restaurants features everything from a raw bar at which oysters, clams, lobsters, stone crabs, and shrimp are bedded down on huge ice-filled scallop shells, to a capuccino-and-croissant bakery, a tropical drink bar, a revolving breakfast buffet, and a long, long luncheon salad bar.

Elevated trains whiz you from plane to the terminal where you'll find baggage pickup, then rental cars, taxis, buses, even a Cadillac limousine will meet you at the door; and everything seems to work with fast-paced efficiency. It's quite a future-step for this once sleepy little conglomerate of villages called Central Florida.

BY TRAIN: Every day Amtrak's shining Silver Meteor and Silver Star streak southward from New York's Penn Station. The **Silver Star** departs at 9:25 a.m., arriving in Kissimmee at 7:29 a.m. the next day. For afternoon travelers the **Silver Meteor** leaves at 3:35 p.m., arriving in Kissimmee at 12:52 p.m. the following day. Official address of the **Kissimmee station** is 416 Pleasant St.

If you're headed for downtown Orlando, you can leave the train at the **Orlando station** located about a mile from the downtown area at 1400 Sligh Blvd. Both trains arrive at that station about 25 minutes earlier than they get to Kissimmee, which is farther south. That is one of the reasons it's a good idea to get an Orlando map from the Chamber of Commerce before you leave home. You'll save yourself driving time and money when you arrive.

Major stops on the New York to Orlando run include Newark, Trenton, Philadelphia, Wilmington, Baltimore, Washington, Richmond, Raleigh, Columbia, Charleston, Savannah, and Jacksonville.

At Jacksonville the Silver Meteor splits, so part of the train can travel to the St. Petersburg/Tampa area, part to Miami. The Silver Star splits just south of Kissimmee for the same two destinations, so it's wise to note which car you're on and where it's going.

From those splits you can deduce that trains also can take you *from* Miami, St. Petersburg/Tampa, and various smaller cities in between to Orlando and Kissimmee.

If you're headed north from Miami, the Silver Star leaves at 2:32 p.m. EST daily and arrives in Kissimmee at 7:21 p.m., in Orlando at 8:07 p.m. You can also catch that train at Hollywood, Fort Lauderdale, Deerfield Beach, Delray Beach, West Palm Beach, Sebring, and Winter Haven stops. Fares in late 1982 were $37 one way, $52 round trip.

To reach Orlando/Kissimmee from Tampa/St. Petersburg, you can take the Silver Meteor, which leaves St. Petersburg at 9:44 a.m. and arrives in Kissimmee at 12:46 p.m., in Orlando at 1:20 p.m. The Silver Star leaves St. Petersburg at 4:04 p.m. and arrives in Kissimmee at 7:21 p.m., in Orlando at 8:07 p.m. Both stop in and can be boarded at Clearwater, Tampa, and Lakeland. Fare on either is $19.90 one way, $28 round trip.

Fares on the major north–south run between New York and Orlando in late 1982 were $143 one way, $286 roundtrip, with a discount special available for $199. Discounts of all kinds and for all reasons (families, senior citizens, students—it goes on and on) are as prevalent on Amtrak as they are on airlines, so be sure to tell travel agents or Amtrak reservationists as much as you can about yourself and your travel plans, so they can help you find the best bargain.

Since the New York to Florida journey takes 24 hours or more, you might consider a "slumber coach," which is the railroad's economy sleeper and has one or two lounge chairs that fold flat at night for sleeping and unenclosed toilet facilities. Supplement for slumber coach accommodations is $45 single and $79 double, one way. Another accommodation level on Amtrak is called a "roomette," a single room with a sofa that unfolds at night to cover bath facilities which are not enclosed. Additional one-way rate is $92. Finally, a couple can reserve a bedroom, which includes a sofa that converts to two berths and enclosed toilet facilities. Supplement for a bedroom is $171 each way.

Meals on Amtrak these days are much the same as airline creations. They're microwaved frozen dinners essentially, although some trains may also include one entrée prepared on the train. Prices top out at about $7.25 for full-course dinners; sandwiches, salads, and the like are also available.

If you're coming to Florida from Europe, you can buy a **USA Railpass** (available only to overseas visitors) for $220 for seven days, $330 for 14, $440 for 21, and $550 for a month of unlimited train travel not only in Florida but throughout the U.S. Children two to 12 pay half price. There's also a family pass on which the head of the household pays full fare, spouse and children 12 to 21 pay half, and children two to 12 get a pass of any duration for $85. Top European travel companies like Thomas Cook, American Express, and Cuoni are among the many agents who can arrange passes for you. Some airlines can too.

Amtrak also has some tour packages which can save you money on car rentals, hotels, and attraction admissions. For information on those packages and for timetables, write to Amtrak Distribution Center, Box 311, Addison, IL 60101, or call the railroad, toll free, in any of the continental states. Toll-free information at 800/555-1212 to discover the number in your state. In New York the number is 800/523-5700; in Florida 800/342-2520.

BY BUS: Buses are often (although not always) the budget way to travel. If you like the idea of leaving the driving to them, you might consider traveling to Orlando on one of the nation's two major bus lines, **Greyhound** or **Trailways.**

Express buses have cut the time you'll spend getting here, but you still should plan at least 36 hours from Chicago to Miami, about 28 from New York, 24 from Washington, and about three days from Los Angeles.

Once you're in Florida, buses can get you from even the smallest village to Orlando.

What's more, both Greyhound and Trailways bus lines offer package tour programs (two- or three-day or longer) that can save you money on hotels, attractions, and transportation costs.

Greyhound, for instance, has a one-day trip from Fort Lauderdale that leaves the station about 6 a.m., whizzes you to Disney World, and gets you back again about midnight, adults for $50, children $31, including park admissions, transportation, and a snack or two on the way.

BY SHIP: By ship, you sneer? Everyone knows you can't get to a landlocked city like Orlando by ship. Ha! While it is true you can't get right downtown by ship, and Disney has not yet arranged a way to sail you across the state, you can indeed get to Central Florida from New York and from Freeport, Bahamas, by ship.

You do that aboard a spiffy new cruise ship, actually two spiffy cruise ships, like this: Scandinavian World Cruises operates a ship called the *Scandinavia,* which sails from New York Harbor to Freeport every week, carrying passengers and cars.

Once on that lively Bahamian island, you can look things over for as long as you like, then catch another of Scandinavian World Cruises ships, the *Scandinavian Sea,* which, according to company plans announced in late 1982, will begin sailings to Port Canaveral by 1983.

Once you (and your car, if you choose) arrive in Port Canaveral, you can take S.R. 528, known as the Beeline Expressway, from there to Orlando. It's about 53 miles, an hour's drive, from Disney World.

So you see—you *can* get here by ship!

BY CAR: To ask several Florida travelers for the best route to Central Florida from your hometown is to discover why horse races are popular: a difference of opinion. Every driver who's ever hit the highroad to the Sunshine State has a special way to get here and is convinced that's the *only* way to go. If you can't decide who's right, you might consider joining the American Automobile Association, which offers members a free route-mapping service. There are a number of other motor clubs, too, offering various services from insurance to maps, breakdown help, even bail bonds if you run afoul of the speed laws. Included among those clubs are Allstate Motor Club, Amoco, Ford, Gulf, Montgomery Ward, Exxon, Mobil, and Texaco Motor Clubs.

Whichever route you select to get you to the state line, once there you'll find friendly Floridians on hand to greet you at **Welcome Stations** set up at key state border crossings. Those stations are located at Yulee (Hwy. I-95); Hillyard (U.S. 1 and U.S. 301); Campbellton (U.S. 231); Jennings (Hwy. I-75); Pensacola (Hwy. I-10); and in Tallahassee in the new Capitol Build-

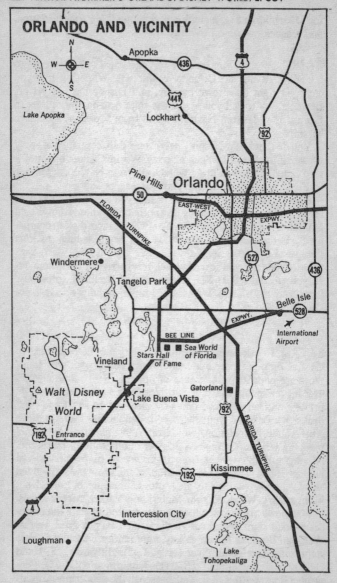

ORLANDO AND VICINITY

ing. Here smiling greeters are armed with masses of helpful pamphlets, friendly smiles, and even a welcoming glass of orange juice!

Costs of automobile travel, by the way, have risen right along with all those other rising prices. AAA in 1982 estimated daily driving costs at about $136 daily for a couple covering 500 miles a day, including meals, lodging, gasoline, and car costs (figured at $8 for every 100 miles traveled, in a car getting 20 miles per gallon). Add $1 a day for each child's meals, and be prepared to vary figures up or down 25% to 75%, depending on the popularity of the region in which you're staying.

Getting Around

Every major **rental-car agency** in the nation has an office in Orlando, and dozens of smaller independent operators do business here as well, making this one of the most competitive markets in the nation. That means you can find rental car rates in Central Florida that are as low—and often lower—than any in the nation.

National Car Rental is the official Walt Disney World rental-car agency and has, or is included in, a number of package tour programs that offer price reductions on attraction admissions and car and hotel prices. Hertz, Avis, Budget, Dollar and other major national chain operations also have package tours that include Disney World.

Two of the bargain leaders in Central Florida and elsewhere in the state are Alamo and Greyhound. Alamo allows you (as do some but not all other car rental companies), to pick up a car from most of Alamo's 14 locations in Florida, such as Miami, Ft. Lauderdale, or West Palm Beach, and drop the car in Orlando at no extra charge. Rates at these two companies in late 1982 were about $75 to $85 a week for air-conditioned, subcompact cars (a two-door Chevette, for instance), including unlimited mileage. Optional Collision Damage Waiver is available for about $6 a day additional.

If you're considering a car rental in Orlando, there are two things you should do. First, ask a travel agent to help you check prices, or make some telephone calls to the toll-free numbers of rental car agencies to ask about rental rates for the time you'll be in Florida. If you're flying to Florida, you might also ask if the company has special price offers in conjunction with any airline. It is getting almost as complicated to work your way through the maze of rental-car rates, as it is to discover all the bargain-flight fares available to Florida, but it is always worth the trouble.

Second, check with your insurance agent to see what insurance coverage you already have, and how much of it covers you in a rental car. If you are covered for collision, for example, and are willing to risk a few hundred dollars in deductible fees if the car is damaged, you can often waive collision insurance and save yourself money. Florida residents who have insurance covering them in a rental car can waive other insurance charges too but must leave a $300 to $500 refundable cash or credit card deposit. You can often waive other insurance add-ons, and you should do so, if you are already insured elsewhere. Read your policy and the small print on the rental contract.

In Florida, by the way, most rental-car companies set the minimum rental age at 21, and a few have set a maximum. You must also have a credit card or be willing to leave a deposit of $300 or more in cash at the rental agency while you have the car. Deposits are, of course, returned when you return the car undamaged.

Here are the toll-free numbers of some of the best-known rental-car companies: **Alamo** (tel. 800/327-9633); **Avis** (tel. 800/331-1212); **Budget** (tel. 800/228-9650); **Dollar** (tel. 800/421-6868); **Greyhound** (tel. 800/327-2501 or in Florida 800/432-1060); **Hertz** (tel. 800/654-3131); **National** (tel. 800/331-4567); and **Thrifty** (tel. 800/331-4200). Avis, Budget, Dollar, Greyhound, Hertz, and National have rental desks in the terminal at Orlando Airport.

A-1 Airport Limousine Service (tel. 859-4667 in Orlando; 933-1808 in Kissimmee) operates airport limousine service to area hotels. You'll find the limousines (which are really 11-person vans) outside the terminal building on the second floor. Prices start at $5 for a one-way ride to the hotels in the Orange Blossom Trail area and rise to $6 to International Drive, $7 to Lake Buena Vista and Walt Disney World hotels, and $8 to downtown hostelries. Farther afield you pay about $13. Children's fares are half-price. You can save $1 on every fare by buying a round-trip ticket.

Some hotels offer free shuttle service from the airport. You can even call many of them free, using telephones at consoles in the baggage claim area.

American Sightseeing Tours now operates regular **bus service** from the airport to hotels. Buses leave from both sides of the second floor of the terminal from about 7 a.m. to 10:30 p.m. It takes about an hour to get to Disney World area hotels. Fares are $5.50 to $6.50 adults, $2.75 to $3.25 for children, depending on where you're going. You can save about 50¢ on each ticket by buying a round trip.

For a taxi, try **Yellow Cab** (tel. 422-4455 in Orlando; 847-2222 in Kissimmee) which charges $1.60 a mile for the first mile, $1 for every mile thereafter. Flat rates are available from the airport and run about $19 to Lake Buena Vista/Disney World, $15 to downtown Orlando, $24 to hotels on U.S. 192 in Kissimmee.

If you'd like to arrive in style, **Prestige Limos** (tel. 827-6105) has a booking booth at the luggage pick-up area too and will bring a Cadillac limousine around for you. Rates are about $4 higher than taxi fares and run from $19 to $25 for most destinations. If there are enough of you traveling together, you might even save money.

Do keep in mind that distances are great in Central Florida's flatlands, so don't expect just to drop into Sea World and walk over to Disney World—it's miles just from Disney's first entrance sign to the parking lot! If you're planning to sample some of the area's great dining spots and lively nightlife, you'd be wise to rent a car, since taxi fares over the distances here can be enormous, and public transportation, great during the day, isn't much after attraction closing-hours.

If Disney World and its fellow attractions are your major interest and you're not planning to do much other exploring, you'll find Orlando has provided plenty of transportation from hotels to the major fun spots. A wide variety of shuttle systems connect the area's attractions, and tour buses by the dozen are available to help you see the most you can in the time you have to spend. In fact, getting to this city's top tourist attractions is almost as much fun as the attractions themselves.

Topping the list of kicky ways to the Worlds is a red British doubledecker bus that rolls the road between Kissimmee and Disney World with stops at Sea World, Circus World, Lake Buena Vista, and Stars Hall of Fame. It's called **Double Dekka Bus Lines** (tel. 847-3222) and will pick you up at any U.S. 192 motel or campground east of Florida Turnpike Exit 65 and take you to any of those attractions for $5 round trip adults, $2.50 children. Double Dekka also picks you up at Disney World when the park closes. Special trips also are available to more distant attractions including Cypress Gardens, Kennedy Space Center, and Busch Gardens for $20 to $30 adults, about half that for children, including admissions. Trips to local attractions are in the $15 to $20 range for adults.

In Lake Buena Vista, **shuttle buses** that operate on an every-15-minutes schedule stop at all hotels and finally at the entrance to the Magic Kingdom and EPCOT. They're free to hotel guests who simply display a pass issued by the hotel. Flags painted on the sides of the buses identify where they're going. Buses operate from 8 a.m. to 2 a.m. so you can take in the nightlife at Disney World.

Gray Line (tel. 422-0745) operates most of what moves on wheels in Orlando. The line's big bruiser buses ply constantly between attractions and area hotels. You can buy an all-day pass that can be used to shuttle to Sea World, Disney World, and other attractions from hotels on U.S. 192 and International Drive for $4 per person. Gray Line also operates trips to attractions throughout Central Florida for varying prices in the $14 to $21 range.

Another tour company operating in the area is **American International Sightseeing** (tel. 859-2250), which runs the airport buses and also has trips between Central Florida and other areas of the state as well as to Central Florida attractions.

Adventurers can rent mopeds at **Moped Rentals** (tel. 351-5566), on International Drive across from Wet 'n Wild, for $29.95 a day including insurance.

You can even **rent a complete motor home** and travel around in style, thanks to **Bomar Corp.** (11251 S. Orange Blossom Trail, about a mile south of the turnpike; tel. 851-4038), which rents the homes-on-wheels for prices beginning at $79 to $89 a week for a 24- or 25-foot Champion. Insurance is $7 a day, and there are no mileage charges, just a $250 refundable deposit. In summer months you'll need to reserve a motor home four to six months in advance.

To toot around in style, rent a spiffy 1929 Model A reproduction. It's fiberglass with a modern motor and automatic or stickshift transmission. These cute little cars are kept shiny as mirrors and are lots of fun. You'll find the rental agency, **Classic Motor Cars,** in the TraveLodge lobby in Lake Buena Vista's Hotel Plaza (tel. 828-8080). Rates are $9.95 an hour, $39.95 for eight hours, $59.95 for a 24-hour day, and $350 a week.

Getting Your Bearings

If there's one place in Florida that really deserves the description "sprawling," it's Orlando. First, there are a dozen or so suburbs large enough to be cities in their own right but too small to be easily differentiated from Orlando's urban sprawl. Second, the city itself sprawls over mile after flat mile of highway-beribboned countryside.

Finding your way around isn't as difficult as it might be, however, thanks to a carefully constructed network of roadways that can speed you from one suburb to the next—and even across the state, east toward Cape Canaveral or west to Tampa.

Here are a few clues to finding your way around this brash and booming territory.

Main east–west artery is **Hwy. I-4**, which runs from Tampa on the state's west coast to Daytona on the east and conveniently zips right through Orlando. If you see the sun dipping off to the west, indicating you're driving north or south, however, don't panic. At times the road does indeed take a north–south twist. Just keep in mind that Tampa to Daytona orientation, take a careful look at an area map, and you'll be all right. Exits from this major expressway take you to Disney World, Sea World, Church Street Station, downtown Orlando, International Drive, Lake Buena Vista, Altamonte Springs, and Winter Park, to name just a few. Hwy. I-4 is likely to be the expressway you'll get to know best, since most attractions and hotels are located on or near it.

The main east–west route past the entrance to Disney World is **U.S. 192** which stretches from Kissimmee, past many inexpensive motels and restaurants, to U.S. 27.

A quick east–west route is a road called the **Beeline**. It intersects with Hwy. I-4, crosses other major arteries like Route 436, Orange Blossom Trail, and the Florida Turnpike, then zips eastward to Cape Canaveral. It's a quick way to the World from the airport, too.

Another east–west byway is the **East West Expressway**, which is north of the Beeline and streaks scenically across Orlando. It can be reached from Hwy I-4.

Route 436 is a major roadway that forms a beltline around

Orlando's east side from the Beeline, past the East West Expressway and Colonial Drive, then bends west to cross U.S. 17/92 and some outlying suburbs.

That street with the picturesque name, **Orange Blossom Trail** (also called Route 441), is a north–south road with plenty of motels and restaurants and no dearth of traffic either.

Another "orange" street, **Orange Avenue,** parallels Orange Blossom Trail but is located farther east and goes past downtown landmarks, as does **Colonial Drive** (Route 50).

Once you've found your way around the city and to Walt Disney World, you'll need to know that the 28,000 acres owned by Disney here are divided into several sections: the magic Kingdom occupies 100 of those acres; brand new EPCOT sprawls across 260 acres; and Disney-owned hotels, shopping plaza, and Discovery Island, River Country, golf courses, and the other sports facilities, all known as the Vacation Kingdom, fill another 2,500 acres.

Chapter III

DOZING IN DISNEY WORLD AND ORLANDO

YOU HAVE PROBABLY NEVER CONSIDERED living happily with a mouse, but when there's magic around, *anything* can happen! What better place to let yourself roll with that magic than in Mickey's Magic Kingdom?

When you stay right here where Mickey, Pluto, and Dumbo are tucked in each night, the magic keeps going from your first morning orange juice until the last glittering firework fades from the sky.

That's the way Walt Disney and his workers planned it when they crowned their Magic Kingdom with two fabulous, fantasy hotels: one a quick trip to your very own Fantasy Island, the other an adventure in tomorrow, capital "T."

Fabulous usually carries a rather high price tag, however, and that's the case at Disney World, where you will pay quite a few pretty pennies for the privilege of proximity. There are mitigating factors, however; the major one of which is the availability of free transportation. When you stay in either of the two hotels owned and operated by Disney, or in four others privately owned but located on Disney World property, you can abandon the trusty auto and leave the driving entirely to them.

Visitors who fly to Orlando intent on spending most of their time at Disney World, with perhaps a tour or two to other area attractions, can find some very comfortable and luxurious places to bunk and forego the expense and hassle of a car.

If, however, you think you'd like to look around this very lovely part of Florida and want to have the convenience of a car at your doorstep, you can find plenty of moderately priced accommodations just a short drive from Disney and from many of the other attractions in the area.

It is crucial to remember that distances are great here in

Central Florida. You cannot spend the morning at Disney World and stroll over to Sea World for lunch. You cannot, in fact, stroll over to Sea World at all unless you're a marathon walker. It is miles just from the first Disney entrance sign to the parking lot, and equally as far from the Sea World entrance to pools where porpoises play.

What I want to emphasize here is that you have several basic decisions to make before you land in Disney World.

If you plan to fly here, you must decide if you want to rent a car and save some money on hotel accommodations, or forego the car and splurge on hotels at Disney World where you do not need a car. You can, of course, see some of the other area attractions on package tours, but without a car you'll probably have to forego a look at Orlando's lovely suburbs and some of the intriguing restaurants and nightlife.

If you're driving here and owe yourself a splurge, there's no better place to take it than at some of the very attractive and interesting hotels on Disney property. If you want to keep your costs down, you can do that by taking advantage of moderately priced hotels and motels that are just a short drive from the park.

Accommodations in Disney World

DISNEY WORLD HOTELS: So what are these fabulous places I've been raving about? Let's take a look at the two hotels owned and operated by Disney World.

If you listen very hard at Disney's **Polynesian Village,** you may hear the plaintive strains of that little character, Tatu, crying "zee plaaaane, boss, zee plaaane." So quickly do you become part of the South Seas atmosphere here, that right at the reception desk you begin wondering why you didn't pack a sarong. Thatched roofs, waterfalls, "longhouses" set amid jungle, lily ponds, tonga torches, grass-skirted maidens, fire dances —one fantastic place indeed to lei your head.

Enter the lobby and stroll into the center of a jungle where perhaps the only thing missing is a volcano! Water trickles over rocks, palms soar to the three-story-high ceiling, anthuriums peek flaming red ears out from behind more than 75 species of tropical flora. Look closely and you'll spot an orchid or two nestled among the greenery. This intriguing spot is called the Great Ceremonial House, and it's where you'll find most of the hotel's sybaritic restaurants, lounges, and shops.

Nine two- and three-story "longhouses" streak down the sides of this complex, which is bounded by a sparkling white beach. Named for Pacific islands, the longhouses are home to 637 rooms. Largest ones are in Oahu, and suites are in Bali Hai, to name a few. South Seas luxury in your room translates to one king- or two queen-size beds, plush carpets, big closets, and dressing rooms. Rooms can accommodate five, even six if the sixth is a toddler. Suites are available for four to eight fantasy-seekers.

Sleeping is the least interesting thing you can do here. There are all kinds of boats to rent, from pedal boats to pontoons to . . . outrigger canoes. There are two super swimming pools, including a Swimming Pool Lagoon, set amid rocks that form a water slide you reach by splashing and spluttering your way through a waterfall!

You'll find a children's playground, a game room called Moana Mickey's Fun Hut, outdoor bars, and a shop in the Great Ceremonial House where you can buy a grass skirt when you really begin to get into the spirit of this place.

You get to this touch of Fantasy Island Orlando-style via the monorail that takes you right to the door. It's just one stop from the Magic Kingdom, so you can see what I meant when I said you don't need a car.

What you'll pay for all this depends primarily on which view you select: pool-view rooms are $85; garden-view rooms, $95; and lagoon-view rooms, $105. There is no charge for guests under 18. Each additional adult in a room is $4.

Onward to Disney's second fanciful creation, the **Contemporary Resort Hotel,** Tomorrowland come to life. For openers, the monorail runs right through the *middle* of this hotel! There are few experiences more awesome than arriving aboard a whooshing monorail and stepping right out into the lobby. (For that matter, there are few experiences more awesome than just riding that monorail through the lobby whether or not you're staying at the hotel.)

A towering A-frame, the Contemporary would have fit right into *Star Wars.* It's sleek, it's practically supersonic, and it most certainly is contemporary.

Largest of the Walt Disney World hostelries, the Contemporary has 1046 rooms in imposing central tower and two garden wings. Just as the Polynesian tends to slow and soothe you, the Contemporary sends your pulses racing, your imagination soaring. That's why some people like it not at all, and others never cease to be awed by its exciting aura of future shock.

Disney doesn't stint on luxury at either of these two hotels. At the Contemporary, you'll find large, luxurious, and spotlessly maintained rooms with two queen-size or one king-size bed. As in the Polynesian, rooms can accommodate five and even six, if the sixth is under three. You can choose rooms in the tower ($105 a day), where some complain that slow elevators are an inconvenience, but where everyone agrees you have a fabulous view of the lake and the intriguing Electrical Water Pageant show on it. From rooms on the other side of the tower, Cinderella's Castle provides an ever-changing, ever-enchanting view complete with fireworks at special times of the year.

Garden Wings flank the main tower, and rooms in these three-story buildings are just as attractive but seem more sedate and relaxed. Prices here are $85 to $95 a day double, and children under 18 are free; additional adults $4 a day.

Suites are also available, and in the Garden Wing they come in several configurations, including studios for two with a parlor and sleeping area with king-size bed; one-bedroom suites which sleep up to six in a bedroom and parlor with two double sleep sofas; and suites which can accommodate seven in bedroom and parlor. Perfect for really big families or several couples.

There's no dearth of activities here. You can send the children off to the game room (or sneak there yourself) where they will disappear for hours, perhaps days, lost in the wonderland of games ranging from skee ball to air hockey, from Space Invaders to whatever other electronic game is new and exciting.

While they're gone, weary parents can try their feet at water skiing, their arms at swimming in two very large pools (there's even a special pool for teenagers), or exercise it all on sailboats, pedal boats, pontoons, shuffleboard courts, volleyball, or jogging at nearby Fort Wilderness. If you're not up to any of that, settle into a good movie—three Disney films are shown daily.

Shopping? Of course, and in some very posh shops located on what the hotel calls its Grand Canyon Concourse.

Both these hotels are very, very popular, and reservations are absolutely necessary as far ahead as possible. If you aren't successful at first, try, try again, since cancellations do happen here as everywhere. Try, try again at **Central Reservations** (tel. 305/824-8000; if you speak Spanish, French, Italian, or German, call 305/824-7900) and don't hang up—the phone often rings five minutes or more before it's answered to keep you from paying while you're on hold. A deposit of one night's rate is required 21 days after the reservation is accepted and will be refunded if you cancel within five days before your scheduled arrival. Reservations are automatically cancelled if a deposit is not received.

If you should arrive before check-in time (3 p.m.) or want to leave after check-out time (noon), you can leave your luggage and go about your play. Both hotels operate luggage-storage areas and will take care of your belongings until you return.

While those two hotels are Disney's top showplaces, there are two more Disney-owned properties here, both of them quieter spots, off the beaten monorail path, and both quite interesting in their own right.

First of these is the **Golf Resort Hotel,** a 151-room spot originally built to serve as a golf clubhouse. Rooms here are a little larger, decorated in muted contemporary colors and located in a two-story building behind the lobby. From a quiet corner of your private balcony or patio, you can gaze out over the golf course or a peaceful green woodland. Here too, rooms can accommodate up to five, plus a sixth small one, in two queen-size beds and a sofa sleeper. Two suites here can tuck in seven sleepy visitors.

You don't golf, you say? No matter, no one will come knocking at your door demanding a starting time, although if that's what you want, it's certainly available on two par-72 courses: the Magnolia, which plays from 5903 to 7253 yards, and the Palm, which plays from 5785 to 6951 yards. Disney doesn't overlook the small ones even on the golf course—there's a Wee Links six-hole, 1525-yard course for the youngsters.

Naturally the resort also has a swimming pool, and for tennis buffs there are two lighted tennis courts open from 8 a.m. to 10 p.m. daily.

Finally there's a small game room to keep the children occupied and a Trophy Room Restaurant for meals, plus a lounge that offers some exotic specialties, including one featuring Kahlùa on the bottom and a tequila sour floating on top. That should help drown 19th-hole sorrows!

Rates at the Golf Resort are $85 a day with a view of the woods, $10 more with a pool or golf-course view. Suites are $210 to $515. As at all the Disney hotels, children under 18 are free.

Last of the four Disney resorts is far from the last resort. It's one of my favorites, and if you like a feeling of seclusion and absolute privacy, this may prove to be your choice, too. Called **Walt Disney World Village Villas,** the resort is several clusters of villas, dubbed Vacation Villas, Fairway Villas, Club Lake Villas, and, most intriguing of all, Treehouse Villas.

All are apartment villas, which means they have kitchen facilities so families, particularly large ones, can save money by doing some of their own cooking. What's more, the apartments are all big, roomy places where everyone can spread out, so you're not tripping over books and shoes on your way to the closet, as often happens in hotel rooms.

Let's start with the **Vacation Villas.** Here you'll find cathedral ceilings in the living room, plush and comfortable furnishings, and plenty of space to roam around. You can choose a one-bedroom villa for four with a king-size bed in the bedroom and a queen-size sleeper sofa in the living room, or a two-bedroom villa for six with king-size or twin beds in each bedroom and that big sofa sleeper in the living room. One additional small person can be accommodated in each of the units (small means under four years old in the one-bedroom, under 12 in the two-bedroom).

A super-elegant part of the Vacation Villas is a section called Grand Vista Suites, which are two- and three-bedroom *homes* where you're treated to bed-turndown service, daily newspapers delivered to your door, refrigerators stocked with staples when you arrive, and lovely furnishings. Whew!

Rates at the Vacation Villas are $120 for a one-bedroom villa, $140 for a two-bedroom; rates at the Grand Vista Suites are $400 to $475, depending on size of the home, and including use of an electric cart and bicycles.

Club Lake Villas were designed for use by conference attendees participating in meetings at the resort's nearby conference center. They're not as large as other villas and don't have full kitchens, only refrigerator and sink. They are, however, very sophisticated and sleek with a wet-bar in a sitting area and a bedroom with two double beds set off slightly from the sitting area.

A one-bedroom suite ($115) also is available and accommodates five with Jacuzzi, two queen-size beds upstairs and a convertible sofa downstairs. All this, by the way is hard by the tranquil waters of a sparkling blue lake. Other facilities at these villas include a swimming pool and three tennis courts as well as a golf course.

Fairway Villas are handsome two-bedroom units located near the tenth, eleventh, seventeenth, and eighteenth fairways of the Lake Buena Vista Club Golf Course. Here you'll find imposing cathedral ceilings in woodsy two-bedroom units with cedar siding on the exterior and rough-hewn wood trim on the inside.

Contemporary furniture pulls it all together and huge expanses of glass bring the outside world inside. They're very impressive places to while away the non-park hours and can sleep six plus a child under 12. Rates for the two-bedroom villas for six are $140 a day.

Finally, my favorites, the **Treehouse Villas,** are fascinating quarters plunked down deep in a shady pine forest. So cleverly do these octagonal creations on stilts blend into their serene surroundings, you may have difficulty finding the forest for the trees . . . er, treehouses. Each has two bedrooms with queen-size bed and comfortable furnishings, a small kitchen, a living room with a convertible sofa, and two baths. All that is on the second floor of the treehouse, encircled by tall glass windows and a wraparound deck where you can meditate on the beauties of the forest around you. On the ground-level floor of the treehouses, you'll find a den and utility room with a washer and dryer.

So lovely is it here, it may never occur to you to look for anything else to do, but if you must, there could hardly be a more entrancing spot for jogging, and the canals that wind about here are a haven for fishing fanatics. Swimmers can head over to the pool at the Lake Buena Vista Club.

Rates for the two-bedroom treehouses for six are $140 a day. There is no charge for additional occupants of the quarters.

Naturally, facilities of this size take up quite a bit of space, so it is helpful to have a car to get around the villas and to get from them to the Magic Kingdom. Although Disney has, of course, provided transportation, you can also rent electric carts for $15 for 24 hours to zip around in the serene style befitting these attractive resorts.

None of the villas have restaurants, but if you want to dine out, you can zip over to the Lake Buena Vista Club or to Walt Disney World Shopping Village.

Once again, Disney people have thought of everything, so you'll find a Gourmet Pantry chock full of goodies right down to pastries. You can pick up groceries or order them delivered to your villa free—if you're not there, they'll even arrange to put them right in your refrigerator for you! Call them at 824-6993 from outside or by dialing a number on your room phone. That, folks, is service, capital "S."

Other facilities include swimming at three different pools, a game room, and one more golf course, the Lake Buena Vista Course, in addition to the two at the Golf Villas, plus tennis courts, and boating on the lake.

At the center of the villa complex is the Pool Pavilion where you can rent those electric carts and bicycles, and use laundry and vending machines, electronic games, and pinball gizmos.

Check-in spot for Vacation Villas, Treehouse Villas, and Fairway Villas is the Reception Center in the Walt Disney World Village Hotel Plaza (more about that shortly) between Trave-Lodge and Americana's Dutch Resort Hotel in Lake Buena Vista. Check in for the Club Lake Villas is at the Walt Disney World Conference Center in Lake Buena Vista.

It is important to note here that while the Villas and the Golf Resort are on Disney property, they are not as close to the Magic Kingdom as the Polynesian and Contemporary Hotels and cannot be reached by monorail. Instead you must get from the villas to the Walt Disney World Shopping Village, the Ticket and Transportation Center at the entrance to the Magic Kingdom, and to the Polynesian and Contemporary Hotels by bus, each conveniently identified with colored flag so you can easily tell which goes where. For a complete look at Disney World's transportation system, see Chapter VIII.

FANCY CAMPING IN DISNEY WORLD: Finally, here are accommodations for those who not only like the great outdoors but like to be right out there in it as much as possible. Number one locale for that at Disney World is a cozy enclave known as **Fort Wilderness.** For some reason this spot is one of Disney's lesser-known attractions and one that's often confused with the Magic Kingdom's other western-oriented area, Frontierland. Fort Wilderness, however, is not an attraction, in the strictest sense, although it is an attractive spot designed for campers and those who like the ambience associated with camping but can do without the drudgery.

Here's how Fort Wilderness works: For campers there are 825 campsites, 200 of them set up for tents and the rest rented to trailer campers. Each of the sites is 25 to 65 feet and located in one of 21 clusters through which roads loop and twist. Each site has 110/220-volt electrical outlets, water, a barbecue grill, picnic table, and disposal hookup. In each cluster you'll find rest rooms, showers, an ice machine, telephones, and a laundry room. Up to seven campers can settle into a site for $19 to $22 a day, depending on location. There's a maximum stay of 14 nights.

Which are the best sites? Well, it depends what you are looking for in a Disney World campsite. Sites numbered from 100 to

500 are near the lakeside beach, the Trading Post, and Pioneer Hall. Farthest away from all that are numbers from 1500 to 1900, which are located amid the loveliest and densest concentration of greenery.

If you can't quite face the idea of a trailer or tent, Disney has thought up a way to provide for you. Throughout the campground you'll find air-conditioned Fleetwood Travel Trailers, 35 feet long and equipped to sleep and feed six. Everything's there, from a can opener to a dishwasher and microwave, from a bedroom with a sink, color television, and double bed or bunks, to a living room with a convertible sofa, television, and sink. There's also a bathroom in each trailer and daily maid service. Quite a "camping" experience, eh? There's just one no-no: You can't have camping equipment on the site, and everyone sleeping there must be doing so inside the trailer. Rates for the trailers are $85 a night.

Rest assured you will not starve at Fort Wilderness, even if you choose not to avail yourself of groceries at the Meadow or Settlement Trading Posts, open from 8 a.m. to 10 p.m. in winter, to 11 p.m. in summer. You can get hot dogs, hamburgers, and the like at the Beach Shack by the lake or the Campfire Snack Bar in Pioneer Hall. For more substantial fare, there's the Trail's End Café, a cozy log cafeteria with beamed ceiling and simple homey cooking, in Pioneer Hall. Later, from 9 p.m. to 12:30 a.m., pizza rolls out of the oven here; and beer, sangria, and soft drinks flow from the taps as happy munchers chuckle over the silent movie or participate in a sing-a-long.

Which brings us to what there is to do here: plenty. Most fun is the Hoop-Dee-Doo Musical Revue which takes center stage three times a night at 5, 7:30, and 10 p.m. So popular is this show that reservations are required. Make them as far ahead as possible by calling Central Reservation Center, 824-8000. If the first show's completely booked, you can get on a waiting list by turning up at the Pioneer Hall Ticket Window prior to the next show and explaining your plight.

While you're watching the antics that occur after the velvet curtain opens, you'll chow on some down-home cookin' in the form of barbecued ribs, corn on the cob, fried chicken, and strawberry shortcake. There is plenty to eat as well as plenty to watch at one of these rip-roaring evenings. Tickets are $17 adults, $14 for youngsters 12 to 17, and $9.50 for children under 12.

City kids who don't get much opportunity to sit around a

campfire will love another of Fort Wilderness's activities, a campfire sing-a-long that occurs near the Meadow Trading Post. Also on the bill there are free Disney movies and cartoons, a marshmallow roast and canoe excursion, called the Marshmallow Marsh Excursion, which paddles off to a special spot where excursionists can watch the Electrical Water Pageant at 9:45 p.m. nightly while less adventuresome campers take up a seat on the beach.

More? You can swim in the lake, pedal around on bicycles, or paddle around in boats, play basketball, baseball, tetherball, softball, or volleyball, jog on a 2.3-mile course, fish, go horseback riding on guided trail rides, try waterskiing, drop in on the village blacksmith, the Petting Farm, or the horse barn, stroll a Wilderness Swamp Trail, and last, perhaps least, play in a games arcade.

Pets, by the way, must be housed in a special kennel here ($3 for overnight stay).

Buses and watercraft connect Fort Wilderness to the rest of the Disney World Kingdom with schedules available at Guest Services. More on the various modes of transport in Chapter VIII's section on transportation in and around the Magic Kingdom.

HOTELS IN WALT DISNEY WORLD VILLAGE HOTEL PLAZA:
Walt Disney World Village Hotel Plaza is quite a mouthful, but it adequately describes four (soon to be five) major Orlando hotels located on Disney property. While they occupy prime land among the thousands of acres owned by Disney World in Central Florida, these hotels are not owned by Disney World but by separate corporations which lease their land from Disney.

All of which means little to visitors except in one particular: These hotels are all very, very close to the Magic Kingdom and have free, frequent, and reliable transportation to the Kingdom, River Country, EPCOT, and, in fact, to all points in Walt Disney World day and night. You can also get reduced rates at Disney attractions, like River Country and Discovery Island, at these hotels, and because they have a rather special status, you can get a seat at dinner shows ahead of the general public.

Just as meaningful, of course, is the quality of these accommodations which is, in a word, top. All offer modern, luxurious surroundings, all the amenities, and a friendly welcome.

There are several ways to get to the hotels, but the easiest for new arrivals is the Lake Buena Vista exit from Hwy. I-4 (this exit also bears the route number SR 535). Signs direct you to the entrance, where you'll know immediately you have happened upon something special. You're transported from flatlands, sand, and scrub palms to a world of emerald-green lawns, median strips filled with greenery and colorful plantings, and best of all, chic, sleek resorts that need not use neon and Day-glo colors to attract your attention. Instead they get that attention in the best way of all, with tastefully decorated, well-maintained buildings and beautiful grounds.

The signs for the properties are subtle announcements, all the same size and color, alerting you to your arrival at these very attractive hotels whose luxury you will find—and pay for—to the tune of about $85 to $110 a night.

Guests' pets can stay at WDW Kennels too for $3 a night.

The first hotel you'll encounter as you enter here is **Trave-Lodge**, Box 22205, Lake Buena Vista, FL 32830 (tel. 305/828-2424 or toll free 800/255-3050). You're greeted in a tiled lobby where a fountain tinkles musically. Home of that now-famous Sleepy Bear, TraveLodge features that chubby charmer. Once the kids are safely tucked in, parents can zip up to the eighteenth-floor Top of the Arc, where they'll have one of the best seats in town for fireworks at the Magic Kingdom.

TraveLodge provides two queen-sized beds in every room and attractive decor. You'll find plenty of smiling service, a game room and swimming pool to play in, and a coffee shop and lounge to retreat to after a long day in the park. Room rates are $79 to $99, year round, for up to four people in a room. In slower months the hotel often features some great bargain package prices. Ask.

Next in line is the **Americana's Dutch Resort Hotel**, 1850 Preview Blvd., Lake Buena Vista, (tel. 305/828-4444 or toll free 800/432-2926 in Florida, 800/327-2994 elsewhere). Royal blue is a favorite color in Holland, and you'll find plenty of that dramatic hue here set off by whites as sparkling as a Dutch kitchen. Huge walls of glass send light streaming across a massive lobby. Nestled on the corner of a lake, Dutch Resort specializes in luxurious extras: big baths, fluffy towels, bedside light controls, rocking chairs in every room, and, of course, that spic-and-span blue-and-white decor. The award-winning Flying Dutchman Restaurant offers breakfast, lunch, and continental cuisine at dinner ($12 to $17), and the hotel's Tulip Café is open

24 hours. For dancing there's the Hague lounge and for cocktails, the Nightwatch.

Outside in the hotel's extensive grounds you'll find a swimming pool shaped like a windmill, a miniature golf course with windmills, a game area, and a children's playground. A room for two with two double beds, and no doubt a windmill somewhere, is $80 to $110.

On the other side of the primped and planted roadway that twists through this complex of hotels is the soaring **Hotel Royal Plaza,** 1905 Preview Blvd., Lake Buena Vista (tel. 305/828-2828 or toll free 800/327-2990, in Florida 800/432-2920), which in late 1982 was deep into a massive renovation designed to modernize every nook of this attractive property.

A 17-story tower houses part of the resort's rooms and is flanked by two 2-story wings. In the center of it all is one very large swimming pool. Every room has a private balcony, and all are tastefully decorated in contemporary colors. You can massage away your aches and pains in a sauna or Jacuzzi, but if you have more energy left after a day at Disney, you can have a go at the game room, shuffleboard courts, or four tennis courts.

For dining, El Cid restaurant offers continental cuisine ($12 to $20 for entrées). There's a coffeeshop called the Knight's Table, plus two bars, La Cantina, and a disco called Giraffe, which happens to be the only disco on Disney World property, so it's quite popular.

Rates at the Royal Plaza are $80 to $110, depending on which location you select, and includes four people of any age in a room.

That mainstay of the tired American traveler, **Howard Johnson's,** Box 22204, (tel. 305/828-8888, toll free 800/654-2000), makes an appearance here, too. So popular did Ho Jo's at Disney World prove, that the company not long ago added a new six-story annex wing. Mainstay of the property, however, is a 14-story tower, which features a glass elevator and a plant-bedecked atrium. Children always seem partial to Howard Johnson's and that is the case here, where the young ones are lured by a whizzing, whirring game room; two swimming pools; a kiddie pool; and a playground.

Rooms are spacious, attractively decorated, and equipped with everything you'd expect to find in a major hotel. This chain has had many years' practice in welcoming weary travelers, and you'll find smiling, responsive service and plenty of it. What's more, you can get something to eat at any hour of the day or night in the hotel's restaurant, which offers all the usual Howard Johnson specialties, including all those flavors of ice cream, of course.

Rates range from $72 to $97 year round; there is no charge for children under 18.

Finally, the new kid on this posh block, is **Buena Vista Palace,** a sister hotel (or is that brother?) to the Royal Plaza. An $85-million creation towering 27 stories over the lake and sporting no less than 870 rooms, the new hotel was just putting on the finishing touches in late 1982, so if you like modernity, you can be sure you'll find the latest innovations here. Buena Vista Palace has four towers, with many rooms that exit right onto a balcony rather than a hallway. Decorated in the latest styles and colors, the hotel features a bridge across a lagoon to a recreation area where you will find two swimming pools set in lush tropical plantings. This new hotel has come up with an interesting architectural innovation: You enter on an upper level of the hotel where a serene, unhurried atmosphere prevails because all the guest services—reservations, car rentals, swimming pool exits, and the like—are located on the first floor. You'll find an interesting Australia-related Outback Restaurant here that's reached by a private elevator; another restaurant, Arthur's Roof, is high atop the tallest tower overlooking EPCOT. Rates will be $98 to $118 year round.

Hotels In and Around Orlando

It did not take long for Orlando's canny entrepreneurs to see that the Mouse might make them rich. Consequently, in what seemed mere minutes, dozens of new hotels and motels sprung up on the flat sands and cow pastures of Central Florida. There are now so many that the first-time visitor may be overwhelmed by the constant assault of a barrage of signs and buildings that stretch out in every direction from Disney World.

On the positive side, however, all that instant competition has provided every level of accommodation in every price bracket. Which means you are likely to be able to find all the amenities from swimming pool to playground, restaurant, game room, and the rest, for just what you want to pay.

What's more, because roads are so many, so good, and move you so quickly from place to place in the Orlando area, you need not feel obliged to settle in right next to Mouseland. If you have a car, there is an enormous range of hotel choices. If you don't, public transportation can whisk you from all but the most remote spots right to Disney World and other attractions. Also several tour companies operate in the area, picking up passengers at most hotels, delivering them to the doors of Disney World, Sea World, Circus World, and the rest, then bringing them safely home again.

To make matters even easier, hotels and motels in the area are clustered in several general locations: along U.S. 192 to Kissimmee, on International Drive in an area called Florida Center, downtown, and near the airport. I've divided them up geographically for you, beginning with those closest to the Kingdom and fanning out to the airport.

JUST OUTSIDE DISNEY PROPERTY: Plunked down all by itself in the countryside just outside Disney World's acreage but still technically in Lake Buena Vista is **Vistana Resort,** on Route 535 at the Lake Buena Vista exit (tel. 305/841-6915 or toll free 800/327-9152, in Florida 800/432-9197). There probably is no quieter retreat outside the Disney Villas than Vistana's own villas, which are one-, two-, or three-bedroom townhouse-style dwellings, complete with balconies or patios.

Designed as condominium homes, these pastoral palaces feature the most contemporary furnishings in living and dining rooms; high, beamed ceilings; attractive woven wall hangings; and an ambience even the most critical traveler is sure to love.

You can settle in here and do some of your own cooking in a fully equipped kitchen, or just settle in and luxuriate in doing nothing at all in tranquil surroundings that include maid service, washers and driers in each villa, a pool, snackshop, jogging trail, and scheduled activities. Tennis is the major focus of this resort, which offers enough courts for Wimbledon, free play, and frequent discounts on tennis instruction and clinics as well as on Disney tickets. Transportation to the park is free.

Rates at Vistana, which has just completed an even more impressive addition called The Falls, that takes water architecture to new heights, are in busiest seasons $150 for a one-bedroom, rising to $195 for larger quarters that can accommodate up to eight people, somewhat lower in other months.

A money-saver just outside Lake Buena Vista's Hotel Plaza entrance (but just a few hundred yards away) is **Best Western World Inn** (S. State Rd. 535, Windermere; tel. 305/976-3636 or toll free 800/327-6954 or 800/628-1234). Two pools here should please youngsters as well as adults, and there's a nice quiet air about the place that's soothing after a long hot day. You'll find 245 rooms here, including five efficiency units with full kitchens, six rooms with king-sized beds, and rooms with refrigerators. Tucked away under rustling pines, World Inn features a coin laundry, game room, a large playground, and movies, as well a bright tropical decor and lots of glass to let in the sunlight you came here to see. There's also an attractive casual restaurant for family dining and a cocktail lounge with entertainment, plus free transportation to the Magic Kingdom, EPCOT, and to Lake Buena Vista Village Shopping Center. Rates range from $48 to $58 year round, depending on season; efficiencies are $65 to $75 and suites $125 to $195.

ON U.S. 192: This is the highway that leads straight to the Disney World entrance, and here you'll find a surprising number of moderately priced motels and a few major resorts as well. I'll start with the Orlando Hyatt Hotel, which tops the price list, and work down to some of the smaller, less elaborate spots for budget-watching vacationers.

The **Orlando Hyatt Hotel** (6375 Spacecoast Pkwy., Kissimmee; tel. 350/846-4100 or toll free 800/396-1234) can be so much fun on its own you may be tempted some days to skip the Magic Kingdom and participate in a little of the magic this hotel goes all out to create. For openers, every building here is painted a different color, delicate pastels all, designed to make it easier to find your way around this massive complex which includes 960 rooms, four (!) swimming pools and four kiddie pools, tennis courts, a shopping mall complete with package store, a game room with electronic toys, and a tot lot for the toddlers. There's even a helicopter on the front lawn if you'd like a bird's-eye view of the *other* Magic Kingdom.

Rooms here are spacious, with big dressing areas fitted out with all the little touches Hyatt so thoughtfully includes, from shower cap to French-milled soap and shampoo. Earthy tones are soothing inside rooms, while outside the attractively landscaped grounds offer shady and sunny spots to while away a few restful hours.

For dining, there's a Big Bicycle restaurant with theme evenings that change frequently but always include entertainment and meals to match the theme. At Limey Jim's, an intimate dining spot that features gourmet cuisine, you can work your way through five or six courses, ending in a finale of specialty liqueur-laced coffees (about $20 to $25 for a full meal).

Double rooms here are $75 to $85, with suites ranging from $240 to $350. Prices drop slightly in slower seasons.

There are two attractive resorts on the west side of Hwy. I-4, Sheraton Lakeside Inn and Orlando Vacation Resort. Both are reasonably close to the Magic Kingdom, and both offer top-quality accommodations.

Sheraton Lakeside Inn (tel. 305/846-3221 or toll free 800/325-3535) has 462 rooms, a seafood saloon, lounge, deli, two heated pools and two pools for the toddlers, a boat dock, paddleboats, mini-golf, tennis courts, and poolside gazebos. Rates here are divided roughly into two time periods, from February to May and June to September, when a couple pays $65 to $70; in other months rates drop to $40 to $50, and children under 17 stay free at any time of year.

Tennis is the focal point of the **Orlando Vacation Resort** (South U.S. 27 in Clermont; tel. 305/656-8181 or toll free 800/874-9064), where you'll find umpteen lighted tennis courts and much, much more. For instance, 225 attractive rooms with plenty of space and bright decor plus a homey little restaurant done up in an antique theme that's fun to explore. Excellent food emerges from the kitchen, too, including fresh bread daily, prices are in the $10 to $15 range. Free shuttle rides to Disney come with the package, for which you'll pay $40 to $50 year round; children under 17 free.

The nearby **Comfort Inn** (7501 W. Spacecoast Pkwy., U.S. 192 West; tel. 305/846-7500 or toll free 800/228-5150) is a pretty place on a strip of highway packed with fast-food restaurants, shops, and chain hotels. Located just one mile from Walt Disney World, the hotel has 282 spacious rooms, each with two double beds decorated in cheerful prints. There's a shuttle service to Disney World, color television, free local phone service, a pool, game room, boutique, laundry facilities, and a cozy restaurant open for breakfast and dinner (prices in the $3 range for big breakfasts, under $8 for steak, seafood, and Italian dinner favorites).

Floridians were born with superlatives in their mouths, so you can expect to find the world's largest, biggest, strangest and all the other "ests" well represented in this competitive locale. Which brings us to a stopping spot the Day's Inn chains call the world's largest **Day's Lodge!** Located on U.S. 192 just east of Hwy. I-4, on a long road sometimes called Spacecoast Parkway (tel. 305/846-7900 or toll free 800/327-9126, in Florida 800/432-9103), this local representative of the Day's Inn chain offers about what you've come to expect in these low-cost but high-quality-for-the-money operations. Day's Lodges, by the way, differ from Inns in that rooms come with cooking facilities. Here in Kissimmee's Day's Lodge, rooms also boast 700 square feet of living space, patios or balconies, and amenities that include a swimming pool, playground, and barbecue. Located just three miles from the Kingdom, the resort charges $55 in summer ($5 more for poolside rooms) and children under 18 are just $1 each. In other months prices drop to $40 to $45.

Back on the east side of U.S. 192, **Larson's Lodge/Kissimmee Red Carpet Inn,** 2009 W. Vine St. (tel. 305/946-2713 or toll free 800/327-9147, in Florida 800/241-3848), is owned and operated by the friendly Larson family that tries hard to give this resort a home-away-from-home atmosphere. You'll first see an imposing wood-and-brick structure at the entrance, backed by a tiled lobby where you'll be greeted with a smile. Resort facilities include a game room, boutique, heated pool, and sundeck—everything right down to a little picket fence around the children's play area. In the resort's three-story wings are 120 attractively decorated rooms, each with two double beds, a sitting area, and picture windows. To make dinner time simple, right next door is a Black Angus Steakhouse where you can chow down on some simple barbecue fixin's for prices in the $5- to $10-range. During most months of the year a room for two at Larson's Lodge is $52, an efficiency $65. In spring and fall rates drop to $35 and $45, and at anytime children under 18 are free.

Red Carpet Inns are represented in another property here, **Terrace Red Carpet Inn,** 5245 Spacecoast Pkwy. (tel. 305/846-7700 or toll free 800/238-6040, in Florida 800/241-3848). A two-story building, this motel has spacious rooms with a view of the pool and patio. Children can amuse themselves on the inn's playground and there's a coin laundry to make quick work of playground results. In the inn's dining room you'll find a sumptuous buffet, and in the Riviera Lounge there's nightly entertainment. Rates are the same here as at Larson's Lodge.

A few rungs down the luxury ladder, you'll find **Colonial Motor Lodge,** 1815 W. Vine St. (tel. 305/847-6121). Furnishings are quite basic, but rooms are neat and clean and big enough for a budget-watching family. There are 40 apartments and motel units with two double beds. You'll also find two swimming pools and a game room. For these simple but adequate accommodations, you'll pay $40 to $48 for two-bedroom apartments, $28 to $32 for motel units in peak seasons, about $28 to $40 double in spring and fall, with no charge for children under 12, $3 each for others.

One of my favorite budget spots is **King's Court,** 4836 W. Spacecoast Pkwy. (tel. 305/847-4762), a small quiet spot that shares a little lake with an adjoining motel called Lakeview (another adequate budget motel). Shady pines drop fat pine cones, and there's a tranquil view of the lake. You can use the resort's boat for a little watery expedition. A swimming pool overlooks the lake, too. Motel units here have two double beds and bright colors, and rent for $32 to $39 year round. Two bedroom apartments are just $35 to $39, and there's no charge for children under 16. Others are $3 each.

Stagecoach Inn, 4311 Vine St., Kissimmee (tel. 305/846-4213 or toll free 800/327-9155, in Florida 800/432-9198), is still another appealing resort on this highway which, despite its different names, is one big road. You'll know you've arrived at the Stagecoach when you see a farm wagon front and center and then spot the rustic resort off the highway. Despite those Old West touches, the Stagecoach Inn has kept its rooms thoroughly modern and colorful. Wide picture windows offer a view of huge, old trees towering over a shady swimming pool. The Old West continues next door at the Gaucho Restaurant, where antique quilts are displayed on the walls, and very inexpensive (in the $5 to $10 range) beef and barbecued items are on the menu. You'll pay $31 to $39 double, year round, and children under 12 are free; others pay $7 each. If you're a member of the AAA, there's a special $25 to $37 rate year round.

If you've got a hamburger fan in your group, you can't go wrong at the **Sunrise Motel,** 801 Vine St. (tel. 305/846-3224)— it's next door to a McDonald's, and there's a Burger King across the street! In quality, the Sunrise Motel fits right into those levels—nothing fancy, just small, simply furnished rooms lined with paneling and decorated in bright colors. Sunrise is about a 15-minute drive from Disney, and room charges are $28 to $35 for two, $35 to $45 for four ("or whatever I can get," meaning it may not hurt to bargain here). Children under 18 are free.

IN FLORIDA CENTER: Florida Center is a name applied to an area that roughly surrounds International Drive, a major thoroughfare near Disney World. With all the attractions, hotels, motels, fast food restaurants, and shops that are located here, Florida Center practically qualifies as a mini-Disney World. I guarantee you won't have any trouble keeping the kids busy on non-Disney days around here. Just send them to the Stars Hall of Fame, Wet 'n Wild, Mystery Fun House—see what I mean? To get here, leave Hwy. I-4 at the International Drive–Sand Lake Road exit and head east on Sand Lake Road (also known as Route 528A).

It won't take you long to spot the **Orlando Marriott Inn**, 6700 Sand Lake Rd. (tel. 305/351-2420, or toll free 800/228-9290). It may, in fact, take you longer to find your way around this sprawling resort. A recent major renovation and construction project has added 439 rooms to the 640 with which it began, making it one of the largest hotels in the area. Strolling around this huge complex, with its rooms clustered into villas named after flowers, is like strolling through a large, showy garden ornamented with little lagoons, ponds, and fountains. Inside the villas you'll find big picture windows, contemporary earthy colors, deep carpets, oversize beds, in some rooms a big, comfy couch and chair and, in some, a kitchenette, too. There are many amenities: lighted tennis courts, two kiddie pools, three pools with sundecks and wooded platforms for scenic sunning, two game rooms and a play area, and a gift and sundry shop. In the handsome dining room, called The Grove, you can dine on seafood and sizzling steaks in the $15 to $20 price range and enjoy nightly entertainment. Marriott has free airport transportation and in peak seasons (January to May or July to September) charges $62 to $90 double; lower rates in other months. Children of any age are free.

Hilton Inns operate three hotels in the Orlando area, but the **Hilton Inn** at 7400 International Dr. (tel 305/351-4600 or toll free in Florida 800/432-5141), is convenient to Disney World and other area attractions. Quite a pretty place it is, too, with a fabulous dome-roofed swimming pool. If you aren't tempted by the golden glow here and want some of that tanning sunshine, you can get that at the hotel's second pool. Suites, kitchenettes, and motel rooms are available at this hotel, which completed a major renovation recently; it now has a cozy contemporary look with lots of greenery to provide a tropical ambience. You can dine inside or outside on a patio under that domed roof (prices in the $10 to $15 range). Children of all ages are free in rooms for which the hotel charges $69 to $99 double in summer and winter months, about $50 to $75 in the less popular visitor seasons of spring and fall.

Another huge resort in this vicinity is the **Ramada Resort Hotel**, formerly the Court of Flags Resort Hotel, 5715 Major Blvd. (tel. 305/351-3340, or toll free 800/228-2828). Located west of Hwy. I-4, the Ramada spreads out over acres of grounds. It's easy to get lost here, but even that can be entertaining, since in your wanderings you'll stumble across three swimming pools, a wading pool for children, an electronic game room, a tour desk, two saunas, lounges, and a popular restaurant, The Glass Garden, which features continental cuisine in the $10 to $15 range. Bright colors accent the 820 spacious rooms, and there are private balconies for quiet hours. Two people pay $43 to $57 year round, and children are free.

One of the newest hotels in the area is the **Sheraton World** at 10100 International Dr. (tel. 305/352-1100 or toll free 800/325-3535). It's right next door to Sea World and at last count had 318 rooms, although that number will be larger soon. Just built in 1980, this very contemporary spot is rigged out in arched wicker headboards and framed prints. A skylight sends rays of sunshine down on the brick-floored lobby, and bright banners add lively touches of color. Families gravitate to the Sunrise Café, while parents often sneak off to the Sunset Saloon. Le Monde Restaurant offers elegant dining on continental cuisine in the $10 to $15 bracket. Sheraton charges $45 to $70 double all year, depending on season, and children are free.

A little farther along International Drive, you'll find **Las Palmas Inn**, 6233 International Dr. (tel. 305/351-3900 or toll free 800/327-2114, in Florida 800/432-1175), right across the street from Wet 'n Wild, a watery wonderland for children and adults. Spain has influenced Las Palmas, which sports lots of dark wood and a red-tiled roof. Spacious rooms feature handsome wall coverings and tasteful floral prints. There's a pool bar for cooling off on hot afternoons, a playground and game room for the youngsters, and an inexpensive restaurant, the Palms. Rates here are $62 to $67 in busy summer and winter months, $50 to $57 at other times of year.

High Q, 5905 International Dr. (tel. 305/351-2100 or toll free 800/228-5151, in Florida 800/327-1366), has a cylindrical tower that soars over Florida Center, and the huge "Q" on top makes it an unmistakable landmark. You can see all over Orlando from the top of this 21-story hotel, which features 300 attractively decorated rooms. Not only do rooms have double beds, they also have couches and dressing areas. To entertain you there are two pools, a game room, saunas and boutiques, a lounge with piano bar entertainment, and two restaurants. There are even a barber shop and beauty salon, and High Q guests have golf and tennis privileges at a nearby country club. Rates here are $38 to $58 depending on season.

Working down to the lower end of the price range, you'll find **Davis Brothers Motor Lodge,** 6603 International Dr. (tel. 305/351-2900 or toll free 800/841-9480), a chain operation with cafeterias whose prices are a budget-watcher's dream. Nice combination of inexpensive rooms and meals here in the heart of Disney territory. Even your canine friends are welcomed at Davis Brothers Motor Lodge, where bright, spacious rooms are $39.95 year round. Buffet-style meals in the cafeteria are in the $3 to $4 range!

Sweden House, home of those bounteous all-you-can-eat buffets, is already a resident of **Gateway Inn,** 500 Kirkman Rd. (tel. 305/351-2000 or toll free 800/327-3808, in Florida 800/432-1179), so if you're traveling with a passel of chow hounds, you are likely to find this a perfect plunk-down spot. An attractive family resort, Gateway Inn wraps itself around a sparkling central pool and features bright and spacious rooms. A playground with swings should keep the youngsters busy, and if that's not enough, there are Ping-pong games, a sundry shop, and, for escapists, a Maid Marion cocktail lounge. Gateway Inn is associated with another moderately priced hotel in Orlando, the **Archway Inn,** 8421 S. Orange Blossom Trail (tel. 305/855-6060), where accommodations and prices are similar. You'll pay $38 to $50 at Gateway Inn and about $36 to $40 at Archway Inn, which is located a little farther from Disney World.

DOWNTOWN: Not too many cities anywhere, and certainly few in Florida can boast, as can Orlando, a sparkling blue lake right in the middle of downtown. Benches set around the lake offer a tempting spot to while away some contemplative minutes as ducks paddle by and fountains shoot skyward. Despite its inviting location, however, the world grew away from downtown Orlando as it has from many cities, leaving behind aging hotels and some imposing Old Florida neighborhoods. In recent years, however, entrepreneurs and hoteliers have begun to cast an eagle eye on downtown Orlando. Some changes are in store, and some have already taken place.

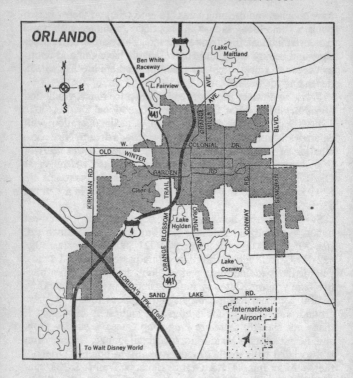

To take a look at this metamorphosis in the making, take Hwy. I-4 to the 17/92 exit and head north to Washington Street.

Here you'll find the star of downtown Orlando's slow but sure renewal: the **Harley Hotel**, 1515 E. Washington St. (tel. 305/841-3220 or toll free 800/321-2323). When I saw what the Harley renovation had done, I could hardly believe my eyes: from the quiet colors, modern prints, and comfortable chairs in the hotel rooms to the entrancing Café on the Park. Plunk down here, gaze out across a smashing view of Lake Eola, and revel in this glamorous atmosphere of brass, leaded glass, deep burgundy velvet, and dark wood. Rates are $53.50 to $63.50 double, all year.

Harley also operates another hotel in the area, **Colonial Plaza Inn**, 2801 E. Colonial Dr., at the edge of downtown Orlando (tel. 305/894-2741 or toll free 800/325-3535), where you will find an extra touch in four of the rooms that you will find in few other spots in the world—a private swimming pool! In 221 other rooms you'll be sans pool, but you'll still have basic accommodations, and you can always nip downstairs and soak in a Jacuzzi. Double-room rates here are $44.50 to $49.50, $100 for suites.

There's a Howard Johnson's in the area, too, and by now you probably know what to expect at this chain. I only mention the **Howard Johnson** at 2014 W. Colonial Dr. and Tampa Ave. (tel. 305/894-2741 or toll free 800/654-2000), because it's owned and operated by Mac Finnane, a very nice man who runs a very nice Howard Johnson's in midtown, near lots of restaurants and shops and only about a 20-minute drive from Disney World. A restaurant with all the requisite Ho Jo flavors is here, too. Rates at the hotel are $43 to $58 in peak summer and winter season, $35 to $44 at other times of the year. Get there on the Colonial Drive West exit from Hwy. I-4.

If you like small places, the **Davis Park,** 221 E. Colonial Dr. (tel. 305/425-9065), may be just what you have in mind. In Orlando just 75 units makes it a small place, so owners Carroll and Toni Chapin like to say they're operating "a village atmosphere in the heart of Orlando." There's a coziness about the place too, from paneled rooms with big dressing areas to a small brick-and-wood restaurant where you'll find inexpensive prices. A few rooms have cooking facilities, and top rates are $33.50 to $37.50 double, about $2 cheaper for singles. Davis Park is about a 20-minute drive from Disney World.

Quality Inns can usually be trusted to have uniform quality and simple but adequate and clean accommodations. In Orlando **Quality Inn West,** 3330 W. Colonial Dr. (tel. 305/299-6710 or toll free 800/327-2016), is even newer than ten-year-old Disney World and proud of its spacious rooms, winding central pool, and attractive grounds. There are two double beds in rooms, and some add couches too. When hunger strikes, head over to the Ranch House Restaurant for inexpensive meals in the $4 to $10 range. If you're looking for a little evening entertainment, stop by Club Escadrille. A couple pays $32 to $39 at this Quality Inn in peak season, $24 to $27 in other months.

Orlando Motor Lodge is a little removed from the usual byways, but you could hardly expect to find a lakeside lodge right on Main Street. This charmer is on U.S. 17/92, North Mills Ave. Take the Princeton exit from Hwy. I-4 (tel. 305/896-4111). You'll also find trim lake-view rooms, a pool, rowboats for a romantic paddle around the lake, a coffeeshop for breakfast, and bargain rates: $24 to $30 double in peak season, $3 additional for rooms with kitchens. Children under 12 are $2 each; others an additional $3 a day.

AIRPORT AREA: Orlando's impressive jetport is not far from the Magic Kingdom and other Orlando attractions, and it's a good spot to begin looking for a room when other motels closer to attractions are filled. There are some very attractive hostelries here, and thanks to plenty of multi-lane highways, they're easy to reach.

Tops among hotels convenient to the airport is the **Gold Key Inn,** 7100 S. Orange Blossom Trail (tel. 305/855-0050), a very special and cozy place. In the lobby there's a brick fireplace flanked by plump couches arranged on a perky flowered carpet. Massive beams dominate the room and there are usually fresh flowers. In your room you'll find comfortable armchairs, reproductions of old English prints, tile baths, and the small touches that make this more an inn than a hotel. For the more active, there are a putting green, tennis, and a swimming pool, and restaurant surrounded by tropical gardens. Shuttle buses stop here to take you to attractions.

Gold Key's Piccadilly Restaurant is an award-winning spot famous locally for its homemade soups, gently seared steaks, delicately roasted prime rib, and excellent seafood, all presented in an atmosphere that glows in the light of candles, stained glass windows, floral prints, and heavy wood beams.

Rates at Gold Key, which is as close as you're likely to come to a country inn in Orlando, are $50 to $56.

Across the street is a **TraveLodge,** 7101 S. Orange Blossom Trail (tel. 305/851-4300, toll free 800/255-3050), with attractive, large rooms in tropical colors and rates of $47 to $59 in fall and winter, $64 to $70 in summer.

WINTER PARK: Winter Park is not right down the street from Disney, but it's such a beautiful hideaway that for my money it's well worth the 20- or 30-minute drive to area attractions. So lovely is this small city, that it is an attraction in itself, a tiny diamond glittering proudly among quite a few rhinestones.

Located just north of Orlando and about 15 miles from Disney World, Winter Park is comparatively easy to find and worth the trouble. Just exit from Hwy. I-4 at Colonial Drive East, turn north at Mills Drive, and east again on Orange Avenue. You can also exit Hwy. I-4 at Fairbanks Avenue and follow that street east to Park Avenue, where you'll turn left.

You'll land right in the middle of a town that likes to call itself "Little Europe" and with good reason: Many of its fabulously beautiful mansions are European in style, its streets are small and packed with shops as elegant and intriguing as any you find in posh European shopping areas, and its ambience is pure Europe, from splashing fountains to tiny courtyards tucked between buildings.

As you roll or stroll down Winter Park's main street, Park Avenue, look up and you'll see an ornate balcony, decked with pots of scarlet geraniums and sparkling white wicker furniture. That's the **Park Plaza Hotel,** 307 Park Ave. (tel. 305/647-1072), a glamorous little hotel recently redecorated but still redolent with Old World, Old Florida touches such as leaded glass windows and a marble desk in the lobby. They've managed to blend antique elegance with modern convenience, using Cuban tile, brick trim, and whirring paddle fans. My favorite is a big room with brass beds, a sitting area, deep plush carpets, pretty pastel colors, and wing chairs. French doors open onto a balcony where you can gaze down on those lesser beings not up there enjoying this luxury, for which you will pay $85 for suite *avec* balcony, $45 to $65 for a room overlooking an enchanting courtyard, $50 to $55 for a view of the park across the street. Worth every hard-earned dime. Additional guests in a room are $5.

A family-owned hostelry, the **Langford Hotel** at Interlachen and East New England Ave. (tel. 305/644-3400), has been around since 1955 but keeps up to date with frequent modernization. Shaded by pines and a deep jungle of plants, the Langford provides a quiet retreat spiritually, if not geographically, in a tiny tropical garden with a little waterfall that glitters at night in the glow of lamplights. Some rooms are downright spectacular, with antique French chairs, crystal chandeliers, a striped silk chaise, patterned carpet, beveled mirrors, and Austrian drapes covering a glass entrance to a private balcony. Another hideaway is covered wall to wall in straw matting and filled with things African from zebra-striped furniture to massive mahogany carvings.

In the hotel's Empire Room supper club, a long menu sports some tempting beef and seafood specialties ($10 to $20 range) and in the lounge the area's liveliest entertainment goes on stage in the form of floor shows and dance bands.

Year-round rates at the Langford are $40 to $45 single, $49 to $55 double.

If my liking for Winter Park has proved contagious but you're watching the $$$, try **Mount Vernon Lodge,** 110 S. Orlando Ave., U.S. 17/92 (tel. 305/647-1166), a pretty place with a soaring Williamsburg facade and pretty interiors. You'll be comfortable here—and near some super restaurants in Winter Park—for rates of $45 to $65. There's a pool, a restaurant, and many of the attractive rooms have refrigerators.

IN SURROUNDING TOWNS: Let me say once more that because it's reasonably fast and easy to get from one place to another in Orlando, there's no reason why you shouldn't stay in one of the attractive small towns that dot the lake-strewn countryside. When you want to spend a day amusing yourself at the attractions, just hop in the car and zip on over there. Just don't forget you'll need a car!

Altamonte Springs is quite a few exits north of Disney World on Hwy. I-4, but it's a pretty town with several very good restaurants. If you don't mind about a 25-minute drive to Disney World, Sea World, and the like, stay here at the **Altamonte Springs Inn and Racquet Club,** 151 N. Douglas Ave., off Hwy. I-4 at Rte. 436 (tel. 305/869-9000). This hotel provides handsomely for the racquet set; it has nine courts, instruction, a resident pro, clinics—the works for tennis buffs. There are also very attractive quarters here, decorated in bright colors and located so you can watch the action on the courts. There's a pool in which to cool off and a coffee shop and dining room to keep you in chow (price range $8 to $15 for dinner entrées). Rates for two at the Inn and Racquet Club are $40 to $49 double all year.

Sheraton operates a resort called **Sheraton Resort Inn** in the little town of Clermont, smack in the middle of citrus country. You'll find it on U.S. 192 and 27 (tel. 813/424-2621 or toll free 800/325-3535). There are 194 spacious, comfortable rooms here on extensive grounds that also harbor an Olympic-size swimming pool, game room, playground, lounge, and dining room with moderately priced offerings. It's just six miles from Disney World, and rates for two are $38 to $52 year round.

Nearby, about four miles south on U.S. 27, is a condominium resort, **Vacation Village** (tel. 904/394-4091), where apartments have lofts, cedar paneling, spiral staircases with bedrooms upstairs in those lofts and downstairs as well. Eight can settle in here and enjoy a sandy beach on Lake Louisa, barbecue cookouts, shuffleboard, badminton, volleyball, and canoeing. Greenery and a woodsy atmosphere make this a restful respite from the miles of neon, and rates are restful, too: $43 to $50 double ($240 to $275 a week) from mid-December to mid-April and $38 to $45 in other months, children under 18 free.

Every time I visit Orlando I find a new treasure for my "memorable places" file. Howey-in-the-Hills is one of those, a little village hidden in the rolling citrus land. Here, too, is a special place called **Mission Inn** (30 miles northwest of Orlando on U.S. 19; tel. 904/324-3101, toll free 800/874-9053), which rises up like a California mirage. Naturally, it has a Spanish theme that permeates the 100 spacious rooms and four suites which feature panoramic views of the countryside or of an 18-hole golf course on hotel grounds.

It's small and a well-kept secret among those who have learned of its charms, as it has all the extras you'd expect to find in a big-city resort from pool to pro shop, from golf carts and tennis courts to games and fishing, boating and water skiing in lakes on the grounds or nearby. Located about 30 miles from Disney World and five miles east of the Florida Turnpike on Route 19, the resort can arrange limousine service from Orlando's airport with 48 hours notice and can see to it you get to Disney World as well. A double room is $64 to $70 in fall, $92 to $98 from February to May. Spacious suites and villas range from $150 to $210 in winter, $25 to $50 less in other seasons. Money-saving golf and tennis packages are available too.

Haines City is a tiny burg near Cypress Gardens, only about a 30-minute drive to Disney World through some pretty country. Here you'll find a posh golf resort called **Grenelefe Golf and Tennis Resort,** 3200 Rte. 546 (tel. 813/422-7511 or toll free 800/237-9459; in Florida 800/282-7875). One of the state's top golf and condominium resorts, Grenelefe has 950 acres of green grounds dotted with shady pines and huge spreading live oaks.

Condominium resorts always offer you plenty of living space in your quarters, and Grenelefe is no exception. All apartments are large, individually decorated by owners who must, nevertheless, meet rigid equipment standards. You'll find contemporary touches like lots of glass, wide dressing areas, big walk-in closets, kitchens equipped with everything from food processors to church keys, high sloping ceilings, and private balconies where you can enjoy some sweeping vistas of woodland paths.

Eighteen of the resort's 36 holes of golf are rated among the top in the state. If you're not a golfer, there are four swimming pools, a spa and sauna, tennis courts, and several restaurants and lounges. Double accommodations are $105 to $240 in peak winter season, $48 to $160 in other months; children under 18 are free. If you'd like to have the resort staff come get you at the airport, that can be arranged for an additional fee.

Last, and in some respects least, is a place for those *really* dedicated to a tan. Called **Cypress Cove**, it's the state's largest nudist resort, located about 11 miles south of Kissimmee on Route 2 (tel. 305/348-5870). No, I have not seen all there is to see here, but there is a lake, tennis courts, canoes, paddleboats, a campground, and rental units. Admission is $3.65, and you can rent a two-bedroom trailer for $37 to $42.

CAMPING: You can't miss **Yogi Bear's Jellystone Park Campground**—the bear's face is on billboards all over town. There are three of these parks in the area, but the closest to Disney World is a pretty wooded 700-site campground just four miles west of the park on U.S. 192 (8555 W. Spacecoast Pkwy., Kissimmee; tel. 305/351-4394 or toll free 800/558-2954). You'll find a lake here, a mini-golf course, boating and fishing, a grocery store, restaurant, and gift shop, not to mention all kinds of special events. Rates of $16.75 include water, electric, and sewage hookup. Tent sites also are available for $12.25.

Second of Yogi's hangouts is a 500-site campground ten miles east of Disney World (9200 Turkey Lake Rd., just off Hwy. I-4, Orlando; tel. 305/351-4394, or toll free 800/558-2954). The third is about 30 miles away in Apopka (U.S. 1, Box 2000, Apopka; tel. 305/889-3048 or toll free 800/558-2954). Rates and facilities are similar at all the campgrounds, with prices about $4 lower at the Apopka site.

Camping World Campground (5175 U.S. 192, Kissimmee; tel. 305/846-3424 or toll free 800/327-9153, or in Florida 800/432-9196), a massive place with a long list of facilities ranging from fishing and shuffleboard to game room, movies, bike and paddle boat rentals, weekend entertainment, and a fancy tropical rock-bedecked swimming pool. It's about five miles east of the gates to Disney World and charges $16.95 for two adults, no charge for children under 18, and additional adults pay $1.50, including water, electric, and the rest of those camping necessities. Tenters pay the same rates.

Chapter IV

DINING IN DISNEY WORLD AND ORLANDO

NOT LONG AGO I heard a stress expert admonish an audience to spend less time worrying, since there's no end to what you can find to worry about and no "cure" for a worry anyway. (No, he didn't say what to do if you're worried about worrying!)

Which brings me to good news for those who may be harboring some niggling worries about the quality, quantity, availability, variety, price, etc., of food in Orlando and Disney World. If you're even a little concerned, here's some advice: Don't be. Finding a restaurant in the price, quality, and atmospheric bracket you're seeking is not a problem in Central Florida; it's finding a square block *without* a tempting restaurant on it that's a real challenge.

If you doubt me, let it be known that in Disney World alone, there were no less than 75 restaurants before they added a dozen or so more at EPCOT—and that's not counting the umpteen popcorn stands, ice cream wagons, chocolate-covered-frozen-banana purveyors, and other vendors in the Magic Kingdom, *and* it's not counting hotel restaurants in Lake Buena Vista's Walt Disney World Hotel Plaza!

Don't think, either, that the restaurants in Orlando are only inside Disney World. The entrepreneurs clever enough to lure a Disney World to a herd of cow pastures in the middle of nowhere were not zany enough to overlook the profit possibilities in the thousands of visitors streaming through the gates of Mouseland who would sooner or later want to exchange silver for golden fried. A large number of those visitors being children, theirs were the first gastronomic desires to be satisfied. Thus in the early days of its boom, Orlando and environs rapidly became hog heaven for fast food freaks.

It wasn't long, however, before burger-and-chicken creators

discovered they could turn their culinary knowledge into even bigger dollars by creating restaurants for the palates of more discerning diners. Thus were born the architecturally impressive and gastronomically top-notch eateries that soon were showing up on respected lists of the nation's best dining spots.

If you want to get your own look at the range from sublime to . . . well, less sublime in dining spots hereabouts, ride over to the suburb of Winter Park, Central Florida's gastronomic capital, and take a look at some enchanting dining spots behind Tiffany glass windows and in tiny courtyards.

Then to satisfy that craving for a double burger, hold the mayo, two orders of fries, and a shake, head for International Drive, where you'll find representatives of what seem to be every fast food chain in the world—there's Pizza Hut, Arby's, Wendy's, McDonald's, Burger King, Denny's, International House of Pancakes, Perkins Cake and Steak, Steak and Ale, Cork and Cleaver, Bennigan's, and Baskin Robbins . . . and more, all on one very short street!

Because Disney World is such a big place, to simplify your selecting I've listed restaurants located within the Magic Kingdom and inside EPCOT in Chapters VII and VIII. That way, if hunger strikes as you tour the Magic Kingdom or EPCOT, you can look right at the walking maps to discover which of the many restaurants is nearest you.

In this chapter, I've listed under restaurants *in* Disney World, those top spots throughout Disney World (including hotels in Walt Disney World Hotel Plaza) that I think you'll enjoy visiting for a leisurely meal, which usually means dinner, but can also be lunch and, at some spots, a sumptuous breakfast/brunch. Reservations are a must at some Disney World restaurants (and may be made up to 45 days in advance!). At the end of this section on "Restaurants in Disney World," I've put together a list of restaurants that take reservations and their phone numbers.

Listed under restaurants in Orlando are some of the best choices in that city and in all the smaller outlying cities in this region—Winter Park, Fern Park, Altamonte Springs, Kissimmee, and more.

Restaurants in Disney World

Let's start right at the top. To my mind that's the glorious, glamorous **Empress Lilly,** a gleaming craft that looms up out of Lake Buena Vista like a ghostly dream. Named after Walt Disney's wife, this glittering tripledecker riverboat is Disney at its best: a fairyland of tiny white lights, the burnished glow of polished brass and mahogany, the sweeping elegance of velvet, damask, gingerbread trim, Victorian furniture, wide staircases, and etched glass. Even if you don't get a chance to try one of the three plush dining rooms here, don't miss stopping by for a visit. Try to go at night, when the twinkling lights that ring the Empress's polished decks turn this permanently moored and entirely fanciful creation into a fantasyland par excellence.

As you stroll the Promenade Deck you'll find one of Disney World's most elegant—and most expensive—restaurants, **The Empress Room.** Lining the room are ornate moldings covered with $8000-worth of gold leaf, and overhead is a massive brass chandelier dripping with shimmering crystals. Damask wallpaper, etched glass, handsome paneling, and a hushed atmosphere broken only by the delicate notes of harp melodies make this room a spot the French kings of Versailles fame would have found quite adequate, *merci.*

There's a handsome forest-green lounge for predinner imbibing and, as you might expect, prices match the upper-crust ambience. Entree prices, for example, can go as high as $32.50 for dishes like oyster-stuffed veal chops or saddle of wild boar, but most entrees fall in the $15 to $20 category—figure $35 to $40 per person for dinner. Other tempters on the menu here include pâtés, chilled avocado soup, smoked duck with creamed horseradish, chicken in a sauce of cream and cider, and fresh mushroom salad; everything's à la carte. The Empress Room is open 6 to 9:30 p.m. daily, and jackets are required.

If you're not prepared to shell out shekels in those quantities, there are two other dining rooms on the Empress Lilly that are almost as tempting: the Steerman's Quarters and the Fisherman's Deck.

In the **Steerman's Quarters** you'll find yourself surrounded by heavy mahogany furnishings set off by a deep shade of red, wainscoting, and flower-sprigged wall coverings. Beef is king here, with several kinds of steaks and prime rib topping the list, and a delicious cheesecake bringing up the menu's aft end. Prices for entrees are in the $10 to $15 range, and the Steerman's Quarters is open 11 a.m. to 3 p.m. and 5:30 to 11 p.m.

Seafood is the center of attention in the **Fisherman's Deck** restaurant. Located on the forward promenade deck, its curving glass window overlooks the glittering lake outside. The decor is blue velvet and the atmosphere is sophisticated and glittering, in this bilevel room where entree prices run in the $12 to $18 range. The hours are the same as the Steerman's Quarters.

Dress aboard the Empress Lilly is dressy, with jackets required for men after 11 a.m. There's valet parking near the boat. No reservations are accepted at the Steerman's Quarters or the Fisherman's Deck, you just give your name to the host or hostess and wait in the Victorian elegance of the lounges aboard. In the Empress Room, however, reservations are required and can be made up to 30 days in advance at 828-3900.

Finally, if you just want to have some fun without food, stop by the **Baton Rouge Lounge,** where banjos twang, guitarists strum, and there's a laugh-it-up good time going until 1 a.m. daily. More on that subject in Chapter V's nightlife rundown.

Running neck-and-neck for top honors in Disney dining is the **Polynesian Village's Polynesian Revue,** often called the Luau. You dine on typical luau cuisine, including a taste of poi, chicken, pork, and spareribs, while graceful hula hands tell tales of the South Pacific. This is one of the best Polynesian shows in the state, since many of the dancers have trained at Hawaii's famed Polynesian Cultural Center. There are two shows nightly in winter at 5 and 7:45 p.m., and in summer a third at 10 p.m., when the culinary offerings are limited to platters of fruit and cheese. Show and dinner prices are $17 for adults, $14 and $9.50 for children at the first two shows, a few dollars less at the last production. Reserve a seat for these popular productions—824-8000.

That's the major production nightly, but you can also feast on roast meats and the flavors of the Orient and Polynesia at the hotel's **South Seas Dining Room,** where prices are $8.25 adults, $4.75 children.

Breakfast is a specialty at **Papeete Bay Verandah,** where you'll find a breakfast buffet that becomes a massive brunch on Sundays. Set aside a little resting and digesting time after one of these gargantuan repasts, which include fresh fruit, crepes, smoked fish, and all the breakfast goodies you can imagine.

Lunch is a sumptuous buffet here, too, and dinner features some interesting tropical touches like coconut milk marinades, entrees steamed in leaves, pork served with peanuts and bananas, and honey-dipped chicken, all served beside the Seven Seas Lagoon, with the turrets of Cinderella's Castle glittering in the distance. You can't match that, even in Polynesia!

Lunch (11:30 a.m. to 2:30 p.m.) is $6 adults, $4.25 children under 12; breakfast (8 to 10:30 a.m.) is $4.50 adults, $3 children;

and Sunday brunch $7.75 adults, $4.75 children. Dinner is $10 to $14 at Papeete Bay Verandah, and reservations can be made at 824-8000.

Similar breakfasts and dinners are available at the **Tangaroa Terrace** dining room near the Oahu longhouse and the hotel's coffee shop, **Coral Isle Café**, which also serves lunch. Duck with macadamia nuts is an unusual dinner specialty at Tangaroa Terrace, and french toast made with sourdough bread and bananas is a breakfast feature at both spots. Prices are similar to those in the Papeete Bay Verandah. Reservations can be made at 824-2000.

Coconut hot dogs? You betcha. At the hotel's **Barefoot Snack Bar** and **Tangaroa Snack Isle**, both open for snacks from lunch through dinnertime.

For sophisticated top-name entertainment and dining combined, the **Contemporary Resort** is the spot. Here in a 15th-floor aerie you feast on American and Continental favorites like steaks, prime rib, and seafood while the lights of the Magic Kingdom glitter in the distance and, at special times of year, fireworks explode overhead.

The **Top of the World** is a popular spot for breakfast, lunch, and Sunday brunch too. Prices for breakfast and lunch buffets are the same as the Polynesian's prices, but a champagne brunch is $9.50 adults, $7.50 children 12 to 17, and $4.75 for younger children.

A favorite of mine in this exciting hotel is the **Gulf Coast Room** where the pace is leisurely. A cool quiet island in the stream of visitors that flows through this hotel, the Gulf Coast Room offers excellent continental cuisine, like New York strip steaks with an herbed butter, veal Marsala, and seafood specialties for prices in the $9 to $13 range. After dinner, settle back with a flaming coffee concoction and let the world roll by as you listen to the quiet music of a strolling guitarist. Reservations are a good idea, since one or two others have discovered my secret hideaway: Call 824-1000.

Buffets are popular at Disney World, and you'll find another one each evening—an all-you-can-eat extravaganza—in the Contemporary's **Terrace Café**, which also is open for breakfast. No reservations are taken for dinner, when the buffet price is $6.50 adults, $4.25 children. At breakfast, Disney characters entertain from 8 to 11 a.m. Prices are $4.85 adults, $3.25 children.

Terrace Buffeteria, which like the Terrace Café is located on the Grand Canyon Concourse of the hotel, caters to early birds and nightowls with its 7 a.m. to midnight hours. Here you find a wide array of breakfast dishes, soups, salads and sandwiches, chicken, fish, and the like for dinner and lunch. It's open for all three meals, and prices are in the $5 range.

Those in search of cholesterol-free diet goodies can find sustenance at the **Pueblo Room,** a quiet spot on the Grand Concourse behind Coconino Cove. Breakfast, lunch, and dinner feature all the usual choices plus seafood, veal, prime ribs, and some fancy poultry dishes for evening dining. There's a special menu for the small fry, too. Prices are in the under-$10 range, and it's open for all meals.

More dining spots in the Contemporary? Of course. The **Outer Rim,** where you can dine overlooking Bay Lake on chicken cordon bleu, shrimp scampi, or prime ribs ($9 to $12); the **Fiesta Fun Center** for snacking; and the **Dock Inn** at the marina for subs and great frozen bananas.

A little farther afield (but not far) from the Magic Kingdom is the **Golf Resort** which sports a Trophy **Room Restaurant.** Sneak off here when things are busy at the other restaurants in Walt Disney World, and odds are you'll slip right into an empty spot and be glad you did. Because the Golf Resort is a little off the beaten track (see Chapter II's discussion of hotels in Disney World), fewer people know about it, so it's less likely to be packed with day visitors. It's every bit as good and as attractive as any of the other restaurants in the World, too, and features more of those gigantic all-you-can-gorge breakfast and lunch buffets (same prices) plus impressive dinner cuisine that can range from fresh oysters, crab, and shrimp, or a platter of vegetable appetizers to entrees of seafood, poultry in creamy sauces, pink prime rib, topped off by a house specialty, french-fried ice cream. What's that? Would I spoil the surprise? The Trophy Room is open for three meals daily, and dinner's in the $9 to $14 range. You can make reservations at 824-2200.

For snacks at this resort it's the **Sand Trap,** a poolside eatery serving lunch and dinner as well as basic survival sustenance.

Finally, at Fort Wilderness the **Trail's End Café** offers a down-home atmosphere of logs and heavy beams with country fixin's to match. Those of you who feel the day's gotten off to a bad start if you haven't launched into biscuits and gravy can satisfy those cravings here for under $4. At other hours of the day, you'll find the likes of chicken pot pie, hot dogs and beans, spareribs, steaks, prime ribs, saucy ham, and roast turkey—simple foods, simply prepared and presented, perfect for those days when you're fed up to here with snacks or haute cuisine. There are specially priced items for children and a make-your-own pizza every night from 9 p.m. to 12:30 a.m.

Snacking spot at the campgrounds is the **Campfire Snack Bar,** where reside all the hot dogs, chili dogs, hamburgers, and such you can consume.

Moving right along now to Walt Disney World Village—when you're at the Golf Resort, you're almost there. When you do indeed arrive at this tastefully designed shopping mall, you'll find a bevy of restaurants as well.

Tops among these is the **Verandah Restaurant,** a plant-filled spot serving breakfast, lunch, and dinner at moderate prices. Bigger-than-a-bite sandwiches are the specialty here at lunch, as are oysters en brochette. At a dinner you can feast on continental dishes like beef Wellington, seafood platters, prime ribs, and veal parmesan. Prices for dinner are in the $9 to $12 range; for lunch and breakfast you'll spend in the vicinity of $5. The Verandah's open from 9 a.m. to 10 p.m. daily.

If you like to see water rippling by as you dine, you'll love the **Village Restaurant,** another gardener's delight, filled with plants and sporting a lovely view of Buena Vista Lagoon. Lunch on a light seafood salad or an omelet stuffed with artichoke hearts, or try a dinner of beef or seafood specialties. After dinner settle into a plump couch in the Village Lounge, lean back and listen to the sound in the area's number-one jazz club. Dinner prices are in the $10 to $14 range, lunch in the $4 to $7 bracket, and there's a $2-per-set cover charge evenings in the lounge. The Village is open for lunch and dinner daily.

A popular place in the village is **Cap'n Jack's Oyster Bar,** which, as you might guess, carries a fair supply of those bivalves plus just about every other kind of seafood treat you can dream up—ceviche (marinated raw fish that's much better than it sounds), clams, shrimp, crab claws, and smoked kingfish. The atmosphere's informal, tropical, and fun. Try one of the special frozen daiquiris or margaritas in monstrous glasses to get things off to a ripping start. Lunch and dinner are served daily, and the price range for dinner is about $10 to $15, for lunch about $5.

Heidelberger's Deli looks just like a Heidelberg spot, but the food tastes like a New York deli, perhaps minus a few of the umpteen selections you find in Big Apple delis. You can choose among several varieties of breads and dozens of cheeses and meats, then chow down on the extras, which include everything

from baked beans to applesauce and imported or homegrown
beers. For the ultimate Florida experience, dine outside on the
terrace under a shower of blossoms from the trees that shade this
cozy spot. Inside ceilings are high, and there are lots of tropical
touches. In either locale prices are in the $5 range. Open for
lunch and dinner daily.

If you like country clubs, you'll love **Lake Buena Vista Club,**
where you'll often find room even when things are jammed at
other hotel and Magic Kingdom restaurants. Here they go all
out to provide enormous breakfasts which, on Sundays, are
brunch feasts ($7.95 adults, $5.75 children 3 to 11). Eggs in all
styles including Florentine (with spinach and Hollandaise
sauce), fruit-filled crepes laced with vanilla sauce, and salads
brimming with crisp vegetables or tropical fruit. Lunches and
dinners are pleasant, too, in this serene spot overlooking a golf
course, and a particular specialty at those meals is a meal-in-a-
bowl onion soup covered with cheeses. Dinner prices run about
$12 to $20 for entrees, and lunch will cost about $4 to $7. For
dinner and brunch, make reservations at 828-3735. Jackets are
required for dinner.

Fast food? Of course, at **Lite Bite,** which has burgers, dogs—
like that. Prices: $1 to $2.

Whether or not you're staying in Walt Disney World Village
Hotel Plaza (which includes Dutch Inn, Hotel Royal Plaza,
TraveLodge, Buena Vista Palace, and Howard Johnson hotels,
see Chapter III), you can pop into these conveniently located
hotel restaurants. Since they're all located on Disney grounds,
they're not far from the Magic Kingdom and EPCOT and make
a pleasant respite from the activities and crowds there.

At **Dutch Inn** you'll find two dining spots, the **Tulip Cafe**
coffee shop, which is open 24 hours a day with the usual coffeeshop fare in the $5 to $10 range, and the much more elaborate
Flying Dutchman. In the Flying Dutchman you'll dine in an
elegant atmopshere on an all-you-can-eat breakfast buffet, fat
sandwiches and the like at lunch, and seafood, steak, veal, and
plenty of fresh fish at dinner. Dinner entrees are $10 to $15.

If you're up at 7 a.m. and still going strong at midnight, you
can find something to eat at **Hotel Royal Plaza's Knight's Table**
coffee shop (prices $3 to $8), which also serves pizza out of the
ovens evenings. For atmosphere and leisurely dining, the hotel's
El Cid restaurant is the place. Heavy on Spanish atmosphere—
carved dark wood, red trimmings, pewter platters, and the like—
El Cid counts among its specialties such beef and seafood special-

ties as steak Diane and Chateaubriand and Maine lobster. Prices are in the $12 to $17 range for dinner, and hours are 5:30 to 11 p.m.

Howard Johnson's needs, as they say, no introduction. You already know that their fried clams are unbeatable, their ice cream a national passion, and their other offerings simple and predictable. Ho Jo's is open 24 hours a day and has a creditable, round salad bar in its restaurant here. Prices are in the $10-and-under range.

Sleepy Bear's Ice Cream Parlor is the favorite of youngsters and not-so-young-sters alike at **TraveLodge.** Breakfast and lunch buffets in the $5 range, and basic beef and seafood dishes ($10 to $15) are served in the **Coral Grotto.**

Finally, **a few tips** on dining at Disney World. If you can, try to avoid the most popular dining hours, 8 to 10 a.m., 11 a.m. to 1 p.m., and 7 to 9 p.m. During those hours, the popular breakfast and lunch buffets at Walt Disney World hotels and at restaurants within the Magic Kingdom and EPCOT are busy. Resign yourself to waiting in line. It will be worth it, though, since the Disney folks do go out of their way to please you.

If you're one of those people who goes berserk in lines, consider leaving the Kingdom or EPCOT at lunchtime and trying some of the restaurants at hotels in the World or in the WDW Shopping Village (although Village restaurants are busy on weekends when local residents come here to shop).

Best bet is to get in on the early or late end of popular dining times, or avoid them altogether by snacking.

At dinner, particularly during the busiest days at the park (see Chapter VIII), make reservations—and at the most popular restaurants (for instance, Polynesian Village's luau show, Top of the World at the Contemporary, Fort Wilderness's show, King Stefan's in Cinderella's Castle, and Liberty Tree Tavern in Liberty Square) make them as far in advance as possible—some shows can be sold out up to a year in advance!

Here's a quick at-a-glance rundown of **Disney World reservation numbers** for those spots which take reservations:

Contemporary Resort: Gulf Coast Room, 824-1000; Top of the World, 824-8000.

Polynesian Village: Papeete Bay Verandah and Tangaroa Terrace, 824-2000; Polynesian Revue (luau), 824-8000.

Golf Resort: Trophy Room, 824-2200.

Magic Kingdom: At King Stefan's in Cinderella's Castle and Liberty Tree Tavern in Liberty Square, reservations must be made in person on the day you're dining, so make that your first stop on arrival at the Magic Kingdom.

Walt Disney World Village: Empress Room on the Empress Lilly, 828-3900, and Lake Buena Vista Club, 828-3735.

Fort Wilderness: Hoop-Dee-Doo Musical Revue at Pioneer Hall, 824-8000.

In general, you can make reservations up to 45 days in advance if you're staying in a Disney World Hotel and up to 30 days if you're bunking down elsewhere. Two exceptions: Reservations for the Top of the World's show can be made no sooner than 21 days before that show, and reservations in the Empress Room may be made 30 days in advance, no matter where you're staying.

Restaurants in Orlando and Surrounding Cities

Dinner in an elegant garden? Or surrounded by the bejeweled glitter of Tiffany glass windows? In an old Florida inn or under the glow of chandeliers in a fountain-trimmed mansion?

You can try all that and more right here in Central Florida, where some of the most glamorous restaurants in the state are waiting to welcome you.

Supplementing those are dozens of small, family-run dining rooms, jeans-and-cotton-shirt spots where the atmosphere is cozy, intimate, and informal, the cuisine homey and all-American.

Because the decision on where to go for dinner is usually made by considering what kind of food you want, I've listed some of the area's most popular options by culinary specialty. You'll have fun trying them and even more fun finding your own candidates for "best restaurant" here in the land the mouse built.

Remember that, unless otherwise specified, the prices I've cited are for entrees, which usually, but not always, include salad, one or two vegetables, and perhaps coffee as well.

AMERICAN CONTINENTAL: Golden light streams through a glass roof and glimmers on formal silver place-settings, etched- and smoked-glass mirrors, lovely linens, and the green leaves of dozens of plants at **Park Plaza Gardens,** 319 Park Ave. S., Winter Park (tel. 645-2475). This small jewel of a restaurant overwhelms you with good things like seafood bisque, exotic shrimp in curry sauce, flounder meunière, wiener schnitzel, and baked Alaska. Open from 11:30 a.m. to 3 p.m. and 6 to 11 p.m.

daily, Park Plaza Gardens is a serene spot. You'll pay about $10 to $15 for dinner at this attractive hideaway next door to the quaint Park Plaza Hotel.

I've already raved about the Gold Key Inn, 7100 S. Orange Blossom Trail (tel. 855-0050), so I'll continue the raves with a review of the Inn's cozy **Picadilly Restaurant.** Long an award-winner for its cuisine and attractive decor, this pretty publike spot serves you on pewter plates, and surrounds you with the gleam of polished wood. The Picadilly is bright with candles and fresh flowers, and provides a charming atmosphere in which to dine on roast beef with Yorkshire pudding, rack of lamb, or baked clam pie. Prices are in the $10 to $15 range. The restaurant is open for dinner from 5:30 to 10:30 p.m. and for other meals from 7 a.m.

Longwood Village Inn can be a little tricky to find but it's worth the map search. Located in a sleepy Old Florida village outside Orlando (take Hwy. I-4 to the Rte. 434 exit, then drive east to Rte. 427, then north two blocks; tel. 834-5555), this inn ranks among the most picturesque in Florida. Built in 1883, Longwood was once a hotel and now is glamorous again under the tutelage of owner Penny Colechio, who sees that the antiques, glittering chandeliers, high ceilings, and paned-glass windows stay sparkling and the atmosphere remains welcoming. Longwood prides itself on its home cooking and bakes its own breads, creates its own salad dressings, sees to it that only fresh vegetables appear on the table, and cuts your steak to order. So charming is this serene and shady spot that it's become a popular wedding site as well. Prices for some very good food in these enchanting surroundings are about $7 to $12. The inn is open for breakfast from 7 to 11 a.m. Monday through Saturday, for lunch from 11 a.m. to 2:30 p.m., and for dinner from 5 to 10 p.m. Monday through Saturday, closed Sundays. There's entertainment in the lounge until midnight Friday and Saturday.

Sometimes the simplest way to get the message across is just to say it right out. That's just what they did at **Two Flights Up,** 329 Park Ave. S., Winter Park (tel. 644-9868), a chic contemporary spot that is two flights up, in a building that was once the old Colony Theater. These days it's celebrating a renaissance as a tiny but fascinating boutique enclave which includes this plant-bedecked restaurant, lighted by skylights and furnished in wicker with sprigged tablecloths. Try one of the mouthwatering veal specialties, the fine seafood selections, steaks, or, my downfall, fettuccine Alfredo, and fudge pie. After that, you'll be thankful for the exercise you get as you go two flights down on the way out. Prices are in the $10 to $15 range, and Two Flights Up is open from 11:30 a.m. to 12:30 a.m.; the lounge is open to 2 a.m. Monday through Saturday.

Not far from Disney World in the Orlando Hyatt Hotel is a spot called **Limey Jim's Restaurant,** at Hwy. I-4 and U.S. 192, (tel. 846-4100 or 422-3106 from Orlando). Just where they got that name is anybody's guess, so spend some time contemplating that enigma while downing all manner of delicacies ranging from steak au poivre to a palate-cleansing sherbet to liqueur-laced après-diner café. You'll pay about $14 to $18 for dinner in a quiet, elegant atmosphere blessed with top-notch service and the soft melodies of a harpist. Limey Jim's is open from 6 to 10:30 p.m. daily.

When Harley Hotels transformed a doddering old downtown hotel into the number-one downtown glamour spot, they didn't stop at the restaurant door. Here at **Café on the Park,** 151 E. Washington, Orlando (tel. 841-3220), you'll find a place with decor as inviting as the food that's prepared in the kitchen. What's more the view out over glittering Lake Eola, with its spouting fountain, is terrific, too. A bevy of mirrors here reflect delicate shades of peach, fresh flowers, shining tableware and many a smiling face chowing down on the likes of steak Diane, veal, lobster, shellfish, and flaming desserts. On Sunday the brunch stretches for a mile or so, beginning with champagne cocktails and working through enough food to keep you going for a week or so. It's $11.50 adults, $6.95 children. Because it's part of a hotel, the dining room is open all day long, but the highlights are the Sunday brunch from 11 a.m. to 3 p.m.; the luncheon buffet 11 a.m. to 2 p.m. ($6.25), weekdays only; and dinner from 6 to 10 p.m. daily.

Step right up and hear all about the fun and frolic at the Rosie O'Grady Church Street Station emporium in Chapter V, but listen here to a word about Rosie's top restaurant, **Lili Marlene's Aviator Restaurant,** 129 Church St. in Church Street Station (tel. 422-2434). Lili Marlene's is a comparatively quiet spot in this never-a-dull-moment entertainment complex. It's pretty, too: full of antiques, including a walnut fireplace once the possession of the Rothschilds, massive furniture trimmed in velvet, lots of oak peneling, and stained glass. Take refuge here for a quiet dinner before you venture into the zany atmosphere that prevails in the rest of Rosie's. Steaks, seafood, and occasional French culinary touches are the fare at Lili Marlene's, where you'll pay about $15 to $20 for dinner, which is served from 5:30 p.m. to midnight daily. Lunch is served from 11:30 a.m. to 4 p.m.

BASQUE: It's rare to find Basque food outside Spain, rarer still to find it here in Central Florida, but here it is at **Meson de España**, 2417 E. South St. at Bumby Ave. in Orlando (tel. 896-9716). A little touch of that interesting northern Spanish cuisine has proven popular, for example: caldo gallego soup (thick with sausage and beans), and shellfish topped with a parsley-laced sauce and served steaming in a metal bowl. Bright red tablecloths and napkins folded like Spanish fans form the backdrop for an intriguing culinary experience at moderate prices in the $10 to $15 range. Meson de España is open from 5 to 10 p.m. Tuesday through Sunday.

CHINESE: Seven stars around the moon, please. What on earth is that? Well, it's lobster, pork, chicken, snowpea pods, mushrooms, baby corn, water chestnuts, bamboo shoots, and bok choy plus seven butterfly shrimp, that's what. And it's all here at **Jin Ho**, 400 S. Orlando Ave., Winter Park (tel. 628-2660), a casual spot that became so popular it was cloned in Altamonte Springs (on Maitland Ave., tel. 339-0790). That Seven Stars Around the Moon dish ($18.75 for two), by the way, is for two of the starving, or one desert-island escapee. Other tasty selections include lots of seafood and a sizzling wor bar with seafood and Chinese vegetables served over crisp rice patties. You won't break the bankroll either: Prices are in the $5 to $10 range. Open from 11 a.m. to 10:30 p.m. daily and from noon on Saturday and Sunday.

Another popular Oriental dining room is **Orient IV**, at 104 Altamonte Ave., Altamonte Springs (tel. 830-4444), where fire lovers will find spicy Szechuan cooking and the less adventurous can try some excellent Hunan cooking. Seafood, chicken, and beef in all those fascinating Chinese preparations are available here for prices in the $5 to $10 range. Hours are 11:30 a.m. to 3 p.m. Monday through Saturday for lunch, 3 to 10:30 p.m. Monday through Thursday for dinner (to 11 p.m. Friday and Saturday), and from 1:30 to 9:30 p.m. on Sunday.

FRENCH: Tiffany glass is worth a small fortune these days in even the smallest quantities, so as you dine at **La Belle Verrière**, 142 S. Park Ave., Winter Park (tel. 645-3377 or 642-02770), you can contemplate the size of the fortune displayed around you. The glowing stained-glass creations you see here are the works of Tiffany, that master craftsman, and they glow in all the colors of the rainbow. You'll glow, too, after lunch or dinner in this dramatic setting sparked by masses of plants and fresh flowers, brick and wood trim, and glimmering candles. On the menu you'll find such delicacies as vichyssoise, escargots bourguignonnes, chateaubriand, roast duck, rack of lamb, creme caramel, dusky chocolate mousse, and fresh oranges topped with rum and honey. The bottom line on your bill will be in the $10- to $15-per-person bracket for dinner entrees, which are served from 6 to 10 p.m. daily, lunch from 11:30 a.m. to 2:30 p.m. Closed Sunday.

Le Cordon Bleu, 537 W. Fairbanks Ave., Winter Park (tel. 647-7575), is not the most elaborately decorated restaurant you'll find in Central Florida, but from its kitchens pour some of the area's best-loved culinary triumphs: things like filet de boeuf royal baked in a puff pastry, pompano with white wine sauce and herbed filets, artichoke bottoms stuffed with crab and covered with Mornay sauce, escargots, duck, crisp breads, and sinful pastries baked right here. Many an award has been bestowed on this restaurant, and every one is well deserved. For a memorable dinner you'll pay about $11 to $17. Le Cordon Bleu is open Monday through Friday for lunch from 11:30 a.m. to 2:30 p.m. and for dinner from 5:30 to 11 p.m.; closed Sundays.

A Winter Park friend of mine swears she owes her Ms America proportions to a diet she pursues at **Maison des Crepes,** 348 Park Ave. (tel. 647-4469). Here's how it works, she says: She downs a couple of these paper-thin delicacies stuffed with creamy rich, incredibly delicious fillings, tosses off a crisp cold salad of spinach, mushrooms, and avocado, and perhaps a chilled glass of white wine . . . then doesn't eat for three days. Knowing what it's done for her, I'd certainly like to give this Winter Park Diet a shot. Perhaps it's not the Beverly Hills solution, but what a delicious way to porkerdom. Maison des Crepes is open 11:30 a.m. to 3 p.m. for lunch and 6:30 to 10 p.m. for dinner daily except Sundays. Prices are in the $10 range or less for dinner.

Last and far from least we come to **Maison et Jardin,** 430 S. Wymore Rd., Altamonte Springs, (take Hwy. I-4 to the Altamonte Springs exit, head west and turn left at the first road on the left) (tel. 862-4410). Be prepared to be swept off your feet by the dramatic beauty of this high-on-a-hill restaurant. Huge trees spread their massive branches over the grounds here, fountains burble, a stream meanders through the woods. From the moment you come up the shady drive, you are transported from the mundane to the marvelous. The "maison" is an elegant old home transformed into a warren of beautiful dining rooms. My favorite's the patio room, where a bay window offers a view of the perfectly manicured lawns bordered by tiny clumps of flaming flowers. Every room has its own delights, be it an ornate chandelier, a painting, or an elegant set of furniture. There's even an Austrian shade in the powder room! From the kitchen comes such specialties as wild rice bisque, mushrooms thermidor, zucchini and hearts of palm salad, veal Strasbourg, and pheasant Souvaroff. There's a wonderful Sunday brunch, too, and on the first Sunday of every month a jazz band entertains. A recent Orlando newspaper survey called this the area's favorite French spot, the restaurant with the best service, the most romantic restaurant, *and* the one with the most atmosphere! That fine service is formal, and your attire is expected to correspond, so jackets please, gentlemen. Hours are 6:30 to 10:30 p.m. Tuesday through Sunday, and from 11 a.m. to 2 p.m. for Sunday brunch. Dinner prices are in the $12 to $20 range, and Sunday brunch is likely to run about $10.

GREEK: You do recall that the world's original epicurean was that Greek Epicurus, so it's fitting that the Greek Jimmy Hansis should have named his **Epicurean Restaurant,** 7900 E. Colonial Dr. (tel. 277-2881) after his famous countryman. If you fancy grape leaves, creamy moussaka, the feta-strewn Greek salads and tangy olives, not to mention sarmades, pastitsio, lamb, and kalamarakia, drop in here. In the background is the soft twang of the bouzouki, perfect counterpoint to a cozy taverna atmosphere. Finish it all off with thick Greek coffee and that irresistible wafer-thin pastry stuffed with walnuts, drenched in honey, and called baklava. Heaven knows what a Greek—or any—chef can do with shark and alligator tail, but those are two of the latest items to join the list here. Epicurean is open from 11 a.m. to 11 p.m., an hour later on weekends, every day except Sunday. Entrees are in the $8 to $12 range.

ITALIAN: My favorite Italian restaurants are La Scala, Gus's Villa Rose, and Spinelli's.

Let's start with **La Scala,** 430 Lorraine Dr. at Douglas Rd., Altamonte Springs (tel. 862-3257), where former opera singer

Joseph del Vento brought both his vocal and his culinary talents some years ago. He named his new stage after an old one, and here he will show you why the Renaissance man was a product of Italy. Not only can del Vento sing, he can cook up veal sautéed with peas, prosciutto, and artichokes; red snapper with parsley, garlic, white wine, oregano, and lemon; fresh pastas; steaks; seafood; and veal. Prices are in the $10 to $15 range, and La Scala is open from 11:30 a.m. to 2:30 p.m. and from 5 to 11 p.m. daily, except Sunday, when hours are 5 to 9:30 p.m.

Next comes **Gus's Villa Rosa**, 5923 Old Winter Garden Rd., in the town of Orlo Vista (take Hwy. I-4 to Rte. 435 and drive north) (tel. 299-1950). Orlo Vista is not exactly a household word, but here in Central Florida Gus's place is well known in many a household. It's a great spot for pastas, veal, seafood, and steaks, all created under the watchful eye of Gus Stamatin, who has rung up a long list of culinary credentials. Your bill will ring on only in the $10 to $12 range, however. Here's a special tip: Try the shrimp Onassis with feta cheese. Mmmmm. Villa Rosa is open 11:30 a.m. to 2:30 p.m. daily for lunch and 4:30 to 11 p.m. for dinner.

Villa Nova Restaurant, 839 N. Orlando Ave., Winter Park (tel. 644-2060), has been holding forth here for more than 30 years. It was started by the D'Agostino family, and now is under the guidance of the skilled operators of Winter Park's very successful Park Plaza Gardens. Villa Nova features the northern Italian cuisine so loved by gourmets. You'll find such delicacies as carpaccio (raw beef filet in a piquant mayonnaise sauce), escargots in a red wine sauce served in puff pastry, mussels poached in white wine, fine steaks, fresh pastas, and a long list of veal and fish favorites from saltimbocca to filet of sole poached in white wine with clams, tomatoes, garlic, lemon, and cream. Very good food is served in several handsome, formal dining rooms for prices in the $12 to $15 range for entrees. They're open 11 a.m. to 11 p.m. daily and there's often entertainment in the lounge.

Spinelli's (1200 Pennsylvania Ave.; tel. 892-2435) is a major contribution to Italian dining in Central Florida and has earned a passel of awards to prove it. This elegant but not overpowering spot evokes the Mediterranean and is especially good at creating innovative approaches to old favorites like osso buco Milanese, eggplant, and pasta primavera topped with fresh vegetables. For a special treat try chicken stuffed with crabmeat. There are more than 100 entrees on the menu here, with most in the $10 to $12 price range for entrees. Spinelli's, which also features a wide variety of continental dishes, is open from 6 to 10 p.m. daily, Sunday 5 to 9 p.m., and for lunch from 11:30 a.m. to 2:30 p.m. Monday through Friday.

MEXICAN: You're already well south of most borders, but for a gastronomic trip even farther *sud,* try **El Torito,** 275 W. Hwy. 436 in Village Shoppes, Altamonte Springs (tel. 869-5061). A sassy margarita or two, a quesadilla, a tostada, perhaps some camarones flores wrapped in bacon and served with grilled pineapple and Mexican corn and, caramba! you'll be warbling en Español. For all this fun you'll probably pay considerably less than the $10 top menu price. The hours are 11 a.m. to 11 p.m. daily, later on weekends, and the lounge is open to 2 a.m.

Chi Chi's, 655 Maguire Blvd., Orlando (tel. 894-0655), is decorated in a contemporary style. A chain operation that's made a name for itself here and in many another locale, Chi Chi's delivers healthy margaritas, whopping tacos and tostados, and wild creations of all kinds. Plenty of choices here, where you'll probably pay well under $10 for chow (I'm not counting your margaritas but you'd better), available from 11 a.m. to midnight daily, later on weekends.

SEAFOOD: Orlando's quite a distance from the sea but that doesn't stop restaurateurs here from ferreting out some good fish, treating them kindly, and serving them up to you in some interesting surroundings.

A newcomer among those is **Brazil's,** 701 Orienta Ave., a block south of Rte. 436 on Maitland Ave. in Altamonte Springs (tel. 331-7260). A young couple, Steve and Lynn Watts, turned their talented hands toward creative seafood cookery only a year or so ago, and since then seafood lovers have been beating a path to their door. The emphasis is on fresh seafood with imaginative touches, creations like shrimp San Francisco (sautéed with fresh ginger, garlic, scallions, soy sauce, and dry sherry) and a crab sandwich on sourdough bread with melted cheese. You'll pay prices in the $9 to $13 range here, and the restaurant is open from 11:30 a.m. to 2:30 p.m. weekdays and 5:30 to 10:30 p.m. daily.

Wear your jeans and an expendable shirt, not to mention an expandable belt, when you try the **Chesapeake Crab House,** 1700 N. Orlando Ave., Maitland (tel. 831-0442). A small spot much frequented by local residents who delight in the informal atmosphere, the huge piles of crabs you hammer into shreds, and the big pitchers of beer. If you're looking for atmosphere, look elsewhere, but if you'd like to latch onto a hammer and pound away at some delectable stone crabs, head for the Chesapeake. Prices are in the $4 to $8 range (plus a $6.95 all-you-can-eat blue crab special). Doors open at 5:30 p.m. Monday through Saturday, close at 10 p.m. most nights, 11 p.m. Friday and Saturday, closed Sunday.

For more of the same atmosphere with a little different seafood focus, try **Lee and Rick's Oyster Bar and Seafood House,** 5621 Old Winter Garden Rd., Orlando (tel. 293-3587). Once again no atmosphere is almost an atmosphere of its own, but the center of attention here is oysters on the half shell, raw or steamed. Trenchermen can order oysters by the bucket and non-fans can choose rock shrimp by the dozen, smoked mullet (definitely an acquired taste), snapper, flounder, snow crab, or scallops, all washed down with pitchers of beer or sangria. Opening hour here is 11:30 a.m. Monday through Saturday, closing 11 p.m. (Sundays 4 to 10 p.m.). Your tab will be in the $6 to $8 range per person.

Gary's Duck Inn, 3974 S. Orange Blossom Trail (tel. 843-0270) has been around a long time and has racked up many awards for good seafood, simply prepared and presented in a casual atmosphere enjoyed by families, singles, couples—everyone. Gary's swears that if you stop here once you'll be back, and they must be right: They're approaching their 40th anniversary. Jumbo french-fried shrimp's a favorite with many habitués of Gary's, but there are plenty of other choices, including brimming seafood platters, lobster, scallops—you name it. You'll pay entree prices in the $10 to $15 range for dinner, which is available from 11:30 a.m. to 10 p.m. daily, later on weekends. Saturdays the doors open at 5 p.m.

Red Lobster, 4010 W. Vine St., Kissimmee (tel. 846-3513), probably won't be much of a surprise to you since this chain has spread far and wide. You'll find a casual comfortable atmosphere, plenty of what the name advertises, lots of other seafood choices, and even a few selections for those who can live forever without seafood. Prices are moderate at this family favorite—in the $8 to $10 range—and the Red Lobster's open daily from 11:30 a.m. to 10 p.m., later on weekends.

STEAKS: Probably the best-known and certainly one of the long-est-lived steak houses in the area is **Freddie's Steak House,** on Rte. 17/92 in Fern Park (tel. 339-3265), where a kind of good-ol'-boy masculinity has determined the decor and the menu. Not much fancy French stuff here, just big thick steaks, a brimming relish tray, crocks of cheddar cheese, several hearty breads, delicately pink prime rib, some seafood selections, ham glazed in rum, bananas, and coconut. You'll struggle out of here as content as the thousands who have preceded you. Bills will run in the $10 to $15 range, and Freddie's is open from 4:30 p.m. to 2 a.m. daily except Sunday. Entertainment in the lounge evenings.

I love restaurants that offer a challenge, and 2.5 pounds of T-bone is *definitely* a challenge. Where? **La Cantina,** 4721 E. Colonial Dr. (tel. 894-4491), where that beefeater's delight is offered on Wednesdays along with salad, bread, and spaghetti. I dare you. This gargantuan eating has been going on here for nigh onto 40 years, in an attractive dining room that features a fireplace, fountain, and sunken conversation pit. Beef is aged and cut right here, and when the butchers are not slashing away, they're stirring the sauce for delicious manicotti, ravioli, and veal. Prices are in the $10 to $15 range, and the restaurant's open from 5 p.m. to midnight Tuesday through Saturday.

Talk of the Town, 6107 S. Orange Blossom Trail, Orlando (tel. 851-7130), has been cloned all over Central Florida in Winter Haven, Lakeland, Clearwater, and St. Petersburg—which means they're pleasing many of the people much of the time with their steak and seafood offerings. You'll find the rarely featured lan-gostinos, tiny rock lobsters, here plus good steak and seafood dinners, which include onion soup, breads, and a hefty salad bar, all for prices in the $10 to $15 range. Even the little ones have a menu here with goodies to their taste and prices to yours. Talk of the Town is open from 11:30 a.m. to 10 p.m. daily (later on weekends).

Kissimmee is definitely not a culinary capital of Central Flori-da and I suspect there are those around this cow town who eat beef three times a day. Ahh, but change is upon us all, even little Kissimmee, where some very creative people have converted an old livery stable into the glittering **People's Place,** 200 Broadway (tel. 847-9327). To find this skylight-lit, gem of a restaurant in downtown Kissimmee is to be surprised indeed. Still there it is, complete with brass and shining crystal, greenery, navy linens, a cozy pub, and an upbeat trendy atmosphere. The owners oper-ate a similarly attractive steak-and-seafood spot, the **Orange**

Quarter, 70 N. Orange Ave., Orlando (tel. 452-2822). At either you'll find potatoes baked in rock salt and served with blue cheese, onions, bacon or crabmeat; sandwiches; crispy salads; and basic seafood, beef, and poultry dishes. Dinner prices are in the $10 to $12 range, and People's is open 11 a.m. to midnight daily, later in the lounge where there's entertainment. Sunday brunch is a special $8 treat, $4.75 for children, that continues as a dinner buffet until 8 p.m.

Barney's Steakhouse, 1615 E. Colonial Dr., Orlando (tel. 896-6865), gets rave reviews for its top-notch steaks and prime rib and seafood creations, and more top marks for a gigantic salad bar with more than 30 offerings to satisfy the rabbit in you. Many, many Orlandoites swear by Barney's which has been serving top-quality beef long enough to win a dedicated following. Try it, and you'll join the throngs. Lunch begins at 11:30 a.m., closes at 2:30 p.m. Monday through Friday, and dinner runs from 5 to 10 p.m. daily, an hour later on weekends. Prices are in the $9 to $14 range.

LIGHT MEALS: A mound of sherbet topped with fresh oranges, grapes, apples, and cantaloupe; crispy pecan waffles; yummy homemade ice cream; a gasp-able banana split; a towering Black Forest cake oozing with chocolate and cherries—do I have your attention? I thought so. The **East India Ice Cream Co.,** 327 Park Ave. S., Winter Park (tel. 628-2305), serves such delicacies by the carload every day of the week. There's no dearth of attendees here, you can bet, for two good reasons. One is those sin-laden desserts supplemented by huge deli sandwiches and crispy, crunchy salads; creamy cheesecakes; and strudels to die for. The other is the decor: brick walkways, an absolute jungle of growing things, paddle fans that cool inside, and a cozy little patio that lures al fresco diners outside. Prices are wonderful, too; most are in the $5 range. The East India Ice Cream Co. is open from 8:30 a.m. to midnight Monday through Thursday, to 1 a.m. on Saturday, and from 10 a.m. to midnight on Sunday.

BUDGET AND FAMILY SPOTS: Many are the fans of **Mack Meiner's Country Store,** 921 N. Mills Ave., Orlando (tel. 896-5902), where you down chili, soups, barbecued specialties, and heavenly hash pie in an atmosphere that's just what the restaurant's name implies. Add oilcloth and kitchen chairs, old movie posters and ads, a player piano and sheet music, and you've got a spot to tie on the feedbag while keeping the young ones amused. Prices are in the $5 range, and Mack's is open from 11 a.m. to 11 p.m. daily. Another operation under the same parasol is called **Café Society,** 120 N. Orange Ave. (tel. 425-6770), and it's in downtown Orlando's French Market area. Here the menu includes crepes, seafood, and eggs Benedict at similarly low prices. (Closed Sunday, however.)

Two longtime favorites in many areas of Florida are **Morrison's Cafeteria** and **Duff's Smorgasbord.** You'll find both in Orlando, Morrison's at 7440 International Dr. (tel. 351-0051), and Duff's at 965 W. SR 436, Altamonte Springs (tel. 862-5092).

Morrison's serves food much loved by many and plenty of it in very reasonable price brackets: $5 to $7 for dinner or less, depending on the state of your gluttony. It's open 7:30 to 10 a.m. and 11 a.m. to 8:30 p.m. There are three other Morrison's in Winter Park, Altamonte Springs, and on Colonial Drive.

Duff's features gigantic buffet spreads for lunch and dinner at outrageously inexpensive prices: $3.25 for adults, $1.75 to $2 for children! Hours are 11 a.m. to 8 p.m. daily.

Pianist George Shearing loves the matzoh ball soup, and jazz stars Count Basie and Maynard Ferguson have stopped by to sample the goodies at **Ronnie's,** 2702 E. Colonial Dr., in the Colonial Plaza Shopping Center, Orlando (tel. 894-2943). At Sunday breakfast you need a shoehorn to wedge yourself into the crowd here. No wonder. Prices in the $5 to $10 range for nearly anything in the place, less for many selections. Bowls of kosher dills and sauerkraut, cheesecake fluffy as cotton, rated the city's best by critics, guilt-spawning pastries—what are you waiting for? Hours are 7 a.m. to midnight daily, an hour later on weekends.

TGI Friday's, at 227 Rte. 436 West, Altamonte Springs (tel. 869-8085), is a place where the waiters are liable to break into song. Bells ring, things whir and buzz, and everyone has a great, if a little crazy, time here. There are several TGI Friday's in Florida, and all of them offer a multipage menu of soups and salads, desserts and appetizers, sandwiches and full-course meals. Things can get pretty weird here, but the food attracts the young with-it set, who munch happily away on potato skins and the like as waiters cavort among the moose heads and old buckets. Prices are in a reasonable under-$10 bracket, and hours are 11:30 a.m. to 2 a.m. daily. An outstanding Sunday brunch is on from 10:30 a.m. to 2:30 p.m.

Here's a place you'll find most anywhere you turn in Central

Florida: **Holiday House.** Therc are 13 of these attractive and inexpensive restaurants around, including one at 1522 Orange Ave. (tel. 425-1521), and another at 2037 Lee Rd., Orlando (tel. 293-4930), more in Winter Park, Mount Dora, and Deland. You eat well here, if simply, and are served likewise. Best news, however, is the price: $4.95 for a dinner buffet, $4.35 for lunch. They're open from 11 a.m. to 9 p.m. daily.

Two near-Disney motels also operate restaurants where the atmosphere is family-casual and the prices are, in a word, wonderful. First of these is the **Gaucho Room** at the Stagecoach Inn, 4311 W. Vine St., Orlando (that's really U.S. 192; tel. 846-4213) where dinner is likely to run less than $7, lunch less than $3.

Second is **Davis Brothers Motor Lodge,** 6603 International Dr. (tel. 351-2900), which has a long and luscious smorgasbord, all you can stuff, for $3 at breakfast, $3.50 for lunch, and $4.25 for dinner, children half price. It's open 7 to 10 a.m., 11 a.m. to 3 p.m. and 5 to 9 p.m.

Village Inn, 345 W. Fairbanks, Winter Park (tel. 645-5767), offers good food at reasonable prices in a quiet, attractive atmosphere. You'll pay about $4 to $7 for a long list of choices that range from steaks to fantail shrimp—and those prices include beverage and dessert. Hours are 6 a.m. to midnight Sunday through Thursday, 7 a.m. to 4 a.m. Friday and Saturday.

Some gourmets, or is that gourmands, of my acquaintance will drive to the ends of the earth for a product born and bred in the Midwest and called Chili Mac. Producer of this delicacy is none other than a chain operation called **Steak and Shake,** which much to the regret of a few, at least, operates in Florida only from Central Florida north. So if you're planning to head south after Disney, get your fix of Chili Mac here at 2820 E. Colonial Dr. (tel. 896-0827), where burger prices are under $2. There are other representatives of these midwestern gourmet delights scattered about town, too, and they're open from 10 a.m. to 11 p.m. daily, to 1 a.m. on weekends.

A SPECIAL PLACE: A restaurant called **Al E. Gator's** obviously doesn't fit into just any category, so I'm putting it in this special one, by itself. Well, on second thought, not all by itself, since Al E. Gator's must share billing with the rest of Sea World's fascinating **Florida Festival.** A maze of boutiques and restaurants, this intriguing creation by the Sea World people features dozens of food purveyors, each of them offering foods Floridians like to consider typically Floridian. That means you'll find a spot selling Cuban black beans and fried plantains; a Key West seafood booth serving glistening clams, oysters, and other raw-bar delights on beds of ice; a rum punch and daiquiri center; the list goes on and on. You can have one thing at one booth, one at another, and just munch your way around Florida without leaving this one fascinating spot. For entertainment while you dine, there's a center stage where lots of fun goes on as well as strolling magicians, clowns, and the like. It's great fun for all the family, all ages and interests. Oh, yes, I almost forgot what started all this: Al E. Gator's is Florida Festival's sit-down restaurant where you can try—are you ready?—a piece of alligator tail. Don't fret. Alligators have been so carefully protected in Florida, they're no longer an endangered species, so Sea World's Florida Festival can sell the meat and never fear the forest ranger. That, of course, is not all they offer at Al E. Gator's, far from it. There are sandwiches and full meals, salads and desserts, plenty of choices from cracked conch to crab quiche, and other exotic specialties like mango muffins and swamp cabbage (in fancy places outside the Everglades that's called hearts of palm!). Open daily from 11:30 a.m. to 11 p.m. (an hour later on weekends), the Florida Festival enclave is at Sea World, 7001 Sea World Blvd. (tel. 351-3326). Prices range from $1 to $3 for booth items, about $8 to $12 for full meals in Al E. Gator's.

Chapter V

AFTER DARK IN DISNEY WORLD AND ORLANDO

MATURE AND ADULT as you think you are, there will come a moment when you seriously consider pushing some little kid out of the way so you can get a better view of Mickey and Minnie as they go cavorting by in the Main Street Electrical Parade. While children love Disney World, adults who have learned all too much about the differences between reality and fantasy tend to worship this place.

Sooner or later, however, the general wear and tear of the crowds, the lines, the hot dogs and popcorn—the sheer thrilling exhaustion of it all—grinds away some of the magic for grown-ups. (Everyone knows those youngsters would go on riding the rides for a week, nonstop, if it weren't for the fun-squelching presence of parents.)

When the consensus finally reaches a no-more-that's-final stage, that is a sign it's time to ease off a bit, to slow down and consider taking a breather. Working on the assumption that parents are people, too, relief can come in the form of some evening entertainment that excludes ducks that quack jokes.

Because Central Florida is an area geared to families, you'll find plenty of wholesome entertainment that's as intriguing for adults as it is interesting to children. Fortunately, that means you can take the children with you, if you like, to many of the top fun spots and, in fact, to all activities inside Disney World where *wholesome* is practically emblazoned on the Disney family crest.

Orlando's not much on razzle-dazzle nightclubs though, so if that's your style, you'll have to travel a little farther south to Miami and environs or wait for a trip to Las Vegas. There is this good news, however: What entertainment you do find here is not expensive, so a night on the town won't cost you two days on the job.

One more thing: Except for the main events, which I'll outline, nightlife in the Orlando area changes frequently, so don't hold me to every word. Hotels and clubs that do offer diverting evening entertainment will always have something going, but you'd do well to give them a call to find out what exactly is happening this week or this season.

Here then is a look at the amusing and amazing ways you can spend an evening in Central Florida. Once again, I've divided all the action up into two parts. That way, if you're staying in or near Disney World and don't feel like straying far from home, you'll be able to see at a glance what's happening in WDW. On the other hand, if you feel like exploring a little, you can turn to the Orlando section of this chapter and—go.

In Disney World

Perhaps the most wonderful thing about fantasies is that you can have them any time, any place, at any hour of the night or day. That's probably part of the reason Disney World keeps its fantasies going from early morning until well into the darkest hours. You'll find everything here, from stirring tributes to a nation those Brits once considered a fantasy to laughing, lollygagging parades of the cartoonist's fantastic characters.

You'll find hula hands telling stories of distant Polynesian lands, ingenuous young faces forming human Christmas trees, Broadway's hottest performers belting it out, jazz artists playing it cool, campfire singers, sparkling parades, and an explosion of fireworks that dazzles your senses as it shatters the silence and sends pinpoints of fiery light into the blue-black skies.

It's all waiting for you in this, the most magic of Magic Kingdoms, so without further ado, let's take a look at all the things there are to do after the sun goes down here in the world Walt Disney created.

Tops among the entertaining possibilities for both youngsters and adults is the Magic Kingdom's **Main Street Electrical Parade,** which takes place at 9 and 11:30 p.m. daily in busy seasons including Easter, summer vacations, and Christmas. Quite a dramatic event it is too: An announcer solemnly says the parade's about to start, the twinkling lights of Main Street suddenly go black, and at the top of the street . . . there they are! Mickey, Minnie, Pluto, Dumbo, and Pinocchio happily waving from their perches aboard 30 floats, glittering wheel to whistle in a rainbow of tiny lights. Slowly the parade, augumented by bands and at Christmas by hundreds of choral singers, winds its glowing way down the darkened street, the towers and turrets of Cinderella's Castle glowing in the dark skies. Everything sparkles, including an occasional teardrop, as the fantasyland's procession moves slowly down the packed street.

Where should you go to see the parade? Well, this is one jam-packed event, so chances are you won't have much choice. The best spot is in the center of the platform at Walt Disney World's Railroad Depot, where you get a fabulous view of the floats as they twist around the Town Square and around the Hub, even if you do have to peek and peer around the trees a little. If you don't manage a good spot there, settle happily for a place along the curb of Main Street, where hundreds of others will be settling as well. If you can, stake out a spot for yourself an hour or so ahead of time, but if you can't keep the squirmers in your crowd busy that long, just join all the others. It doesn't matter all that much since the floats tower over the crowds, and it's the general impression of light and music and laughter that's the magic of it all anyway.

Naturally, the 9 p.m. parade is the busiest, since most of the small fry need to be tucked away before the 11:30 p.m. extravaganza. If you're looking for the least crowded conditions, opt for the later parade. It's every bit as glittering.

There's one more possible viewing spot: a stool at Pecos Bill's restaurant in Frontierland. It's right on the parade route, which incidentally, begins at Main Street, goes around the east half of the Hub, across Liberty Square Bridge, and through Frontierland.

More electrical magic? Step right up to the beach and see the **Electrical Water Pageant,** featuring 1000 feet of illuminated creatures floating merrily across the lake on which the Polynesian Village, Fort Wilderness, the Contemporary, and River Country are located. This watery wonder wends its way around the lake, appearing at the Polynesian about 9 p.m., at River Country about 9:35, at Fort Wilderness at 9:45, at the Contemporary about 10 p.m., and in the park itself about 10:20 p.m., on nights the park is open late. Check at Guest Services of City Hall to see if the show's going on while you're there and when and where you can go to get a look.

If you've read the section about hotels in Disney World, you've already discovered two other major evening events here, the **luau at Polynesian Village** and the every-evening show at the **Contemporary Hotel's Top of the World show.**

That luau is a touch of exotica that provides a different kind of fantasy altogether, the fantasy of desert islands, waving palms, seductive music of the South Seas, graceful dancers and brave warriors. Presented every night at 5 and 8 p.m. with a third show added at 10:30 p.m. from the end of March through late August, the luau features a rib-sticking dinner of Polynesian treats for the first two shows, lighter fare of fruit and cheese for the final performance. Here's your chance to try some poi and wash away the taste with pineapple, to watch beautiful dancers tell island stories with graceful hands and assorted other parts, and to listen to the hypnotic thudding of the war drums. Cost of the show is $17 adults, $14 children 12 to 18, and $9.50 children 3 to 11.

Meanwhile, over at the Top of the World in the Contemporary Hotel, there's a razzle-dazzle **Broadway show** in full swing. Often featuring some of the top names in show biz, the Top of the World packs them in for its dinner and entertainment, which goes on stage at 8:15 p.m. and 11:30 p.m. nightly (dinner seating at 6:30 and 9:45 p.m.). Entertainment changes frequently, so call to find out what's going on this week. Cover charge for the show is $7.50 adults, $3.75 children 3 to 11 and dinner at the Top, where you can really look down on the world from a glamorous vantage point, is about $10 to $15 for entrees, about half that for children's meals.

You and/or the youngsters can have dinner with the Disney characters at the Trophy Room in the Golf Resort. You'll dine on prime rib, chicken, or fish, served family style, then giggle away the evening with the characters as they tower over you with their funny faces. Youngsters get a souvenir to take home, and adults get a present too—the starry eyes of those little ones. Dinner is $12 adults, $10.50 children 12 to 17, and $7.50 children 3 to 11. Reservations are required for the dinners. Make them at 824-5029.

More moon over the Magic Kingdom? How about a **moonlight cruise** aboard a sidewheeler that takes you on an hour-long sail across the waters of Bay Lake and the Seven Seas Lagoon? You can imbibe something soothing, watch the lights sparkling around you and the stars overhead as you dream yourself back into the days when civilized people lived like this *all* the time. Cruise times vary, so check with City Hall on the day you'd like to take the cruise. An extra bonus is a waterside look at the Electrical Water Pageant as it glitters across the waters. Fare is

$2.25 for adults, $1.75 children. You can also call for reservations at 824-1000.

An evening aboard the **Empress Lilly** is among the more memorable events you can pencil in for your visit to Disney World. Dine in one of the handsome restaurants aboard this fairy-tale craft, then stop in for some rip-roarin' fun at the Baton Rouge Lounge, where you may be treated to some lively banjo-strumming entertainment, a guitarist, a group of entertainers—who knows what? Always funny and always fun, this is an amusing way to while away some evening hours. Things keep going until 1 a.m. here, where you can order specialty drinks by the pitcher. There's no cover charge or minimum either.

Those who prefer to keep their entertainment on an informal jeans-and-plaid-shirt level will love the **Hoop-Dee-Doo Musical Revue** at Fort Wilderness campgrounds. An every-evening event that goes on stage at 5, 7:30, and 10 p.m., this is one of the park's most popular shows and is often booked far in advance. Got the hint? Good, call 824-8000 and don't waste any time doing it. It's so popular partly because children will love it, partly because adults love it, and partly because it's so good. First they feed you to a fare-thee-well with ribs and chicken, corn on the cob, strawberry shortcake, and the like, and then they get you laughing so hard you don't know whether you're choking from laughter or all that food. Vivacity they've got, these performers, and enthusiasm they've got—and get—from an appreciative audience that joins right in for these whoop-and-holler evenings. Join them. Show and dinner price is $17 adults, $14 for youngsters 12 to 18, and $9.50 for children 3 to 11.

One other good time in Fort Wilderness is a good old-fashioned campfire evening. Called the **Marshmallow Marsh Excursion,** this novel evening of activity begins with a canoe excursion through the waterways, moves along to a campfire sing-a-long, and winds up with a marshmallow roast at a lakeside vantage point from which participants ogle the 9:45 p.m. Electrical Water Pageant. Cost is $4.25, and reservations are necessary for the show which takes place only in June, July, and August. Call 824-2788 or go to the ticket booth at Pioneer Hall.

There's also a nightly **Campfire Program** at Fort Wilderness's Meadow Trading Post, complete with sing-a-long, Disney movies and cartoons, and Chip and Dale often on hand to keep 'em giggling. It's free.

Movies? Of course. For evenings when the feet simply will not go a foot farther, head over to the Contemporary Resort where

WDW guests can watch Disney features in the theater near the Fiesta Fun Center. Hours are 4:30, 7, and 9 p.m. most evenings, but you might check at the hotel to be sure and to find out what's playing.

Although there's a no-liquor policy in the Magic Kingdom itself, there are a number of cocktail lounges in the four Disney resorts areas and in the Walt Disney World Shopping Village in Lake Buena Vista. Here's a look at some of the lounges where you might find a respite from the activities around you.

You'll find that Polynesian theme right in your glass at Polynesian Village Hotel. There's a long list of exotic tropical drinks, ranging from basic piña coladas and Mai-Tais to creations with names like the Blue Lagoon—it really is blue—Seven Seas, and Chi Chis. All these and more are stirred up in **Captain Cook's Hideaway** in the Great Ceremonial House where there's nightly entertainment as well (8 p.m. to 1 a.m.); the **Tambu Lounge** beside the Papeete Bay Verandah (nightly entertainment here too), and the **Barefoot Bar** out by the swimming pool.

In the Contemporary Resort a Mexican atmosphere prevails at **Coconino Cove.** South of the border goodies are on hand at cocktail hour, and there's nightly entertainment. Two other lounges at the Contemporary are the **Monorail Club Car**, a tranquil spot for some quiet conversation, and the **Sand Bar**, down by the marina, which features a piña colada with a twist—ice cream.

Special concoctions are a feature at the Golf Resort Hotel's **Player's Gallery,** where you can gaze out over the greens while you sample a Double Eagle—that's tequila sour floating on Kahlúa—or an Unplayable Lies—champagne and Southern Comfort nestled around a whole frozen apricot. Whew!

In Lake Buena Vista at Walt Disney World Village Hotel Plaza, all five hotels have cool hideaways, some with entertainment, some just for sitting.

At Dutch Resort **The Hague Lounge** has entertainment and dancing, while the **Nightwatch** is a quiet spot where you can do pretty much what the name implies.

Hotel Royal Plaza's **La Cantina** sparks cocktail hour with an oyster, shrimp, and crab raw-bar specialties, and the **Giraffe** disco maintains a frenetic pace to the wee hours. That disco, by the way is the only one in WDW, thus making it a popular spot for Disney employees. Its new look features a purple, yellow, and deep-green color scheme that's a dazzler, plus substantial happy-hour hors d'oeuvres that make the Giraffe a popular spot for early evening snacking too.

TraveLodge's **Top of the Arc** offers a Magic Kingdom view that is nothing short of spectacular, and there's dancing and entertainment to boot.

Howard Johnson's Resort Hotel has a cozy lounge, too.

Finally, there are a couple of lively locales in Walt Disney World Shopping Village. **Cap'n Jack's Oyster Bar** produces a happy combination of potables and seafood treats, and the **Village Lounge,** which features excellent jazz entertainment in comfortable surroundings.

The *Empress Lilly* has two lounges in addition to the lively Baton Rouge Lounge mentioned earlier: the **Promenade Lounge** and the **Starboard Lounge.**

Orlando Nightlife

To start at the top of Orlando's evening entertainment offerings is without question to start at **Rosie O'Grady's,** (Church St. Station; tel. 422-2434), the Disney World of Orlando's nightlife. Rosie's is funky, Rosie's is—here comes that word again—wholesome, and, above all, Rosie's is *fun.*

From the first moment you hear the wheezing wail of the huge calliope that occupies center stage outside Rosie's, you'll know you've landed somewhere special. Rosie's and all the wacky fun that now surrounds it, got started a few years back after Orlando lured Disney World here, thereby giving the city a hearty shove into Tomorrowland. That successfully accomplished, Orlando began to seek its roots. It wasn't long before developers discovered Church Street, where a decrepit but historic hotel and railroad depot somehow remained standing after years of neglect. Here began a concerted effort to bring the past back to life. That aging railroad station, topped by a shining silver cupola, became the center of redevelopment, and Rosie O'Grady's moved in to become the center of the center.

Today you'll find here a rip-roarin' Gay 90s (or is that Roaring 20s) atmosphere in the restaurants, the saloons, and even a whirling dervish of a disco. Step in the door and you're surrounded by an array of plants, antiques and brass, stained glass and skylights, and a rabbit warren of fascinating places to prowl. Peek around a corner and you come face to face with an ornate confessional from a French monastery (it's in the pub). Turn a bend and stumble on train benches from an old railroad station, cast-iron tables from an English pub, huge brass chandeliers salvaged from a Boston bank, teller's cages vintage 1870 from a Pittsburgh bank.

When you've absorbed all that, move on to Rosie's four fun centers. First there's Rosie O'Grady's Good-Time Emporium, complete with a red-hot mama in a slinky dress, a crooning minstrel singer who dances his way around the room—across the tops of the benches you're sitting on—and kicky can-can girls clacking across the bar. Then there's Apple Annie's Courtyard, where you can dine on fat sandwiches, salads, and plum daiquiris to the sounds of bluegrass music. Next there's Lili Marlene's Aviator Pub and Restaurant (see Chapter IV on dining in Orlando) for dinner in smashing surroundings.

If you love that foot-stompin', clog-cloggin' get-down country sound, you'll find it in a new addition at Rosie's, the Cheyenne Saloon & Opera House, where those twanging sounds reign supreme and cloggers tap out those fascinating rhythms.

Finally, you can hit the heights—literally—with a hot-air balloon trip under the auspices of Phineas Phogg's Balloon Works ($96.50 per person) and a stop at ole Phineas's other hangout, a trendy disco complete with a balloon-basket balcony from which you can watch dancers cavort amid flashing strobes and puffs of fog.

Open from 11 a.m. to 2 a.m. daily, Rosie's is the top star in the Orlando firmament, a not-to-be-missed winner for fun and frolic. The evening cover charge is $4.75, and drinks are in the $2.50 range. If you have dinner at Lili Marlene's, you can get a refund on the cover charge, so try a late dinner and predinner entertainment, if you're on a tight budget. That refund can also be applied to a drink on your way out, and speaking of drinks, you can take the huge glasses your drinks come in with you as a souvenir or turn them in at the gift shop for a $1 refund.

A new addition to Rosie's is the Cheyenne Saloon and Opera House, which features a whoop-de-doo country and western evening complete with twanging guitars, soulful singers, and stomping cloggers.

Children are welcome at Rosie's, and they won't feel a bit out of place, since many parents bring their youngsters here for a big night on the town. Skip the disco with the young ones, however.

Sea World lets very little seaweed grow under its feet in competition with Disney World for the tourist dollar. That's part of the reason you'll find, here, at the second most popular attraction in the Orlando area, a nightly Polynesian luau with everything from poi to pulsating Polynesian music and those talented dancers with 78-rpm hips. This show is very popular, so take the time to make reservations at 351-3600 (ext. 442) for the 7:30 p.m. event, for which the dinner and show charge is $13.75 adults, $5.95 children.

As you might have noticed, theater plays a big part in everything that goes on here in Orlando, including nightlife, so you'll find three theaters in the area.

Once Upon a Stage, 3376 Edgewater Dr., Orlando (tel. 422-3191), features a buffet dinner at 6:30 p.m. and a Broadway musical at 8:30 p.m., Tuesday through Sunday, for $15.75 to $17.75. Dark Mondays.

Theater on Park at 401 Park Ave., Winter Park (tel. 645-5757), is Winter Park's dinner-theater operation and features good local theater in a small intimate setting. Tickets are $17 to $19 weekdays, $18 to $21 on weekends, and Theater on Park is also dark Mondays. If you get an attack of the munchies before the show, you can curb it with sandwiches, soup, pastry, and cheese accompanied by beer or wine for about $5.

Edyth Bush Theater (1010 E. Princeton St., Orlando; tel. 896-7365) occupies very impressive quarters in Orlando and features a series of childrens' plays as well as adult fare performed by the Central Florida Civic Theater. Tickets are $7 to $8.

Many, make that most, hotels in the Orlando area feature regular entertainment, ranging from country and western music (especially popular in this section of Florida) to easy listening and dancing music to a little comedic touch here and there.

Included among the most popular evening stopping-spots are the **Ramada Inn Central** (4919 W. Colonial Dr.; tel. 299-8180), which at last check was featuring western music; the **Hilton Inn Gateway** (7470 W. Hwy. 192; tel. 828-8125), where you can dine on homemade cornbread, barbecued ribs, and corn on the cob at a western cookout that's served with country music every Tuesday night from 8 to 10 p.m.; two other **Hilton Inns** (at 7400 International Dr., tel. 351-4600; and on W. Colonial Dr. at John Young Pkwy., tel. 295-5270), both of which feature music for listening and dancing; **Limey Jim's** at the Orlando Hyatt (Hwy. I-4 and U.S. 192; tel. 846-4100); and the **Piccadilly Pub** in the Gold Key Inn (7100 S. Orange Blossom Trail; tel. 855-0050).

More? Of course. The **Langford Hotel** (at Interlachen and East New England Aves. in Winter Park; tel. 644-3400) is among the top hotel entertainment spots in the area and features music for dancing as well as showy entertainment and dazzling revues. There's a varying cover charge.

Winter Park has a couple of other special entertainment spots too. One is called **Two Flights Up** (329 Park Ave. S.; tel. 644-9868), a popular gathering spot and a well-known dining emporium. Another is **Harrigan's,** 310 Park Ave. S. (tel. 628-1651) where there's always a with-it crowd chowing, chattering, tuning in on the sounds of bluegrass or jazz. Finally, but certainly not least, is the **Park Avenue Disco** (4315 N. Orange Blossom Trail; tel. 295-3751), where the dazzle goes on and on from swirling rainbows of light to a spooky fog and silver snowfalls. In this two-story dance center the music begins at 7 p.m. nightly except Monday. Admission is $3 per person (except Wednesday, when ladies are free). Just behind Harrigan's you'll find another Winter Park "in" spot, **Uncle Waldo's** (325 Moody Way; tel. 645-5214). Le Cordon Bleu Restaurant's bar, **Harper's,** is popular with students at a nearby college and has entertainment every night except Sunday and Monday.

Young-but-getting-older white-collar types can be found in droves at **Bennigan's** (6324 International Dr., Orlando; tel. 351-4435) and at **Valentyne's** (54 N. Orange Ave., Orlando; tel. 849-0862) where happy hours are well-attended events.

For urban cowboys the spot is **Dallas** to ride the mechanical bull or shoot it with some good ol' boys and girls who hang out here for atmosphere and country-and-western sounds.

On a slightly more esoteric level, the **Orlando Symphony Orchestra** (tel. 841-1280) performs in winter months and the **Orlando Opera Company** (tel. 423-9527) warbles from about November to February for ticket prices in the $10 to $25 range.

Rollins College, one of the state's loveliest campuses, has theater productions regularly during the school year and a concert series as well. Ticket prices vary but are in the $5 to $10 range. Information is available at 646-2233 or 646-2145.

Top-name singers, dancers, and stars of all kinds appear here, too, at the **Bob Carr Performing Arts Center** (401 W. Livingston St., Orlando; tel. 849-2363). To find out what's going on there and elsewhere, check the entertainment section of the *Orlando Sentinel* or several tourist-helper publications including *Orlando Magazine, Florida Tourist News,* and *See Orlando.*

Not far from Disney World, **The Worst Bar** (at Ramada Resort Hotel, formerly Court of Flags, tel. 351-3340) has turned out to be one of the best in town. Now open a year, it's jam-packed almost all the time and features drinks in the $1.50 to $2 range and plenty of outrageous party happenings. Top-40 entertainment is the style produced here by live bands that begin about 9 p.m. and keep things lively until 2 a.m., Monday through Saturday.

Café on the Park in the Harley Hotel (151 E. Washington St.; tel. 841-3200) is a somewhat more sedate atmosphere—and a beautiful one—for dancing. It's open Monday through Saturday from 7 p.m. to 2 a.m.

A guitar player and live band alternate to keep things moving at **Orange Quarter** (Orange Ave. at Washington St.; tel. 425-2822), and there's a $1-buffet at happy hour that will stave off the munchies. Entertainment's on from 4 p.m. to 8 p.m. Wednesday and from 7:30 to 11:30 p.m. weekends.

A disc jockey spins 'em nightly at **Goodlife's** (359 Park Ave. N. in Winter Park; tel. 534-0062), and on Monday from 7 to 11 p.m., a local radio station broadcasts live from here.

You never know what will be going on—musically, that is—at **Halsey's** (216 Park Ave., Winter Park; tel. 647-9868) and discovering what's happening may be half the fun. Whatever it is, it will be taking place on weekends at this popular seafood eatery.

It's bottom-to-bottom on the dance floor at **Vibrations** (Lee Rd. at Hwy. I-4 in Howard Johnson's; tel. 644-6100) and knee-to-knee at the bar Monday through Saturday, when a dance band entertains. A popular place for slightly more mature singles in search, so they say.

There's contemporary jazz every night from 9 p.m. to 1:30 a.m. at **Brazil's,** a much-admired seafood restaurant, (Maitland Ave. and S.R. 436 in the Orienta Shopping Plaza; tel. 645-2475) and **Freddie's,** the popular steak house in Fern Park (Hwy 17/92, tel. 339-3265), has a locally well-known female vocalist entertaining every night but Sunday in the Lamplighter Lounge.

At historic **Longwood Village Inn** (Hwy. 427 off S.R. 434, Longwood; tel. 834-5555) there's a nostalgic sock-hop some evenings, live '50s music on others, and a disc jockey on still others. Nostalgia and this beautiful old home are an unbeatable combination.

The elegant **Maison et Jardin** (430 Wymore Rd., Altamonte Springs; tel. 644-4410) has a warbling Italian vocalist who entertains at dinner hours here and will serenade you with your favorite love song. You'll be enchanted. On Sunday there's a jazz band for Sunday brunch entertainment.

Chapter VI

SPORTS IN DISNEY WORLD AND ORLANDO

YOU DON'T THINK for a minute, do you, that those same Disney creators who invented a lovable mouse would stop at that? Certainly not. Once they'd figured out how to entertain you in their fanciful world, they sat down again and figured out ways to keep golfers, tennis players, swimmers, joggers, and even professional shoppers happily occupied. Now there are so many sports available, in so many locations around this vast acreage, you nearly need a scoreboard to keep track.

Sports in Disney World

Since there's everything here to play on and with, from golf courses to outrigger canoes, let's start with that most popular of sports, golf, and see if we can't find a sport for everyone.

GOLF: Those links take up plenty of space in Walt Disney World's huge complex. For openers there are three golf courses here, the **Magnolia**, the **Palm**, and the course at **Lake Buena Vista Club.** All three started life as desert sands but have been miraculously converted into tree-lined, water-dotted, hilly areas, interesting enough to challenge golfers on the PGA Tour route which visits here each year. If you're a golfing fan, you'll find them challenging but not terrifying. All are par-72 courses in the 7000-yard range. Carts are required on the courses; the fee for which is included in the $22 greens fee for guests of Walt Disney World Resorts, $29 for visitors. Several area hotels also offer a golf membership card that gets you on the links for a few dollars less. If you really want to save money, plan your outing for the hours after 3 p.m., when a twilight rate of $14 goes into effect for all golfers, resort guests or not.

If you're staying at a Disney World resort, you can confirm starting times as soon as you have a confirmed reservation. If you're not, you can make reservations up to seven days in advance from January through April, when the courses see the most play. Guests at hotels in the Walt Disney World Village Hotel Plaza, by the way, are considered day visitors. Starter's telephone number is 824-3625.

If you've got a young golf fanatic in your crowd, Disney can provide. Called the **Wee Links,** this youngsters' golf course features six holes and a total of 1525 yards. It comes complete with all the nail-chewing difficulties of any golf course—traps, water hazards—but they're just a little easier to escape. Composed of an artificial turf, the course is measured in yards especially designed for the youngsters: Two feet equal a yard. Financed by the PGA in the hopes of encouraging more young golfers, the Wee Links charges a $3 fee for youngsters under 18, and that includes clubs, a lesson on basic golf rules and etiquette, and 12 holes—that's two rounds—of golf. Those special lessons are at 8:30 and 11 a.m. and 2 and 4 p.m. daily. All the traveling done on the course is done on foot, so there are no cart charges. Adults needn't feel left out here: They can play, too, for $6.

If you'd like to get in some lessons while you're here, sign up for the **Walt Disney World Golf Studio** (tel. 824-3628). You'll be part of a small class in which instructors highlight your skills and help you add to them. After class you get a look at the lessons on videotape and are treated to a critique of your style, which is recorded on a tape you can take home. Disney's Golf Studio operates at 9 and 11:30 a.m. and at 2:30 p.m. Monday through Friday, at 9 and 11:30 a.m. on Saturday, and lasts for about two hours. Fee is $30 for guests of Disney resorts, $34 if you want to play nine holes after the lesson to practice what you've learned. Day visitors pay $35.

Private lessons are also available for $15 a half hour, $20 to $30 if you want advice from the club pros, who also will take to the links with you for for $50 to $75. Book private lessons at 824-3628 for the Golf Resort courses—the Magnolia and the Palm—or 828-3748 for instructions at Lake Buena Vista Club.

Rental equipment is by Spalding and Top-flight and costs $8 for clubs, $1.95 a bucket for balls, and $2.50 for shoes. Get them all at the Pro Shop.

If you've always dreamed of playing in a **tournament,** you may even be able to satisfy that dream à la Disney. Local tournament play is organized by a Tournament Coordinator (tel. 824-4602), who may be able to include you in one of the local play-offs. If you're *really* into this thing and have the bucks to back it, you can play in the annual Walt Disney World National Team Championship Golf Classic each fall. To play with two pros during the tourney you must join the Classic Club for a $2750 one-year membership fee, which includes six nights' hotel fees, greens fees for a year, and admission to the Magic Kingdom for a week. Details on the club are available at 828-3692.

TENNIS: Those who want their contact with a small white ball to include strings and a net can chase that elusive orb at several interesting locations around Walt Disney World. You'll find three courts at the **Lake Buena Vista Club,** two at the **Golf Resort,** and six at the **Contemporary Resort Hotel.** At the latter you'll also find a speedy ball machine that will keep you running, plus a backboard. All are open from 8 a.m. to 10 p.m. daily and are lighted hard courts. Fees are $4 an hour for singles, $6 for doubles for WDW hotel guests, with others charged $1 more. Those ball machines and the practice alleys that go with them are $5 an hour, but you can use the backboards free unless the courts are very busy, and then you'll pay regular court fees. Reserve court time at the Contemporary at 824-1000 (ext. 3578), at the Golf Resort at 824-2200, and at the Lake Buena Vista Club at 828-3741.

If you'd like to improve your tennis, there are lessons available for both adults and youngsters 4 to 16. Video cameras help the pros show you how to expand your talents. Fees are $15 for the adult clinic, $8 for younger players. Private lessons are $12.50 a half hour, $3 more if you want instruction from the club pro. Add $5 to that if you'd like to see yourself on videotape. Details on the instructional programs are available at 824-1000.

If you want to rent a racquet, you'll pay $1 an hour, and you can buy a can of three tennis balls with the mouse's visage emblazoned on them for $4.

BOATING: So many watery activities are there at Walt Disney World, your only problem may be drying out wrinkled finger-tips. There are all kinds of boats, from speedy little craft to outrigger canoes, plenty of places to swim, and some favorite fishing holes.

If you like to stay atop the water while exploring, roam the byways of lovely, 450-acre Bay Lake and the adjoining 200 acres at the Seven Seas Lagoon. Marinas at Contemporary Resort, Fort Wilderness, and Polynesian Village will rent you small, two-sailor sailboats called Sunfish ($5 an hour), one to six-passenger Capris ($7 an hour), or 14- or 16-foot catamarans for $7 to $9 an hour.

If you prefer power, you can start small and slow with motor-powered pontoon boats topped by canopies. Rental rates are $12 a half hour. Similar canopy boats accommodating up to ten people are $10.50 a half hour.

If you're *really* not in a hurry, you can provide your own power on pedal boats that rent for $5 an hour. Canoes get you around in leisurely style, too, and cost is just $7 a day, $2 an hour. If there are eight of you, canoe in style aboard an outrigger canoe ($1 per person per hour).

When speed's the thing, zip off across the waters on small boats called Water Sprites that fly like the wind and rent for $7.50 a half hour (children must be over 12 to rent or drive the boats, although younger sailors may ride in them accompanied by an adult). For even closer contact with the water, attach yourself to the back of a ski boat and waterski for $31.50 an hour, including equipment, boat, and captain.

You'll find sailboats and speedboats, pontoon boats and pedal boats at Contemporary Resort, Polynesian Village, Fort Wilderness, and the marinas in Walt Disney World Village, where you can explore three more small connected lakes named Club Lake, Lake Buena Vista, and Buena Vista Lagoon. Canopy boats are available at Walt Disney World Village Marina, canoes at Fort Wilderness Bike Bar, outrigger canoes at Polynesian Village Marina, and waterski boats at Fort Wilderness and Contemporary Resort.

You'll need a resort identification card, a driver's license, or a Magic Kingdom passport to rent the craft. Can you sail a privately owned craft in Disney World? No.

SWIMMING: One hardly expects to find a sandy white beach here in the landlocked center of Florida, but as usual Disney creates—with five miles of soft white sand. You can't miss that silica, in fact: On a monorail journey you'll spot the sands at Polynesian Village and behind the Contemporary, stretching around to Fort Wilderness.

As for swimming pools, there are nine of them on the grounds, one or sometimes two at every hotel and villa area. Although there's no charge for using them, they are not open to day visitors, only to guests of the WDW resorts. More pools for hotel guests are at the Walt Disney World Village Hotel Plaza hotels (Dutch Inn, Royal Plaza, Buena Vista Palace, TraveLodge, and Howard Johnson's). Most interesting of the swimming holes is the pool at Polynesian Village, a fanciful creation with a waterfall and slide set among huge man-made rocks.

Pools and beaches are only for the use of guests staying at the Disney-owned hotels or campground, so if you're intent on watery fun, head for River Country where Disney has created another Magic Kingdom using water as the main ingredient. Read more about that watery wonderland in Chapter VIII.

FISHING: Fishing is another guests-only sport at Walt Disney World and can be done in two ways: on your own in canals near the villa areas or at Fort Wilderness on a special Disney-organized expedition. Those expeditions leave at 8 a.m. and 3 p.m. daily from the Fort Wilderness campgrounds and are $52.50 including equipment, boat, guide, and snacks. If you're staying in a Disney accommodation with a kitchen, you can keep your catch—usually bass—and cook it, but if you don't have a kitchen, just sigh a contented, triumphant sigh and toss it back into the deep. You don't need a fishing license.

HORSEBACK RIDING: Trail ponies carry you off into the lovely wooded countryside here on daily treks that take off at 9 and 10:30 a.m., noon and 2 p.m. Quiet rides with a guide are $5.25 a person, and both day visitors and resort guests are welcome, although the kiddies must be at least nine years old. Reservations can be made at 828-2734.

JOGGING AND WALKING: Perhaps the best way of all to see the wondrous world Disney has created is on foot, walking or running. If you're a runner, all the hotels in WDW and in the Hotel Plaza carry jogging maps that show you how to plan the run (or walk). It's wise to do these activities early in the morning or after dusk, since other times of day can feature more Florida sun than you can handle. Fort Wilderness has an official jogging trail, 2.3 miles of it, complete with exercise stations. Otherwise you're pretty much on your own, so it might be wise to take a look at your prospective jogging or walking area by car or bus before you set off (or at least be very sure of your directions). If you miss a turn, a leisurely two-miler can become a sweating six-mile morning. Follow *that* with a visit to the Magic Kingdom or EPCOT, and your feet are liable to make their displeasure known.

Walkers should head to the River Country area, where you can stroll down a nature trail or over to Marshmallow Marsh at Fort Wilderness where a mile-long path takes you along the lake and through the woods.

BICYCLING: You can rent a bike at the Fort Wilderness Bike Barn or at the Pool Pavilion in the Vacation Villas ($1 an hour, $4 a day, $2 and $6 for bicycles built for two), then pedal along miles of bike paths in Walt Disney World Village and at Fort Wilderness.

WORKING OUT: Contemporary Resort has a health club complete with most of the usual exercise equipment, a sauna or whirlpool, and massage artists. The fee is $2, whirlpool $3, massages $15. Hours for women are 9 a.m. to noon Monday, Wednesday, and Friday, to 1 p.m. on other days; for men 1 p.m. to 6 p.m. Monday, Wednesday, and Friday, from 2 p.m. other days. Closed Sundays. Massage appointments can be made at 824-1000.

VOLLEYBALL, BASEBALL, HORSESHOES: Facilities for these sports, plus tetherball, are available at Fort Wilderness but only to guests of Walt Disney World resorts. You need your own equipment for softball and baseball.

In Orlando

Although Disney World has some of the best in Orlando sporting life on its grounds, you'll find plenty of places to play in the rest of Orlando as well. You have quite a range of choices, too, from wild rides on airboats that skim across the water to—are you ready—hot-air balloon rides high into the air.

Let's start with the nation's most favored sports, golf and tennis, and work up to the more unusual activities available.

GOLF: Golfers staying within range of Disney World can head for Kissimmee's **Buenaventura Lakes Country Club** (301 Buenaventura Blvd.; tel. 847-3457), a par-30, nine-hole course with greens fees and cart charges of $4 to $6.

Another nearby course is **Poinciana Golf & Racquet Club,** on U.S. 17/92 west of Kissimmee (tel. 348-5300), where you can play 18 holes, a total of 6697 yards of par-72 golf for $10.

Closer to downtown Orlando is **Fairways Golf Club** (14205 E. Colonial Dr.; tel. 273-9815), an 18-hole, par-70 course of 6162 yards, which charges $8 plus $10 for an electric cart.

In Winter Park the **Municipal Course** (644-8195) is right downtown and offers a nine-hole, par-35 course that's 2651 yards long. Fees are $5 weekdays, $1 more on weekends and holidays, and just $3.50 after 3 p.m. in winter, 4 p.m. in summer. Juniors pay $3.50 and pull carts are permitted.

TENNIS: Tennis players should head for the **Orlando Vacation Resort** (west of Hwy. I-4 on U.S. 192; tel. 904/394-6171), where you'll find 17 clay and asphalt tennis courts for $2 to $5 an hour, or **Vistana Resort** (east of Hwy. I-4 on Rte. 535, the Lake Buena Vista exit; tel. 846-1200) where there are 14 clay courts that rent for $5 an hour. Vistana offers a free tennis clinic at 10 a.m. daily except Sunday, and they even throw in a free racquet. Private lessons are $15 a half hour, group lessons and tennis clinics $10 an hour. Court hours: 8 a.m. to 11 p.m.

Up in Altamonte Springs the **Altamonte Springs Racquet Club and Resort** (151 N. Douglas Ave., off Hwy. I-4 at Rte. 436; tel. 869-9000) has plenty of courts; lessons are $14 for 45 minutes with a tennis pro, plus a clinic to improve your skills.

Orlando Tennis & Racquet Club (825 Courtland St., Orlando; tel. 644-5411) offers private lessons for $22 an hour and is open for play daily from 7 a.m. to 11 p.m., with earlier opening and closing hours on weekends.

Orlando Tennis Center in Exposition Park (W. Livingston St. in downtown Orlando, tel. 849-2161) has 15 lighted courts, open from 9 a.m. to 10 p.m. daily (earlier closings on weekends) and charges $2.

Free asphalt courts are available at **Oak Street Park,** (Palm and Oak Sts., Orlando; tel. 847-2388). More free courts are located in parks in Orlando and Kissimmee. To find out just where they are, call the Orlando Recreation Department at 849-2288 and its counterpart in Kissimmee at 847-2388.

BOATING: Kissimmee was carved out of flat sands and cypress swamps, some of which have been kept intact with huge cypress trees dripping eerie Spanish moss into the black water. It's quite a sight, and you can see it in some interesting ways—aboard a canoe, an electric boat, or an airboat. Rent any of those from **U-Drive Airboat Rentals,** 4266 Vine St., six miles east on U.S. 192 (tel. 847-3672). Fees begin at $5 a half hour for airboats, $3 for canoes.

For first-class travel, rent a houseboat with galley, bath, and air conditioning, and tour the crystal springs of St. John's River. Boats are provided by **Sunline** (tel. 736-9422 or toll free 800/874-7004). The company's located at Holly Bluff Marina in Deland, and the boats are $645 a week in busy season, $520 in other months.

PARIMUTUEL SPORTS: Watch those canine racers streak after the electronic bunny at **Seminole Greyhound Park,** Rte. 17/92 in Casselberry (tel. 841-3480), and at **Sanford-Orlando Kennel Club,** Dog Track Road (tel. 831-1600). Seminole is open May to September; Sanford, December to May, with racing nightly (except Sunday) from 8 p.m., matinees on Monday, Wednesday, and Saturday at 1:15 p.m. Admission is $1.

Orlando-Seminole Jai-Alai Fronton in Fern Park (211 S. Hwy. 17/92; tel. 339-6221) gives you a look at that unusual and thrilling sport nightly (except Sunday) from October through February. Admission begins at $1 and games start at 6 p.m. daily, with noon matinees on Monday, Wednesday, and Saturday.

From April to September harness racing trots off nightly except Sunday at 7:30 p.m. at **Ben White Harness Raceway,** (1805 Lee Rd.; tel. 293-8721). Admission is $1. In other months you can watch them train those sleek trotters for free.

BASEBALL: In March and April the **Minnesota Twins** play at Tinker Field, the Tangerine Bowl, at the corner of Tampa and Church Streets (tel. 849-6346). Tickets begin at less than $10.

If you'd like to see whether you might just qualify for a team yourself, go hit a few at the **baseball batting range** (on U.S. 441, two miles east of Kissimmee; tel. 847-6502). There are three pitching machines plus a golf driving range and miniature golf course.

SWIMMING: There are lakes and swimming pools scattered about. The Orlando Recreation Department (tel. 849-2288), the Orange County Parks Department (tel. 420-3640), or the Kissimmee Parks and Recreation Department (tel. 847-2388) can tell you where the best swimming's located.

I can tell you there's much water fun to be had at a local attraction called **Wet 'N Wild** (6200 International Dr.; tel. 351-3200). You can ride bumper boats and speedboats, or paddle around a surf pool in which constant four-foot waves are created by a machine. Slide down white-water slideways or careen down a Kamikaze slide that sends you into a pool from a platform six stories high! There are squirting games and other fun for kids, a Corkscrew Flume that spirals you through a figure-eight and a tunnel, even a Bonzai Boggan water-rollercoaster that races at 30 m.p.h. then plunges you into a pool. You can picnic along the lake, snack at snackbars, and just generally spend an uncomplicated day in watery surroundings. Admission is $7.95 adults, $5.95 children 3 to 12, free to toddlers, and the attraction's open from 10 a.m. to 5 p.m. daily. There's usually a bargain-rate discount after 3 p.m. too.

FISHING: With lakes everywhere you look, there's certainly no dearth of fishing holes. **Bass** is the big catch in these parts, and a favorite spot to fish for them is Lake Tohopekaliga (much easier to get around than to pronounce). Kissimmee River's another spot that's good for fishing, and the Kissimmee-St. Cloud Convention and Visitors Bureau (Box 2007, Kissimmee, FL 32741; tel. 847-5000) can send you a list of fishing camps, boat rentals, bait shops, and the like in the area.

If **deep-sea fishing** is more to your taste, you'll naturally have to head to the sea in the Cocoa/Port Canaveral area where the Cocoa Chamber of Commerce (431 Riveredge Blvd.; tel. 636-4262) headed by one very friendly Floridian, Joe Smith, can supply you with directions to marinas. Deep-sea fishing on charter boats is likely to run about $150 a day, higher in busy seasons.

If you're looking for an **inexpensive fishing trip,** try the *Miss Cape Canaveral,* an 80-foot party boat that sails at 8 a.m. daily, returns at 5 p.m. from Port Canaveral, about an hour's drive due east of Orlando. Price is $25 adults, $20 children under 12, plus $5 for rod and reel. The boat's docked at Commercial Road behind Fisher Seafood (tel. 783-5274).

Pier fishing is available at Canaveral Fishing Pier, just north of Cocoa Beach.

HORSEBACK RIDING: This is horse country, so it's not difficult to find equine entertainment. **Devonwood Farm,** 2518 Rouse Rd., Orlando, about a half mile east of Alafaya Trail & Hwy. 50 (tel. 273-0822), for instance, offers horseback riding for $7 an hour, lessons and riding trips by reservation only. They're open 9 a.m. to 4:30 p.m. Another trotting spot: **Stonehedge Stables** (about six miles east of S.R. 436 on Red Bug Rd.; tel. 365-6191), where rentals are $6 an hour, reservations are required, and riding is available from 9 a.m. to 4:30 p.m., Monday through Friday and from 8:30 a.m. to 6 p.m. on weekends.

ICE SKATING: Never let it be said that we did not provide you with every option. If you can't bear to be without a little of the cold stuff, try the **Orlando Ice Skating Palace** (3123 W. Colonial Dr., in the Parkwood Shopping Plaza; tel. 299-5440). It calls itself an Olympic-size arena and is open every day, charging $3.95 adults ($4.95 weekends), $3.45 for children under 13 ($4.45 weekends). Skate rentals (in case you forgot to pack those for a Florida vacation) are $1.

BALLOON TRIPS: Phineas Phogg's, part of the amazing Rosie O'Grady's complex (tel. 422-2434), takes you up, up, and away early in the morning at 6:30 a.m. when the winds are breezes gentle enough to waft you across the countryside on a 3½-hour journey which includes picnicking on bread, fruit, and cheese. The fee is $96.50 per person for an experience you'll never forget.

WATERSKIING: Dee's Ski School and Camp (Rte. 1, Box 595, north Lake Juliana in Auburndale; tel. 813/984-1160) sports a lakefront clubhouse, five regulation slalom courses, and two fiberglass jumps. About a 30-minute drive from Disney World, the ski center is open year round and offers camping, cottages, a pro shop, and a fishing pier as well. To get there, take Exit 21 (S.R. 559) from Hwy. I-4, go one mile south toward Auburndale, and turn right on Lundy Road. A half hour of skiing is $15.

Chapter VII

SHOPPING IN CENTRAL FLORIDA

IF YOU LIKE SOUVENIRS, you will *adore* Orlando and environs, where there are more—and more bizarre—interpretations of that word than you could conjure up in your wildest dreams—or nightmares!

Where else in the world could you find a high-powered executive discussing millions of dollars on a telephone receiver lifted from the firm grip of a white-gloved Mickey Mouse telephone? For that matter, how many places do you find people strolling the streets wearing black plastic mouse ears?

It's contagious, this junk-abilia fever that hits Orlando visitors, so don't think for a minute that you're immune. Rare is the soul that can head home without a picture of the mouse—or Shamu the Killer Whale, or one of their fanciful buddies—triumphantly emblazoned somewhere on the body or the possessions.

So if you're a collector of almost anything, you can be sure you'll find something here in Orlando to collect. If you're not a collector, you probably will be by the time you leave here, since there are few places to escape the barrage of sales pitches.

Despite appearances, however, real people do live in Orlando, and some of them have taste good enough to produce some interesting treasures you may enjoy after the mouse mania has faded.

Because there are so many hundreds of places to buy typical souvenirs, including every hotel gift shop and hundreds of shops in Disney World and EPCOT, Sea World and Circus World, I'm going to trust you have enough ferreting ability to find those yourself.

What you'll find in this chapter instead are tips on some spots to seek out for bargains on souvenirs that do not scream "souvenir!" Interestingly, Orlando's accent on families, supplemented by its comparatively youthful population, has led to the rise of many cut-rate and discount shops that offer interesting bargains on name-brand items. What's more, some area shops are in locations so intriguing they're as interesting to visit as they are to explore for your special kind of treasure. Finally, best of all, there are some fascinating boutiques, particularly in the nearby suburb of Winter Park, that feature exotic creations difficult to match anywhere.

Let's take a look then at some of the top spots for a shopping break from the fun and frolic of Orlando's attractions.

Right **on Disney World grounds** in Lake Buena Vista is one of Orlando's favorite shopping spots, **Walt Disney World Shopping Village.** Throngs of locals sweep in here on weekends to raid this interesting conglomeration of 27 boutiques, featuring everything from delicate handcrafted Christmas ornaments to gourmet kitchen necessities. There's a candle shop; a shop featuring the finest—and most expensive—in crystal, china, and silver; a card and gift shop; and a shop that can engrave your photograph on a platter. Spain contributes its wood, metal, and porcelain products to a shop called Toledo Arts, and there's an around-the-world boutique with treasures from everywhere.

Toys of all kinds turn up at Pooh's Place and Toys Fantastique; there's a photo studio where you can have your picture taken in turn-of-the-century clothes; and there are stores featuring children's clothes, men's clothes, and women's tropical outfits. You can buy fancy bathroom accessories, perfumes, gourmet goodies including freshly roasted coffee beans and straight-out-of-the-oven pastries, exclusive and expensive chocolates, sundries and cards, liqueurs and liquors, wines and things to serve them all in, shoes, batiks, brass goodies, and ships in bottles.

All those treasures are interspersed with some intriguing restaurants (see Chapter IV on dining) and spiced with some attractive architecture. At night tiny white Italian lights twinkle in the trees, turning this shopper's haven into the kind of fairyland even Tinker Bell would approve. One final don't-miss here: In Toys Fantastique is a dollhouse so elaborate and so fabulously appointed you'll gasp at the crystal and etched glass, miniature treasures of such beauty they're not for sale, although you can acquire reproductions with determination and money.

In Disney World's Magic Kingdom and EPCOT, you'll find

dozens, nay hundreds, of shops which I've outlined in Chapters VIII and IX.

Downtown Orlando is just beginning to come into its own as a shopping area. The prettiest parts of it to date are the **Orange Quarter & Shops,** Orange Ave. and Washington St., and the **French Market** on North Orange Avenue. There are just nine shops and two restaurants in the Orange Quarter, but the setting's a delight of cedar and brick elegance, much of it preserved from days long gone. At the French Market an enticing European flavor prevails.

Over in **Winter Park,** Central Florida's Little Europe, you'll find 'silk scarves spilling over a counter, pearls and diamonds dramatically displayed in glittering windows, small treasures and large ones, all presented in shops so tasteful and elegant you'll think you're wandering in Zurich or on Paris's Rive Gauche. All this elegance is centered on Park Avenue, one of the state's poshest shopping streets, ranking right up there with Palm Beach's famed Worth Avenue.

There's a tiny jewelry shop here with a royal-blue enameled bracelet I covet, another pretty little shop selling scented and intricately designed candles that look almost lovely enough to eat, and some boutiques that do indeed sell things to eat so appetizingly displayed you're likely to make one of the village's elegant restaurants your next stop. One especially interesting shop here is operated by Ted Dobbs, a heraldist, who will research your family name and, with the help of his wife, Pat, a calligrapher, inscribe it on a crest. He created one of those for the Reagan-Davis clan, a/k/a the First Family, and earned an invitation to the inauguration.

If you like **shopping malls,** you will be thrilled with Orlando, where Altamonte Mall (on S.R. 436 between Hwy. I-4 and U.S. 17/92, Altamonte Springs exit from Hwy. I-4) sports no less than 150 stores that will help separate you and your greenbacks. Quite an attractive setting in which to spend, too.

Colonial Plaza Mall (E. Colonial Dr. at Bumby St.) has more than 100 stores to wander among, and **Orlando Fashion Square** (E. Colonial Dr. at Maguire St.) has 92 shops in all price brackets.

If you feel like a little drive, whiz over to the village of Brooksville, where **Rogers' Christmas House Village** (103 Saxon Ave.; tel. 904/796-2415) keeps Christmas going all year long. Billboards all around Central Florida lure you here—where it's always December 25 except on December 25, when they celebrate what they sell all year long. Open 9:30 a.m. to 5 p.m. daily, this extensive shop shimmers with Christmas lights, multitudes of animated displays, and ornaments so entrancing not even Scrooge could resist them. You'll find the shop at the intersection of U.S. 98, Rte. 40, and U.S. 41, about 10 miles west of Hwy. I-75.

Multitudes of bargain seekers have moved Orlando's entrepreneurs to provide in the form of **factory outlet shops.** So popular has this form of shopping become in Central Florida, that there's now even an entire shopping center composed solely of shops billing themselves as factory outlets.

One of the best-known and best-advertised of the factory outlet stores is **Dansk** (7000 International Dr.), importers and creators of sleek Danish contemporary pottery, gorgeous teak trays and other teakwood ware, stainless steel, and glassware.

Supplement that with a trip to **Fostoria** glassware outlet (105 W. Colonial Dr.), where you'll find that company's wares at discounted prices, plus George Briard barware and ice buckets; Imperial, Viking, and L. E. Smith glassware; and crystal and well-designed plastic dinnerware. Or try the **China & Glass Factory Outlet** (62 W. Colonial Dr. or 6811 Visitors Circle, across from Wet 'n Wild on International Drive), where there's more of the same with a number of companies, including Wedgwood, Royal Doulton, and J.G. Durand represented.

Tennis buffs will find big discounts on brand-name tennis and sportswear at **Second Serve** (1121 N. Orlando Ave.), and **Polly Flinders** (in Casselberry Square, S.R. 436, Casselberry) carries those much-loved handsmocked dresses that look so cute on little girls.

Leotard lovers can fit themselves out at a fraction of retail prices at the **Danskin Factory Outlet** (Interstate Mall in Altamonte Springs) which offers tights, skirts, tops, and all the rest of those elasticized products essential to the survival of female athletes and fashion-plates.

Kingpin of the discount delights is **Fitz and Floyd Factory Outlet** (at the end of International Drive at Oak Ridge Road intersection, follow signs on International Drive from Sand Lake Road, exit on Hwy. I-4). Here you'll find 70 cut-rate shops open seven days a week and positively jammed most any day you choose. Housewares, perfumes, gifts, entertainment items, shoes, clothes—you name it, they're all here at prices they say are 25% to 75% lower than retail prices.

Finally, let's not forget the one thing that distinguishes Florida tourists at airports all over the nation: bags of grapefruit and oranges. You can stock up on those mandatory purchases at hundreds of small shops scattered around Orlando. One of the best known is Stuckey's (there's one just off Lake Buena Vista, Rte. 535, exit of Hwy. I-4). There are also several citrus sellers on International Drive including **Citrus Circus** (across from Wet 'n Wild at 6813 Visitors Circle).

A biggy in the business is **Orange Ring** (two locations, one on U.S. 27 north at Haines City and the other at U.S. 192 four miles east of Disney World). Here you can even pick your own orange on 10,000 acres of groveland and tour a packing and juice plant as well. While you're at it, indulge in a free glass of OJ and try a piece of citrus candy or some orange jelly.

Another similar spot is **Benson Groves** (3315 N. Orange Blossom Trail, also known as U.S. 441, one block north of Silver Star Road), where you can sample the various kinds of oranges— Temple, Parson Brown, Navel (don't they have the greatest names?)—and ship home your favorites. Avocados and mangoes here in season too.

Citrus Tower (25 miles west of Orlando and a mile north of the intersection of S.R. 50 and U.S. 27) does indeed tower over the miles of groves surrounding it. You can go up to the top of the tower for a fabulous view of silver-blue lakes and emerald-green groves, or visit a citrus packing plant, a citrus candy factory, and a glassblower's workshop at this citrus store-cum-attraction. (Tower rides are $1.75 adults, $1 for students 10 to 15, others free.)

Last, perhaps least, take note of **Flea World,** where you can roam no less than 12 acres of treasures and trash—one person's treasures are another's trash, remember—everything from tomatoes to gas masks. You'll find it at U.S. 17/92 in Sanford (tel. 645-1792). Tell them to send a search party if you're not back in 12 hours. An hour an acre seems reasonable, no?

Chapter VIII

EXPLORING THE MAGIC KINGDOM

AT LAST YOU'RE HERE, in a place so captivating more than 12 million people visit it every year, a place sprinkled with stardust and glittering with the prestidigitation of imagination.

It's a special place, the Magic Kingdom, a place where reality remains at the ticket booth and fantasy goes exploring, as the mantle of maturity lifts, to be replaced by that starstruck child who lives deep inside all of us.

Jaded as you may be, cynical as you are about this man-made magic, you too will feel the effect of this place when you step onto the macadam of Main Street. It doesn't matter that a child is crying, that you're a little lost, that bells are clanging on the horse trolley, and hooves are rattling on the cobblestones. In one heart-stopping moment distractions disappear, and the days of innocence gone, those cloud-filled moments long forgotten, and people and places that can never return are, in this moment of awe, recaptured, remembered, relived.

Into the sky above you, Cinderella's Castle soars, and on the street before you, a grinning mouse looms into view. All around you the homes, hearths, and hopes of another era transport you from a spinning twentieth century to the era of your imagination, into a time when anything can happen, if you let it.

Let it.

Orientation

Enchanting as are these opening moments—and quite a few of the intermediate ones—in the Magic Kingdom, reality does have a way of intruding. There are things with which you must cope, chief among them the exigencies of entry, arrival, and survival. To help you do that, let's take a look at some of the things you'll need to know before you go and when you get there.

WHEN TO GO: Disney World is a *very* popular place, and that translates into crowds, all the time, all year long, at all hours of the day and night. Lest you panic at the thought, however, let it be known that the Magic Kingdom is a huge place and can absorb thousands and leave you feeling there's hardly anyone around. Also, there are ways to avoid the most crowded times and days. One of the easiest is by getting to the park quite early, say 7 or 8 a.m., during the busy holiday and summer seasons. At less crowded times of year (hold on, I'm coming to that), a 9 or 10 a.m. arrival will help you avoid traffic and lines.

What are the **hours** of the park? Well, they vary by season, but in fall and winter—that is September, October, most of November, the early part of December, and January—hours generally are 9 a.m. to 6 or 7 p.m. At Thanksgiving, Christmas, New Year's Eve, and Easter, holiday hours are extended to midnight. During the week of Washington's Birthday—that's February, in case you forgot—and college spring-break weeks toward the end of March, the park is usually open to 10 p.m. Park operators sometimes decide to change hours, for some reason, so it's a good idea to call Disney information, 824-4321, to find out what's happening today.

Most people expect to find the **biggest crowds** at Disney World in the summer, when children are out of school and everyone's vacationing. Actually, however, the really monstrous crowds come at Christmas, when this fairyland becomes even more magical than usual. From Christmas through New Year's Day, 60,000 to 80,000 people *a day* troop through the turnstiles here.

Next most popular visiting days are in late November around Thanksgiving, two weeks at Easter, during college spring breaks in late March or early April, Washington's Birthday week in February, and finally those summer holidays June through August. At any of those times, you can expect to find 40,000 to 65,000 people sharing the magic.

If you're intent on avoiding crowds, slowest days at the park occur from the beginning of January to mid-February, March, September, October, and most of November, when the crowds ring in at a low of 15,000 a day to a high of about 40,000.

As panicking as those figures are, it may ease your mind to know that this is a very big place. When you and all those other people are moving about on 100 acres of ground, even a crowd of 40,000 is not an uncomfortable mass and often doesn't even mean interminably long lines. When, however, the numbers get into the 60 to 80,000 range, you can be sure you will wait in line for everything from a hot dog to a hot-dogging ride on the Space Needle (which I'm convinced would have a long line even in the middle of a hurricane).

Whether you can bear up under the crowd strains or not is a decision only you can make. Some people think it's well worth it—and Christmas at Disney World does indeed have many memorable moments—while others won't come within miles of the park at those super-busy times.

If you'd like to narrow your choices even more scientifically: In summer the busiest day at the park is Tuesday, followed by Monday, Wednesday, Thursday, and Saturday, pretty much in that order. In fall Saturday is the busiest day. Just about all year round you'll find the smallest crowds on Friday and Sunday.

WHAT TO WEAR: Let's start with the hour or so preceding your departure for the Magic Kingdom. Let me into your bedroom for a moment while you decide what to wear. What to wear may not sound important—this is just a day in a park, for goodness sake—but, believe me, four or five hours of sunshine and miles of steps later, what you have on, or off, will become all-consumingly important.

Wear comfortable clothes and layer them on, so you can add or subtract without multiplying stares. In Florida's sunshine you may think a minimum of clothing is best, but keep in mind that desert dwellers do not by chance wear long, enveloping gowns and head-covering turbans. Clothes keep *out* heat too and ward off sunburn, a condition that can inflict itself on you with great rapidity in Florida—even on cloudy days.

I'm not quite sure how to put this next suggestion tactfully, but those with less hair atop their domes will appreciate—make that, need—a hat. Even the hair-endowed are likely to appreciate a hat's shade on hot days.

Disney officials say shoes and shirts must be worn at all times in the Magic Kingdom, but I'm afraid that rule, especially as it applies to shirts, is broken as often as it's kept. You must have both aboard transportation vehicles, however. They'll insist.

Shoes? Definitely, and comfortable ones, shoes you've come to know and love and absolutely no new ones, whose idiosyncrasies have not yet made themselves known. You will walk . . . and walk . . . and walk . . . and just when you think you don't have to walk another step, you discover you have to walk another step. There's a strong possibility that no matter what you do, your feet will be aching at the end of the day, but you can reduce the groans by getting as comfortable as possible before you take the first step.

One more accoutrement, sunglasses. Glare is everywhere.

GETTING THERE: Now let's get on the road and get on over there, which you do by taking Hwy. I-4 (west in the direction of Tampa) or U.S. 192 east or west, depending on where you're staying. Huge signs on both roads make the Magic Kingdom so easy to find, even the White Rabbit could get there on time.

As you follow the entrance road leading to the Magic Kingdom, you can tune into a radio station, 640 on the AM dial of your car radio, for some basic information on entry to Disney World grounds. On very crowded days, signs also indicate how long you may be stuck in traffic approaching the Toll Plaza. Beyond that Toll Plaza, where you pay a $1 parking fee (waived if you're a guest of a WDW resort), are two miles of attractively landscaped roads to the parking area.

On the way you'll pass the Disney Car Care Center (tel. 824-4813), where you can buy gas and have minor repairs done from 7 a.m. to 10 p.m. AAA cards are accepted. Employees there will drop you wherever you need to go in Disney World and pick you up later, so you don't lose the day babysitting your car. In and around the parking areas, there are tow trucks with emergency equipment available for minor troubles, like dead batteries or empty gas tanks.

Once you reach the parking area, you'll find a multitude of Kids of the Kingdom on hand to wave you into a parking spot. Be sure to note the name of the parking lot you're in—they're named for the Seven Dwarfs and other assorted Disney characters—and the number of your parking line. On busy days there can be 80,000 people in the park, and that's a lot of light-blue station wagons. (If you don't trust your memory, there's a place to write parking information on the back of your parking stub. Keep the stub if you leave the park with plans to return that day—it's good all day long.) Handicapped visitors can park in a special lot adjacent to the Transportation and Ticket Center. Ask at the Toll Plaza for directions to the special lot.

Now, collect all the things you've brought (cameras, jackets, sunglasses, this guidebook, of course), step out of the car, look around, and you will shortly see a jeep-drawn tram snaking its way around the parking lot. Board the tram, and in a few minutes it will deposit you at the Transportation and Ticket Center, where you buy tickets for entrance to the park. Those who arrive *very* early may be lucky enough to find a space in Bashful, Sneezy, Donald, or Daisy parking lots, which are within walking distance of the Ticket Center.

Back to business, if you arrive at Walt Disney World by bus, you'll alight at the bus stop near the Transportation and Ticket Center. That's where you will reboard the bus at the end of the day, too. You'll also find lockers here, if you'd like to stash some of your belongings and pick them up before you leave.

BUYING A TICKET: So here you are at the row of ticket booths where you'll have to make another decision: How many days can you spend exploring the Magic Kingdom and taking a look at the wonders of the future at Disney's brand new Environmental Prototype Community of Tomorrow, otherwise known as EPCOT?

Since that may take some consultation, I've allotted a special section a little further along in this chapter to a discussion of ways to see Disney World. Recommendations on how many days it takes to see it all, or the parts of it in which you're most interested, come from the best brains at Disney and from my own assessment, acquired after walking many a mile around both the Magic Kingdom and EPCOT. Take a look at that section on making the most of your (one, two, or three) days in the Magic Kingdom. Then, make some decisions, and then turn back here for a look at the prices.

A few years ago Disney World simplified life for us all by abandoning its former ticketing system which involved separate tickets for "A," "B," "C," and "D" attractions. In its place the park now sells one-, three-, four-, and six-day tickets called "World Passes," which can be used at any attraction in the park and allows you aboard all the park transportation from the monorail to the horseless carriage. When EPCOT was completed in October 1982, that massive section of the park was included in passports so you can travel around at will skimming back and forth, if you like, between the Magic Kingdom and EPCOT.

Here are the prices of those World Passes (as compiled in late 1982):

A one-day World Pass to *either* the Magic Kingdom or EP-COT, but not both, is $15 for adults, $14 for children 12 to 17, and $12 for youngsters 3 to 11. Children under 3 are free at both attractions.

There are no two-day World Passes available, but a three-day passport permitting admission to both the Magic Kingdom and EPCOT is $35 for adults, $33 for children 12 to 17, and $28 for those 3 to 11.

A four-day World Pass, again including admission to both the Magic Kingdom and EPCOT, is $45 for adults, $42 for children 12 to 17, and $36 for youngsters 3 to 11.

Finally a six-day World Pass also is available for $60, $56, and $48 and is good for a year.

Tickets must be paid in cash or by traveler's checks, no credit cards. Personal checks are accepted with proper identification, and WDW resort guests may charge tickets to their rooms with proper identification.

You can order tickets by mail by writing to Admissions, Walt Disney World, Box 40, Lake Buena Vista, FL 32830, but do allow 15 working days for processing of your request.

If you leave the Magic Kingdom and want to return the same day, have your hand stamped at the exit.

If you're staying at one of the Walt Disney World resorts or in one of the hotels at the WDW Village Hotel Plaza, you can buy tickets right at your hotel. Villa guests can get them at the Reception Center. WDW hotel guests save $1 on each one-day pass, $3 on a three-day ticket, and $4 on a four-day World Pass.

GETTING TO THE MAGIC KINGDOM: Once you've bought your tickets, you still have another journey ahead, and an exciting one it is, too. To get to the door of the Magic Kingdom, you must find your way around or across the Seven Seas Lagoon (really a big lake). There are two kicky ways to do that: Whoosh over on a monorail or slosh over on a ferryboat. Either one can be boarded at the Transportation and Ticket Center, and both let you off right on the threshold of the Magic Kingdom.

On the five-minute monorail journey to or from the park, you'll ride alongside that sparkling lagoon, pass right through the lobby of the Contemporary Hotel and beside Polynesian Village, so you can get a look at both resorts. Peer below you as

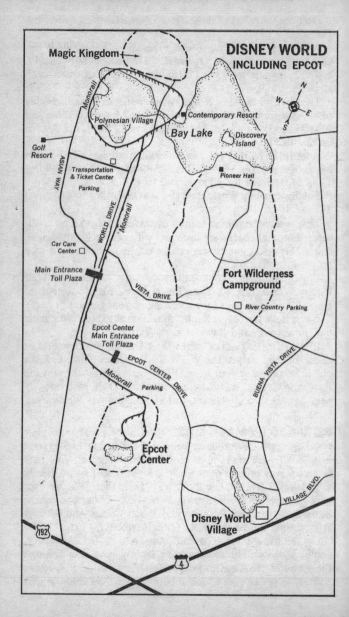

DISNEY WORLD
INCLUDING EPCOT

Magic Kingdom →

Polynesian Village

Contemporary Resort

Bay Lake

Discovery Island

Golf Resort

ASIAN WAY

Transportation & Ticket Center

Parking

WORLD DRIVE

Monorail

Monorail

Pioneer Hall

Car Care Center

Main Entrance Toll Plaza

VISTA DRIVE

Fort Wilderness Campground

River Country Parking

Epcot Center Main Entrance Toll Plaza

EPCOT CENTER DRIVE

Monorail

Parking

BUENA VISTA DRIVE

Epcot Center

Disney World Village

VILLAGE BLVD.

192

4

the monorail streaks along the water, and you'll spot bushes and trees shaped by talented gardeners into fascinating animal topiaries. My favorite's the Nessie sea monster whose curving backbone rises up from, and disappears back into, the ground. Try *that* with your yew tree!

On the ferryboat you ride merrily across the water and get a fascinating look at the Magic Kingdom as it rises up before you like a mirage. It's about a five-minute trip, not much longer than the monorail, but you do have to walk a little farther to the ferry dock. On crowded days, however, you can sometimes find a spot on the ferry faster than you can wait out the line to the monorail. Handicapped guests can use either form of transportation, although holding a wheelchair in line at the ramp to the monorail could be a bit tedious when the line's long, as it often is.

SPECIAL NEEDS—CHILDREN, HANDICAPPED, FIRST AID, AND MORE:

Having faced all those decisions and gotten yourself to the entrance of the Magic Kingdom, now what? Well, if you have **toddlers or small children** with you, you can be sure an exciting day with Mickey and Minnie will tire them out. To save your shoulder, your energy, and perhaps your temper, rent a stroller at the Stroller Shop for $1 a day. The shop's located at the far right of the Magic Kingdom entrance.

If that tiny one is a baby with a **baby's needs,** things like diapers, bottles, formula, and pacifiers, you can satisfy those at the Baby Center, a Gerber-sponsored endeavor. It's not far from the entrance to the Magic Kingdom, just off Main Street, U.S.A., next door to the Crystal Palace Restaurant. Here you'll find disposable diapers and a place to make the change, baby bottles and a place to warm them, pacifiers, baby food, and formula.

If you think you or one of your party might have trouble maintaining the pace, you can **rent a wheelchair** for $1 a day plus a $1.50 refundable deposit. You'll find the chairs at the Stroller Shop, too. If you have your own wheelchair, that's fine too, of course.

Just a note here about wheelchair travel: You can go just about anywhere in the Magic Kingdom in one, but wheelchair guests can't get off or on the monorail at the Contemporary Hotel. All the attractions except Space Mountain, Peter Pan's Flight, Swiss Family Treehouse, the Skyway, and the WEDway PeopleMover are accessible to guests who can be lifted from wheelchairs. Attractions that can accommodate guests right in their wheel-

chairs are Main Street Cinema in Main Street U.S.A.; Tropical
Serenade in Adventure Land; Hall of Presidents, Liberty Square
Riverboats, and Diamond Horseshoe revue in Frontierland; and
Mission to Mars, Circle-vision 360 "Magic Carpet 'round the
World," and Carousel of Progress in Tomorrowland. Many rest-
rooms in the Magic Kingdom also are equipped for people in
wheelchairs.

Disney World visitors who are **blind** or have difficulty seeing
should stop by City Hall on Main Street, U.S.A., and pick up a
free tape cassette and a portable tape recorder which will help
them find their way around the Magic Kingdom via sound and
smell descriptions. There are Braille keys on the tape players.

One would hope the need for **first aid** won't arise, but if you
need a Band-Aid or an aspirin or even something more complicated, head for the first-aid station beside the Crystal Palace,
just off Main Street, U.S.A., or a similar facility at the Transportation and Ticket Center. There's a registered nurse there to help
you. If you need certain kinds of pills, however, be sure to take
them with you. There's no pharmacy at the park.

It's possible that soon after you arrive, you will find that some
of the things you thought you would need have become needless
burdens. Naturally this book will not fall in that category. For
those things that do, however, go over to the **lockers** located
directly under the Main Street Station (and at the Transportation and Ticket Center as well), and for 25¢ or 50¢ you can keep
your extra baggage secure while you traipse around the park. If
you have something so large it won't fit the lockers, they'll take
care of it for you at City Hall or Guest Relations at the Ticket
and Transportation Center.

One thing you can't take into the Magic Kingdom is **pets**, be
they parrots, poodles, ocelots, or a lovable turtle. Despite Disney's love for mice, dogs, elephants, ducks, and the like, you
must park *your* Pluto here at the kennels, just next door to the
Ticket and Transportation Center. Your pet will be cuddled,
loved, kept fed, watered, and so pampered in air-conditioned
quarters that you may need a week to unspoil the little darling.
If you have exotic pets, you must bring their cages or containers
with you, and pets must have a certificate of vaccination just in
case they bite someone. If you're just at Disney World for the
day, you can't leave Fido in the kennel overnight, but if you're
staying in a WDW resort or in a WDW Village Hotel Plaza you
can. Kennels close an hour after the Magic Kingdom and EP-
COT.

Some of us could lose things in an empty room. If you recognize yourself in that description (as I do), relax, Disney has the problem handled. Lose it, then rush over to **Lost and Found,** where you can retrieve everything from your sunglasses to your sister. You can also report the loss at City Hall in Main Street, U.S.A., or at Guest Relations at the Ticket and Transportation Center.

As for **lost children,** you may find them here or over at the Magic Kingdom Baby Center (by the Crystal Palace Restaurant), where hostesses will calm you down and find the missing little one.

If the **missing person** is an adult who's strayed or failed to show up at noon as you'd agreed, etc., etc., then head for City Hall where Kingdom Kids keep a message book. It might be a good idea to tell your whole group about this handy service, so you'll all know where to look if you get separated somehow.

You can find **telephones** directly beneath the Main Street Train Station and at the Transportation and Ticket Center. Calls from within the Magic Kingdom are just 10¢.

Then we come to the matter of **money.** Did I not tell you Disney thinks of everything? They thought, of course, of money and provided for it in the form of the Sun Bank, located just inside the Magic Kingdom on Main Street. It is open daily from 9 a.m. to 4 p.m. and can help you with all the details of traveler's

KEY TO THE NUMBERED REFERENCES ON THE MAGIC KING-DOM MAP: (Main Street, U.S.A.)1. EPCOT Center Preview; 2. Main Street Cinema; 3. Magic Kingdom Baby Care Center; 4. First Aid Center; 5. City Hall; (Tomorrowland) 6. Swan Boats; 7. Circle Vision 360 "Magic Carpet"; 8. If You Had Wings; 9. Mission to Mars; 10. StarJets; 11. WEDway PeopleMover; 12. Tomorrowland Stage; 13. Carousel of Progress; 14. Skyway; 15. Space Mountain; 16. Grand Prix Raceway; (Fantasyland) 17. Mad Tea Party; 18. Mr. Toad's Wild Ride; 19. Snow White's Adventures; 20. Dumbo, the Flying Elephant; 21. Cinderella's Golden Carousel; 22. Cinderella's Castle; 23. 20,000 Leagues under the Sea; 24. It's a Small World; 25. Peter Pan's Flight; 26. Skyway; (Frontierland & Liberty Square) 27. Haunted Mansion; 28. Mike Fink Keel Boats; 29. Liberty Square Riverboats; 30. Tom Sawyer Island; 31. Hall of Presidents; 32. Diamond Horseshoe Revue; 33. Frontierland Shootin' Gallery; 34. Country Bear Jamboree; 35. Frontierland Railway Station; 36. Big Thunder Mountain Railroad; (Adventureland) 37. Pirates of the Caribbean; 38. Jungle Cruise; 39. Swiss Family Treehouse; 40. Tropical Serenade.

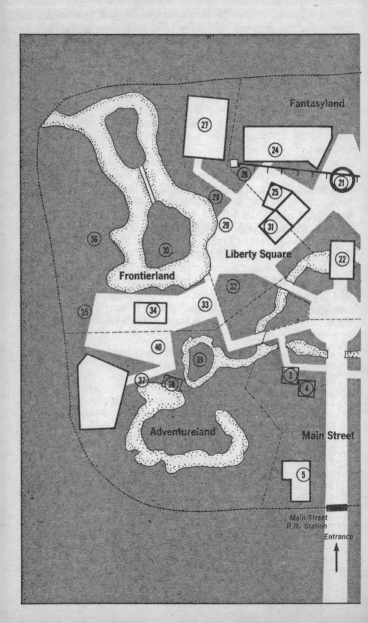

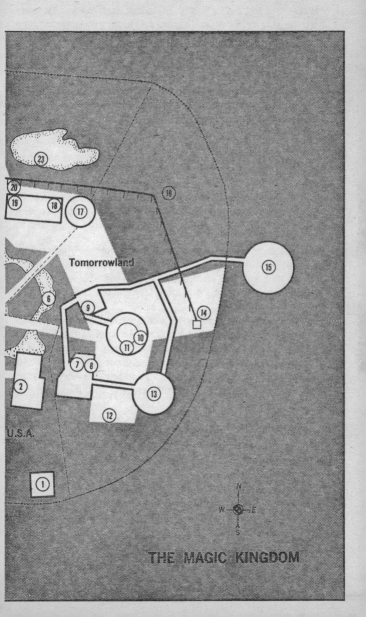

THE MAGIC KINGDOM

checks—selling, cashing, and refunding lost checks. Bankers here can also issue cashier's checks and money orders, exchange foreign currency, provide emergency check-cashing for those with American Express or bank-issued credit cards, and cash personal checks up to $25, if you have a driver's license and major credit card. There are two other Sun Banks in Disney World at Lake Buena Vista and in Walt Disney World Village.

Foreign currency can also be exchanged at City Hall, at the Guest Relations window at the Transportation and Ticket Center, and at the ticket booth in the Train Station on Main Street.

More on money. You can receive money by wire through Western Union offices at the Contemporary and in Kissimmee (tel: 847-4838) and in Orlando (tel. 841-4733).

You can pay for purchases in Magic Kingdom shops with cash, traveler's checks, or American Express, and for meals in the Magic Kingdom's sit-down restaurants with cash, traveler's checks, or credit cards, but in the fast-food dining areas, cash is the word.

Everything you ever wanted to know about the day's **entertainment** is available at the City Hall Information Center, where you can pick up maps and information on just about every facet of the Disney operation including transportation facilities and times.

If you forgot or didn't bring a camera and have an urge to remedy that situation, head for **camera rental** in the Polaroid Camera Center on Main Street, U.S.A. They'll rent you a Sonar One-Step or Polavision Camera free. All you do is leave a $50 to $100 deposit (cash or MasterCard) and buy $10 worth of film. You can rent other kinds of cameras here, too, for about $5, including a roll of film.

You'll find **film on sale** here in the Camera Center and at Tropic Toppers in Adventureland; Frontier Trading Post in Frontierland; Heritage House in Liberty Square; and Castle Camera or the Royal Candy Shoppe in Fantasyland. All hotels carry camera supplies too.

Postcards and stamps can be bought at The Card Shop, Emporium, and Penny Arcade on Main Street and mailed in antique-looking olive mail-boxes. They'll be postmarked Lake Buena Vista, however.

If you buy **plants** in one of the shops and don't want to carry them around, park them in the kennels at the Ticket and Transportation Center or at Fort Wilderness.

Alcoholic beverages are not permitted in the Magic Kingdom but are available at all the hotels and in EPCOT. You must be 19 in Florida to buy alcoholic beverages. Younger travelers are permitted into hotel lounges but can't sit or stand at the bar.

If you run out of **cigarettes,** you can buy them at the Tobacconist on Main Street, Tropic Toppers in Adventureland, the Trading Post in Frontierland, the Royal Candy Shoppe in Fantasyland, Heritage House in Liberty Square, and Mickey's Mart in Tomorrowland. There are vending machines at Columbia Harbour House in Liberty Square, King Stefan's in Cinderella's Castle, Pinocchio Village Haus in Fantasyland, Tomorrowland Terrace, and the Mile Long Bar in Frontierland. Hotels have them too, of course.

Finally, if you somehow forgot to buy those **mouse ears** for Aunt Tillie, don't despair. Once you're back home, just call (tel. 305/824-4718) or write Walt Disney World, Box 40, Lake Buena Vista, FL 32830, Attn. Mail Order Dept., and they'll send you what you want by mail.

Getting Around in the Magic Kingdom

There's no doubt about it: The fanciful mind of that creative cartoonist has given new meaning to transportation. Here in the Magic Kingdom you can get around in fascinating ways that range from an antique horse-drawn trolley to a flying futuristic monorail.

Not only are those clanging, tooting conveyances fun to look at and to ride, but they save your feet from the tortures of pounding pavement. At the end of a long day in the Magic Kingdom, you'll look upon *any* step-saver with gratitude. What's more, all the transportation in the Magic Kingdom and in all of Disney World is free.

Let's start our explorations of Magic Kingdom transport with the most exciting way of all to go: **the monorail.** This sleek bullet-shaped train, with "fronts" on both ends, runs in a circle around the Seven Seas Lagoon, stopping at the Transportation and Ticket Center, Contemporary Resort Hotel, Polynesian Village, and the Magic Kingdom. You can now also board a monorail at the Magic Kingdom's Ticket and Transportation Center and zip over to EPCOT. To ride in the very first car, just ask the driver.

Inside the park, an old-time steam train makes a wide circuit around the perimeter of the park with a stop at Frontierland.

If you're a railroad buff—as was Walt Disney—and even if you're not, you'll enjoy a look at and a ride on these **railroad cars** that have an intriguing history stretching back to the turn of the century when they were constructed. Disney creators found them in Mexico, where they had been converted from coal- to oil-burning trains. Overhauled then and constantly, as is everything in Disney World, the colorful trains now operate on clean diesel fuel, and have lots of shining new parts to supplement the original equipment. Several different kinds of engines, named after Disney and his family and friends, pull the cars.

It's a lovely, breezy ride on a warm day and gives you a good introductory look at all the lands plus a glimpse of some of the animated creatures operated by the complex computer system WDW calls AudioAnimatronics.

I've already mentioned the ferryboat alternative to the monorail, but a little repetition never hurts, so: You can catch a **ferryboat** to or from the Transportation and Ticket Center to the Magic Kingdom. Although it takes just about the same time to traverse the water as the monorail takes to make its circuit, the ferryboat seems longer to most people, so lines for the boat are often shorter at the busy opening and closing hours of the park. What's more, it's a cool, relaxing ride across the lagoon and offers you an unusual view of this wonderland.

A quick and relaxing way to get from Peter Pan's Flight in Fantasyland to the center of Tomorrowland is the **Skyway to Tomorrowland.** A cable-car-in-the-sky ride, the Skyway gives you an eagle's-eye view over the Magic Kingdom before landing you in Tomorrowland. You can also take the ride from Tomorrowland and back to Fantasyland, but you'll first have to get off and get in another line to go back again. In short, the Skyway's a one-way trip in either direction.

In Main Street, U.S.A., there are several ways to travel. My favorite's the **horse-drawn trolley** that rattles its way down the middle of Main Street pulled by the rippling muscles of European plow horses. Those equine heavyweights haul visitors down Main Street to the Town Square and back up Main Street to Cinderella's Castle all day long and live in a fancy barn at Fort Wilderness on their days off. You can see them there and watch them being shod if you're staying at Fort Wilderness.

You can almost feel the shock—not to mention the disdain— people felt at the turn of the century when you first spot a

horseless carriage clipping merrily along Main Street. What a sight those first automobiles must have been to people who had never seen a motorized vehicle! In fact, those antique cars remain a strange sight today, but that doesn't make them any less fun to ride. What's more, you'll never have to get out and crank, since the cars sport modern engines and chug around the Main Street area with considerably more confidence than those early models could boast.

Doubledecker buses ply that busy Main Street thoroughfare too, joined by a merrily clanging, bright-red fire engine that's the stuff of many a youngster's dreams. You can ride both of them, but if you miss an actual ride on the fire engine, you can go look it over at the Firehouse, a sight in its own right. It's next door to City Hall.

Land-Hopping

It's time to start trekking, so let's take a look at the "lands" of Disney World. Attractions, restaurants, shops, and service centers are described as you explore each land, and you can see where the attractions are located by matching the number in the description with the numbers that appear on map.

GETTING ORIENTED: When you enter the Magic Kingdom you will pass underneath the railroad station and find yourself in Town Square. Stretching out in front of you is Main Street U.S.A., and way at the end of that picturesque turn-of-the-century street looms the grandeur of Cinderella's Castle, turrets glistening in the sunshine.

Just in front of the castle is an area known as the Hub, although its official designation is Central Plaza. Like Town Square, the Hub forms a circle. Think of it as the center of a wheel whose spokes run off left and right to the other lands in the Magic Kingdom. As you face the castle, the streets to Tomorrowland and Fantasyland are on your right; the avenues which will take you to Liberty Square, Frontierland, and Adventureland are on your left.

Since there are waterways circling the Hub, there's also a bridge to each of the lands. Again, as you face the castle the first bridge on your right goes to Tomorrowland. Moving counterclockwise, the second one to your right goes to Fantasyland, the next one which you'll find on your left goes to Liberty Square and Frontierland, and the final one on your left goes to Adventureland.

That may seem a little complicated, and an abundance of waterways, trees, flowers, curves, bridges, and dazzling distractions does complicate things a bit, but don't worry. Just keep an eye on the Magic Kingdom map, and if you still begin to feel a little lost, ask directions of any employee—you'll see hundreds of them cleaning, selling, and helping all over the grounds—and you'll soon be back on track again.

A LOOK AT THE LANDS: Okay, oriented and anticipatory, off we go for a gleeful romp among fat bears and leering pirates, mysterious haunted houses and runaway railroad cars. . . .

Main Street, U.S.A.

It's the queen of Main Street, U.S.A., the first thing you'll see and the last thing you'll remember. It's none other than Cinderella's Castle, and it towers over the far end of Main Street in glittering magnificence. Somehow it fits there, despite the juxtaposition of medieval upon the turn-of-the-century prettiness of Main Street.

Here in the shadow of Cinderella, bells clang, horseshoes clatter, painted gingerbread façades sparkle, and there you are, suddenly cast out of the racing bustle of the 20th century, back into a time when life moved more slowly. Glittering gaslights trim the curb, flags flutter atop widow's walks, bay windows jut out over a sidewalk, wrought-iron intricate as a spider's web rims a roofline, and an attic glass is carefully trimmed in ornate woodwork white as snow.

It is doubtful any Main Street in the U.S.A. was ever so picture-pretty. You'll want to explore every one of the emporiums here, and there are plenty, for each of them has something fascinating to show you.

To help you tour the Magic Kingdom's attractions, shops, and restaurants, I've numbered the attractions beginning at Main Street, U.S.A., and working around counterclockwise to Tomorrowland, Fantasyland, Frontierland and Liberty Square, and ending in Adventureland.

To make a systematic tour of Main Street, you can start by turning to your right in the Town Square and heading over to a wide verandahed porch where an **EPCOT Center Preview (1)** will give you an idea what's in store over at that newest Disney addition.

Right next door is the **Town Square Café,** a Victorian delight gleaming with brass trim and woodwork. Breakfast is popular here, since you can sit outside in the relative cool of early morning and watch the square come to life. Simple home cooking, baked chicken, crisp salads, hefty sandwiches, chocolate cake, and the like also keep the Town Square Café crowded at lunch and dinner. Table service is available here, by the way.

One of my passions is hats, so I never miss a visit to the next shop along the way, **The Chapeau.** Here you'll find some frothy confections of lace, ribbons, and feathers incongruously paired with the monogrammed Mousketeer ears you'll see everywhere. Great place to stock up on costume-party accessories or to pick up a little something for those people whose favorite cliché is "Now let me put on my other hat for a moment. . . ."

Next door, just at the corner, is that helpful place I mentioned earlier, the **Polaroid Camera Center,** where you can borrow one of those quickie cameras by leaving a refundable $50 deposit and buying a roll of film for about $10. Lots of other camera companies display their products there, too, and there are film, flashcubes, and various camera needs for sale. You can also have a Polaroid shot taken of you and the gang in Victorian costume making a whistlestop visit to the park aboard the back of a caboose.

As you continue along the right-hand side of the street, you see the **Main Street Cinema** (2). Chortle over some of the classic silent films of a bygone era and stars like Charlie Chaplin and Fatty Arbuckle. Don't miss the early Mickey Mouse cartoon, *Steamboat Willie,* first cartoon with sound and with the famous mouse and his mate.

If you like delicate china, you'll love **The Cup 'n Saucer,** where the best-known china purveyors have assembled their wares. Prices run from bargain to billionairedom, so you will find plenty to ogle.

It's December 25th all year round at **Holiday Corner,** and you may find just the perfect little mouse to hang on your tree. Mickey's here, too, napping while he waits for Santa in a tiny living room full of tiny furniture. Candlemaking's a talent on display here, too, and some lovely scented ones roll from the talented fingers of the dippers.

More Disney World souvenirs—it's amazing how many

things people can theme dream—at the **Disney & Co.** shop next door. It may be hard to drag the kids out of this one.

Even harder to drag the distaffers out of the next shop along this side street: **Uptown Jewelers** carries a captivating line of antique-looking jewelry and some Disney character charms that may be among the more long-lasting souvenirs of your visit here.

Everything's old-fashioned everywhere you look on Main Street, but the **Market House** gets my vote for best "old" interpretation. Here a potbellied stove of the general-store variety is the center of things, surrounded by oak cases full of goodies that aren't old-timey but seem that way—Smucker's jams and jellies, Cracker Jacks, and other old favorites.

Shadow boxes, those black profiles created with an artist's eye and a sure hand on the scissors, are made as you watch at **The Shadow Box**—and there are always plenty of watchers. Plenty of buyers, too, since the paper portraits are just $3, complete with frames.

Everytime I see a glassblower at work I wonder what would happen if he *took* a deep breath instead of exhaling one. Somehow those artisans always manage to keep their mind on their work, which is just as well since they're working on molten glass so hot one misstep would require lots of burn remedy. Watch them twist their fiery product into fascinating forms at **Crystal Arts**, where you can also see a glass engraver at work.

Back on the main part of Main Street, cool off from watching that fiery glass at the **Main Street Bakery**, a charming little tearoom, where you can pick up some delicious coffee cake and Danish pastry. Then go next door to combine it with an ice cream creation at the **Sealtest Ice Cream Parlor.**

If it's meal or snack time, you're right in place for a stop at the **Plaza Restaurant.** You can sit down, soak up the art noveau decor, and let a waitress bring you a sundae dripping with sweet things or a substantial lunch or dinner that might include a hearty casserole or a pasta selection, a fat sandwich, or an over-stuffed salad. For something lighter, there's a wildly colored pavilion next door that raisin-lovers should adore: everything you order comes with a little side treat of raisins!

Or cross the street and have a jumbo hot dog and a soft drink in the pleasant, airy, red-and-white decor of the **Refreshment Corner,** a spot that will be appreciated by anyone who's hooked on old Coca-Cola memorabilia. Lots of it here.

If you continue on down the side street, you'll come to another popular Main Street, U.S.A., stopping spot, **Crystal Palace Res-**

taurant. This glass-domed barn of a restaurant is a cafeteria with some lovely views out over a courtyard or across the flower-bedecked sidewalks. Breakfast is a popular meal here, since there's a wide selection of goodies, usually plenty of room, and not much waiting time at early hours.

Here, too, is the **Magic Kingdom Baby Care Center** (3) and the **First Aid Center** (4) (see the beginning of this chapter for a description of the services available at both centers).

You can now work your way down the opposite side of the street (that is, the left side as you face the castle, the west side of the street for those with a good sense of direction) aiming back toward Town Square.

An irresistible medley of aromas wafts through the door of the next shop along the avenue, **The Tobacconist.** This shop sells all flavors of pipe tobacco and some unusual cigarettes, cigars, and smokers' accessories.

Think you can't buy anything for a penny anymore? Ha! You can at Disney World where the **Penny Arcade** is the perfect place to lighten the load of coppers in your pocket. Use them to watch the first "movies," which were flipping cards that moved fast enough to fool your eye into thinking the characters were moving. Some slapsticky humor and some fun things like a kiss-power tester will keep you laughing.

If you know someone who's a practical joker—or are one yourself—you won't want to miss the next shop, the **House of Magic.** Well stocked with the gag items so loved by the world's lampshade wearers, this emporium also answers the dreams of would-be Merlins with things that pop up, disappear, reappear, and turn up in someone's ear. You can even find a monster mask here that may bear some resemblance to your boss.

If there's someone you'd like to send a greeting card, stop by the **Hallmark Card Shop,** just around the corner from the House of Magic. Attractive stationery here and some unusual wrapping papers and party supplies.

Don't get your hair cut before you leave home. Wait until you get to the Magic Kingdom, and get those locks shorn in the style provided by **Harmony Barber Shop** (tel. 824-4550 for appointments). Likely as not you'll be serenaded during your shearing by—what else?—a barbershop quartet. If there's a moustache in the crowd, buy him his very own moustache cup.

Here in this well-manicured and planted side street, you'll also find **The Greenhouse,** specialists in silk flowers so realistic you'll occasionally catch yourself sniffing a noseful of silk. There are plenty of the real things here, too, plus pretty pots to put them in. If you want to buy a live plant, but wonder how it—and you—are going to make it through a sunny day in the park, drop it off at the kennel near the Ticket and Transportation Center. A plant-sitter will keep an eye on it for free until you retrieve it. Little replicas of those terrific animal-shaped topiaries you see from the monorail are on sale here too.

Entries and exits wind all around these stores, and The Greenhouse is really a part of one of the largest stores in the Magic Kingdom, **The Emporium.** Its towering façade makes it a good landmark on Main Street, U.S.A., and inside you'll find zillions of souvenirs from T-shirts to towels to those ubiquitous ears.

Tick, tick, tick, it's the **New Century Clock Shop.** There's every kind of horological hardware you can dream up here, including those famed Mickey Mouse watches. This is a great place to send habitual latecomers.

When you walk out the door of The Emporium, you'll see **City Hall** (5), number-one information center in the Magic Kingdom and the place to go when you need help with just about anything. The **Sun Bank** is right next door to provide you with financial services (see beginning of this chapter where those services are outlined).

Now you're back where you started at the Town Square and the **Railroad Station.** Here are two more possible stops, a snack bar called the **Station Break** and a **Newsstand** that's really a souvenir shop, no news.

From here in Town Square you can grab a ride on the railroad, if you're planning to make Frontierland and Liberty Square your next stop. Or jump on the horse-drawn trolley, an antique jitney or horseless carriage, fire engine, or the Omnibus doubledecker. Pick one and hitch a ride up to the Hub in front of Cinderella's Castle, where you can decide which of the lands to visit next.

Tomorrowland

Ah, future shock. Here at Disney World you can see what that means by walking a few steps from the old-time atmosphere on Main Street, U.S.A., across a bridge, and there it is—the crystal ball of tomorrow gleams before you, inviting you to take a peek, if you dare.

Here you can play on an intriguing new transportation system, go on a mission to Mars, and soar through the black hole of infinite space on an innovative rollercoaster.

What are we waiting for? Let's leave yesterday behind and race off into tomorrow. Once again, the attractions are keyed by numbers to the Magic Kingdom map.

As you cross the bridge to Tomorrowland (it's the first street on your right just as you end your walk up Main Street toward the castle and reach the beginning of the Hub area), you'll see a lovely blue canal. Floating serenely on it are enchanting craft called **Swan Boats** (6). Float down the waterways of the Magic Kingdom on one of these graceful creatures, and you'll feel a little like that mythological goddess, Leda, who got to know quite a bit about swans in her lifetime. These Swan Boats are a popular summer cooling-off spot.

Once across the waterway you'll find on your right one of the all-time favorite exhibits in the park, **Circle Vision 360 "Magic Carpet 'round the World"** (7). The wonders of the world roll out before you, behind you, and all around you as you watch a film that encircles the entire room. What a strange feeling it is to stand there in the center of the room and watch waters stretching out in front of you and see those same waters rolling away behind you. Reams of equipment are used to show this most unusual 20-minute film which many Disney-goers consider a must every time they visit the park. Some of the stops on the film's journey are Denmark's Tivoli Gardens, London's Thames River, Rome's crumbling Coliseum, the Sahara Desert, the Nile Pyramids, and a vast array of U.S.A. landmarks.

Next door is Eastern Airlines' exhibit **"If You Had Wings"** (8), a five-minute film that first takes you to tropical wonderlands in the Caribbean then ends with some swooping special effects that make you feel as if you are actually there. Exciting. At the entrance to the exhibit, Eastern, the official Disney World airline, has a ticket sales booth that can help you out if you want to catch the next plane to the tropics.

On your left as you enter Tomorrowland is **Mission to Mars** (9) where for a moment you become an astronaut heading off into space after a briefing by Mission Control. McDonnell-Douglas created this attraction, which includes some bizarre sounds, seats that shudder as you take off into space, and satellite photos of Mars' surface. Young explorers with good imaginations may like this one better than adults, who have become inured to it all after watching many a rocket launching on television.

Next door is a spacey gift shop junior astronauts will find

irresistible. Called **The Space Port,** it's filled with wire sculptures, "rain" lamps, and lots of chromey futuristic items.

Once you manage to drag yourself away from the glittering wonders of The Space Port and get back on the sidewalk, look up in the air and you'll see two other Tomorrowland attractions, **StarJets** (10) and the **WEDway PeopleMover** (11). On a StarJet you pilot your own spacecraft, a bullet-shaped car that moves in a circle as you "pilot" it up and down a few degrees—breezy and fun if you're a ride enthusiast.

As for the PeopleMover, it's a series of small trains moving on a track, a story or so above the grounds of Tomorrowland. Relaxing if you're footsore by now, the PeopleMover is an innovative concept in transport in that it is powered by a motor that has no moving parts, uses little power, and discharges no polluting chemicals. You travel about a mile on the trains enjoying views of the monorails zooming by, some racing cars zipping along below, and, at one point, you even get a preview look at that scary Space Mountain rollercoaster. Good place to decide whether Space Mountain is going to be part of your future.

Right here, too, by the PeopleMover and the StarJets, is a snack bar called **The Space Bar,** offering a variety of sandwiches and snacks, soft drinks, and desserts.

Since this area forms a rough circle, let's move to the right (as you face StarJets and Space Mountain, that futuristic volcano-shaped building that towers over Tomorrowland). Back of the beaten path tucked away in foliage around the corner from Eastern's "Wings" exhibit is the **Tomorrowland Stage** (12) where Kids of the Kingdom present a show called "Walt Disney World Is Your World."

Next door you'll see a saucer-shaped building that houses the **Carousel of Progress** (13), a General Electric show which was first presented at the New York World's Fair. This 20-minute production features those life-sized, animated, computer-controlled figures Disney does so well. At this exhibit the AudioAnimatronic characters are a family group that tells you about the ways in which electricity has changed the history of this nation.

Moving along to your right you'll find the **Skyway Station Shop** filled with more mouse ears, T-shirts, and typically Disney souvenirs.

Beside the shop is the **Skyway** (14), a very popular attraction I mentioned earlier as a clever way to save your feet the journey from Tomorrowland to Fantasyland. Skyway's a cable car suspended high over the lands, and you move at a slow pace from Tomorrowland to Fantasyland, getting a marvelous view of the goings-on below. Lines here, they tell me, are often considerably shorter than Skyway lines at Fantasyland, so it might be a good idea to see all of Tomorrowland first, then take the five-minute Skyway ride to Fantasyland.

Here we are at last, the one Disney attraction every thrill-seeker is determined to ride: **Space Mountain** (15). Enter here, and an eerie outer-space feeling descends upon you as you spot Disney employees in a control room from which a strange blue glow emanates. Trepidation mounts as you hear the shrieks of riders and culminates in some serious second thoughts when you see the bullet-shaped cars that are about to rocket you into this black hole journey. It's comforting to have a companion on this ride since you sit directly in front of your companion, more or less on his/her lap. Both of you are buckled in together and off you go into the wild black yonder, accompanied by wonderfully spooky sound-and-light effects. Meteors hurl themselves at you, stars shoot through the darkness, white lights zap. Slowly, slowly, you roll off into the blackness, then your speed increases, and suddenly you're whizzing through the inky darkness, your rocket tearing off at what seems to be 90-degree angles, flying up and down inclines.

Scary it is, but not as terrifying as some of the more diabolical rollercoaster rides in amusement parks these days. Disney's Space Mountain thrills lie in spooky sounds and lights and the disorienting psychological effects of rapid, unexpected movement in darkness. It's also a short ride, just a little over two minutes at speeds of about 30 miles an hour. You're advised to pass this one up if you are subject to motion sickness, have a weak back or heart condition, poor health, physical limitations, or are pregnant. It's also a good idea to leave glasses, packages, and the like with a companion, since they can fly out of the car when you will be in no condition to attempt a retrieval. Lines here are enormously long almost all the time. This is a ride much loved by youngsters, who take it over and over despite the wait, often an hour or more. You'll have to decide whether a two-minute ride is worth an hour-long wait. Thousands think it is.

Walk straight ahead as you leave the Space Mountain, and near the StarJets ride you will see a good snacking spot, **The Lunching Pad,** my candidate for Disney World's best pun. Here you can stoke up on some nutritious goodies like yogurt, trail mix, juices, sandwiches, salads, and natural foods, including carob-flavored treats.

To your right as you face The Lunching Pad is **Mickey's Mart,** filled with more Disney-theme treasures.

Next door to that a little farther along is **Tomorrowland Terrace,** a fast-food dining spot featuring performances by Michael Iceberg, who makes strange sounds on electronic musical instruments. You can chow on some ordinary fare like hamburgers and hot dogs with extraordinary names like Moon Burgers and Galactic Pizza, a creation on sourdough bread.

Across the sidewalk is the **Grand Prix Raceway** (16). Racing-car buffs can get behind the wheel here and zoom in cars that run on a single metal track and seem to be racing even if they're only going about seven miles an hour. Kids (you must be taller than 4'4" to ride) love it, but they aren't the only ones. The trick to steering, an aficionado tells me, is to turn the wheel all the way over in one direction or the other.

Fantasyland

Cloud pictures in the sky, rabbits with monocles, dwarfs and witches, glass slippers and little boys with wings. That's the stuff of fantasies, those glorious moments when imagination is unfettered by reality and dreams are released to fly free.

Nowhere will you find the stuff of fantasy so faithfully portrayed as in the Magic Kingdom's Fantasyland. Here colors glow, architectural ornaments glitter, and even the flowers seem to grow with a little more vigor. You would expect children to love Fantasyland's rainbows of colors and never-ending surprises—and they do—but I often think those who love it most are adults, who know too well the fragility of fantasies.

You can get here several ways: By coming straight up Main Street and around the Hub, you enter in the most glamorous way of all, right through the middle of Cinderella's Castle; from any of the lands, just follow the streets around in the direction of Fantasyland (any Kingdom Kid, and plenty of signs, can tell you which direction to go); and finally, the way we'll go, right around the bend from Tomorrowland.

Since we're trying to do this systematically, let's start where we left off in Tomorrowland and just keep on going into the land of fantasies. Right in front of the Grand Prix Raceway, you'll see the first Fantasyland attraction you can visit, and it's a crazy one, **The Mad Tea Party** (17). You do remember that wacky soul in

EXPLORING THE MAGIC KINGDOM 131

Alice in Wonderland who invited Alice over for some un-birth-day party tea, don't you? Well, join the Mad Hatter here and go round and round in a king-sized teacup that spins crazily about a huge teapot.

Stagger out of your cups and just ahead you should see another wacky ride, **Mr. Toad's Wild Ride** (18), based on a Disney film about a toad who trades his manse for a car. This one reminds me a little of an electronic game, since you ride in a car past all kinds of thrills—a chicken coop filled with protesting cacklers, a haystack, down a railroad track, and through the dark where you're threatened by all sorts of falling, banging things.

If you need a little something to calm your nerves, stop in right next door to Mr. Toad's hangout at **The Round Table** for a soft ice-cream cone to soothe you, or at the adjoining **Lancer's Inn** for pizza and other assorted treats.

Think some gum drops or a peppermint stick will provide enough soothe? Get one next door to Lancer's at **The Royal Candy Shoppe**, which also dispenses Disney memorabilia.

Between the candy shop and another souvenir store, **The Aris-toCats,** is an adventure that takes you to the fairest of them all, Snow White. Go deep into the dark, forbidding forest of **Snow White's Adventures** (19) to meet that wicked witch and shed a tear for gullible Ms. White. Just keep an eye out for the evil sorceress—she's got some surprises in store for you!

Around the bend from Snow White's Adventures, on the other side of The AristoCats gift shop, is **Merlin's Magic Shop.** Would-be tricksters can pick up the things they'll need to turn rabbits out of hats and one scarf into a rope long enough to save Rapunzel. If you don't have a dummy with you, you can buy one here or become one yourself with the addition of some ghastly monster masks.

Across the sidewalk from Snow White's place is darling Dumbo, the elephant world's answer to the Flying Nun. At **Dumbo, the Flying Elephant** (20), you'll see that fat little crumpet whirling young riders up, down, and around in a simple ride that will thrill the little ones but is pretty tame for adult riders.

As you wander on in the shadow of Cinderella's Castle, you will pass—or if you're like me, you will *not* pass, you will get on—**Cinderella's Golden Carrousel** (21). What can you say about a merry-go-round? It's wonderful and yes, I have a favorite steed, but I'm not telling which one. You'll take it, and it's mine. Besides, there are 89 others on this remodeled early-1900s carousel that once resided in a Detroit park, all of them glamorous equines that will carry you off in style. No expense was spared on this glittering creation which is something to see, whether or not you ride.

While you're right here, take some time to wander through the crowning glory of Disney World, none other than **Cinderella's Castle** (22). This is Disney magic at its best, a fairyland structure crowned with needle-pointed spires and trimmed with turrets, chimneys, and lacy woodwork. Taller than Sleeping Beauty's manse in California's Disneyland, it seems to float through the clouds, its towering loveliness reflected in the waters that surround it.

Modeled after the architecture of medieval France and the incredible Bavarian palace of Mad King Ludwig (who may have been crazy but had the eyes of a Michaelangelo), the castle hides an interesting secret: Beneath it is the center of the labyrinthian corridors used by Disney characters to traverse the park so they can turn up wherever they wish like magic. Down here beneath the ground are stored the thousands of glittering costumes worn by Disney performers who move through the corridors on electric carts. That's how Mickey and Minnie are able to be on Main Street one moment and turn up two "lands" away just a short time later.

You can't explore the whole castle, which also contains broadcasting facilities and an apartment meant for, but never used by, the Disney family, but you can walk straight through it and across the moat.

On your way through, marvel at the enormous mosaic murals composed of thousands of tiny slivers of glass in all colors of the rainbow, plus real gold and silver, relating the woes of lovely Cinderella and those nasty step-relations of hers. It's not hard to imagine her living happily ever after, here in this glittering monument to fairy tales. Who wouldn't?

Here in the castle is one of the Magic Kingdom's best and most elaborate restaurants, **King Stefan's Banquet Hall.** To dine here is to be served by lasses clad in ornate medieval gowns, in a setting of heavy wood beams and high ceilings, to drop back into another century, a time of royalty and riches, of knights in shining armor. King Stefan, by the way, was Sleeping Beauty's papa. Lunch and dinner are served here, and the preparations are more elaborate than you'll find elsewhere in the Magic Kingdom. You must make reservations at the door, and you'd better do that as soon as you arrive at the park, as seats go quickly.

Here, too, is an interesting gift shop, **The King's Gallery,** where you'll see fascinating chess sets and some lovely, if expensive, items ranging from music boxes to enamelware, lidded German beer steins, pewter and wood-work, and a special metalwork done with silver and gold etched onto steel and called Damascene work after the Damascus creators of this skill.

Back in Fantasyland and behind the castle, you'll see a body of water dotted with boulders that reach rough fingers out of the water and impede the progress of a submarine. A submarine? Yes, indeed, it's Fantasyland's **20,000 Leagues under the Sea** (23), in which you board a submarine piloted by that dreadful Captain Nemo of *20,000 Leagues under the Sea* fame. These submarines carry you through millions of gallons of water in which dwell all kinds of imaginary sea creatures that loom up out of the blue. You even pass a polar ice cap before returning once again to terra firma.

Along the edge of Captain Nemo's playground is another snacking spot, the **Tournament Tent,** named for the tentlike enclosure from which are dispensed fruit drinks, ice cream, and submarine sandwiches.

Beyond that you'll see another tentlike structure, **Fantasy Faire,** where Mickey himself appears, accompanied by other characters who sing and dance for you several times a day. You can find out what hours they'll be performing at City Hall or on signs posted outside Fantasy Faire.

As you might have noticed by now, there is absolutely no chance of starvation in Disney World. One more spot dedicated to staving off hunger pangs is **Pinocchio Village Haus** just across from the carousel. There's a European flavor about this warren of rooms that has cuckoo clocks tweeting away the hours. More of the usual child-pleasing fare here: fried chicken, hamburgers, hot dogs, and soft drinks. You can have breakfast here, too, if you decide to start your day in Fantasyland.

Hard by Pinocchio's hangout is another all-time park favorite, **It's a Small World** (24). Some parkgoers tell me they stop here every time they visit Disney World. They just can't get enough of the hundreds of tiny dolls dressed up in folkwear of every nationality and singing their little hearts out. As you ride through this one, you're serenaded by the dolls, moving hands, feet, eyes, and assorted other parts. There are Hawaiian hula dancers, toy London Beefeater Guards, wooden-shoed Dutch dancers, Greek terpsichoreans, herds of singing animals, plus dozens more. Definitely one of Disney's cutest AudioAnimatronic displays. You'll love it. Everybody does.

Directly across the walkway from Small World is a big enclave which houses a number of shops and restaurants plus another favorite Disney attraction, Peter Pan's Flight.

Straight across from where you're standing when you exit Small World is another camera shop, **Castle Camera Shop,** which is convenient if you've run out of film; a juice bar, **Troubador Tavern,** and another hat shop, this one sponsored by that **Mad Hatter.**

Here, too, you'll find **Peter Pan's Flight** (25), on which you'll fly over the rooftops of London, Big Ben, Thames, and all, just the way Peter and Tinkerbell did. Watch out for that vicious Captain Hook, and cheer on the crocodile who's got a taste for captain-meat.

You can see more of these characters at **Tinkerbell's Toy Shop,** where pirate ships and their crews are the theme. Buy an Alice in Wonderland or Snow White costume here, who cares if Halloween is a year away?

Finally, on the very edge of Fantasyland near It's a Small World is the other end of that **Skyway** (26) I mentioned earlier. Board here and ride through the sky on a cable-car trip to Tomorrowland.

Frontierland and Liberty Square

Americana in all its glory comes to life in these lands as Disney World, in its inimitable style, honors the American battle for liberty and the frontier spirit of those who fought and died in the subsequent struggles to expand the nation's boundaries.

Here America's legends, real and fictional, become the themes of rollicking entertainment, cozy cafés, and shops packed with the regalia of those bygone days. It's sometimes corny and sometimes commercial, but beneath the surface runs a recollection that the nation we all share today is the gift of those who shed their blood on icy battlefields or fought their way through the wilderness to hack out a tiny piece of tomorrow for us all.

Just as Fantasyland merges imperceptibly into these two lands, Frontierland and Liberty Square flow together around a tranquil waterway that provides a setting for the re-creation of legends and legendary times in American history.

At the center of it all is a massive tree of such impressive girth and stature no one could bear to destroy it, so the giant live oak was dubbed the Liberty Tree and moved to its present location between The Hall of Presidents and Liberty Tree Tavern where it has become the focus of these two lands. In its ancient branches are 13 tiny lanterns honoring the 13 original colonies that ignited the lamp of freedom in this nation.

You can enter these two lands from several directions, including the roads leading off to your left as you walk down Main Street toward the castle. Let's work on the assumption, however, that you're moving right around the park, counterclockwise, so you'll be near the Main Street exit when you've seen everything.

Okay, on we go then making our way from Fantasyland through Frontierland and Liberty Square.

As you leave Fantasyland past the Skyway ride, keep to your left and you'll pass right through to these two Disney lands. Happy will be the cooks who spot **Yankee Trader Gourmet Culinary Aids,** a shop packed with all the kitchen accoutrements you can think up and perhaps a few you've never seen. Big wooden spoons, gadgets that cut french fries and flute radishes, mashers and mills, specialty foods, and lots and lots of cookbooks. No pioneer chef ever had it so good.

From there keep to your right and . . . shiver . . . it's the **Haunted Mansion** (27) rising in spooky splendor at a curve of the waterway. All the elements of horror are here—tombstones, cobwebs, see-through ghosts, and creaky noises—but you'll find it more fun than faint-producing.

As you enter a hall lined with portraits, you'll hear us dedicated cowards shrieking as the walls rise (or does the floor drop?). Once past that little thriller, you get a look at a most civilized, if somewhat ghostly, banquet where the transparent departed nod and chatter happily beneath spider webs and layers of dust. Bats swoop, creatures appear and disappear, and you'll love every ghastly, or ghostly, minute of it. This one's a top park attraction and definitely a don't-miss. (An interesting side note here: Workers have to struggle to keep this place *dirty* by importing dust and spreading it around. Call me, fellows, I know where you can get some cheap and I'll even lend you my vacuum.)

Back outside (sigh of relief) in the security of daylight, wander back the way you came and focus on water. That shouldn't be difficult, since you'll see quite a lot of it streaming by. To get out there on it, choose one of three ways: by keelboat, doubledecker riverboat, or on a Tom Sawyer-inspired raft.

That brings us to three adventures located right here. **Mike Fink Keel Boats** (28), was named for a riverboat captain of the early 1800s. One of the keel boats is named *Gullywhumper,* and the dock where the boats are moored is flanked by the **Keel Boat**

Shoppe, where you can buy some of the magic they make at the Haunted House.

The **Liberty Square Riverboats** (29), moored nearby, sail up and down the waterway here, so to avoid a repetititive trip, pick one or the other. Along the way on either boat you'll see Disney-created animals and pioneer adventures in action, not to mention more of the beautifully manicured grounds that you've been seeing all over the park. These paddlewheelers are real riverboat replicas run by a steam-driven paddlewheel. Hidden underneath the water, however, is a rail that keeps the boat on course.

If that youthful adventurer, Tom Sawyer, captured your childhood imagination, here's your chance to follow in his wake, so to speak, aboard a **Tom Sawyer Island** (30) raft journey that takes you across the river to Tom Sawyer's own island, where there are caves to explore, a rope bridge to traverse, and a shudder-causing water crossing made of barrels—a barrel of laughs for thrill-seekers.

This island is a wilderness of deep tropical jungle growth that creates a restful serenity. There's plenty for kids to explore, ranging from **Fort Sam Clemens** guarded, in a manner of speaking (you'll see what I mean), by more AudioAnimatronically controlled characters and fitted up with toy guns the kids can blast away on to their heart's content. There's a dark tunnel to call echoes in, and for parents who want a moment's quiet, there's a pretty resting place called **Aunt Polly's** where you can munch on some basic sandwich and soft drink selections.

Back at the riverboat dock and across the street from it you'll find a cluster of shops and eateries surrounding another premier attraction at Disney World, **The Hall of Presidents** (31). A favorite of history buffs, this production features life-sized and lifelike figures of every president of the U.S., including the current one, answering a roll call while his predecessors listen, make notes, squirm about a bit, and even whisper to each other in the background.

Each president is dressed in the clothes of his time. All the duds were carefully researched, as is everything about this show, from the furnishings to the minutest details of hair, eyes, cuff links, and tie pins. Preceded by a film outlining the importance of the Constitution to America, the Hall of Presidents' roll call provides a stirring show and one so realistic you will hardly believe your eyes.

On a side street here you'll find a cluster of shops and fast food shops including **Heritage House,** where historical memorabilia

—authentic-looking copies of historic documents on parchment paper make attractive souvenirs—and Early American-replica housewares are sold; **Mlle. Lafayette's Parfumerie,** purveyors of famous perfumes and special scents custom-made in any combination you like; **Olde World Antiques,** which is jammed with antique furniture and bric-a-brac, the real thing plus reproductions; **Silversmith,** where you'll wonder how they keep all those polished silver spoons, pitchers, bowls, and candlesticks shining; **Sleepy Hollow Refreshments,** where you can find munchies and try a special Lengendary Punch; **Columbia Harbor House;** and finally **The Fife and Drum,** an ice cream shop (or shoppe).

That brings us to **Liberty Tree Tavern,** which is just a little too special to lump in with all the snack shops and quick stopping spots in the Magic Kingdom. Here pillars soar at the wide entrance, and inside early Americana comes to life. You'll spot a spinning wheel waiting for its mistress to continue her work, a writing desk worthy of Ben Franklin, a tiny cradle, pewter, copper, and a fireplace. You'll feel as if you stepped right back into time in this wallpapered and draperied dining room where waitresses stride from the kitchens carrying heaped-up platters of food every bit as typically early American as the atmosphere: apple brown betty, pumpkin pie, pot roast, beef stew, and a very special walnut bread that's not to be missed. You can have lunch or dinner here but do anticipate a crowd, since this lovely dining room ranks right up there with King Stefan's Banquet Hall in popularity.

As you stroll along the street where Liberty Tree Tavern is, you'll be moving right into Frontierland, where there's more fun in store.

Just beyond the Liberty Tree Tavern is one of the park's best-loved show spots, the **Diamond Horseshoe Revue** (32), where leggy, beruffled damsels kick up their heels and some corny comics deliver punch lines that wouldn't play even in Peoria but are so silly you laugh anyway. All together, it makes a lively vaudeville show reminiscent of a frontier saloon performance that wouldn't raise even a schoolmarm's eyebrow.

There are several shows each day, and you need reservations, which you can make by presenting yourself at the door of the attraction in the morning of the day you want to attend. Reserved seats are on a first-come, first-served basis. First arrivals usually show up minutes after the park opens, so get there early. If you don't make it, drop by 45 minutes or so before a show and hope for a cancellation.

Next door to the Revue is another chapeaux chateau, **Tricornered Hat Shoppe.** This one's big on frontier headwear—raccoon caps, cowboy gear, and the like. Once you've invested in the perfect ten-gallon topper, stride next door, pick up a gun, and mow 'em down at the **Frontierland Shootin' Gallery** (33), where you can fire away at toy buffalo, rabbits, and other frontier dinner fare. A dozen shots are 25¢ at the Shootin' Gallery, one of only a few attractions in the Magic Kingdom that charge a fee.

To complete the outfit you started at the Tricornered Hat Shoppe, stop at the **Frontier Trading Post** and stock up on all the things an urban frontiersperson needs—sunbonnets, belt buckles, moccasins, a six-shooter, even an Indian drum you can use to pound out a come-home-to-supper message for the kids.

One Disney visitor I know so enjoys the next attraction you'll see in the Magic Kingdom that he's seen it no less than nine (!) times and says he can't wait to get back again to make it ten. He is not alone in his feelings about the **Country Bear Jamboree** (34), a rocking-and-roaring good time presented by some of the fattest, funniest roly-polys your imagination could conjure.

Performed in Grizzly Hall, this grin-and-bear-it, western hoedown is entirely peopled by bears (AudioAnimatronic all) who have exchanged hibernation for jubilation. Hear Five Bear Rugs, a country and western group, lay it on thick; watch Teddi Bearra flirt and flutter her boa; and Big Al, well, you have to meet Big Al to understand why he's become a park folk hero.

As the bear buffs exit the Country Bear Jamboree, many of them head right next door to the **Mile Long Bar,** which isn't quite a mile long but looks it, thanks to tricky mirrors and a gleaming brass rail. Mooseheads and the like offer some glassy-eyed stares as you munch away on Frito-Lay products.

Next door the **Pecos Bill Café** sports a rustic interpretation of Old West atmosphere with stick-and-twig ceiling and indoor and outdoor dining areas that serve hamburgers and hot dogs.

At the end of this boulevard is the **Frontierland Railway Station** (35) mentioned earlier under ways to get around the Magic Kingdom. You can board the steam train here and travel back to Main Street, U.S.A., scenically circling the park, or, of course, get off the train here after boarding on Main Street.

There's still one more choo-choo you won't want to miss: **Big Thunder Mountain Railroad** (36). Board this train and whiz off over hill and dale, past a towering red stone outcropping, a flooded mining town, waterfalls, cackling chickens, hee-hawing donkeys, and authentic mining equipment. Just watch out for the sharp curves and at that last bend—prepare to get a little damp!

Adventureland

Even the meekest among us harbor secret dreams in which we challenge a whitewater rapid or stride across an African veldt roamed by lumbering elephants and racing gazelles.

No matter that we trudge off instead to offices where the biggest adventure is a jaunt to the watercooler and the only roars are disapproval. No matter that we use the down payment on a Tahiti-bound sailing yacht to reseed the front lawn and relegate our fantasies to vicarious video excitement.

No matter, for in our secret dreams we're off sailing the seven seas, brandishing a sword, swigging rum from a gold chalice, and daring our enemies to fire at will. We hear the low growls of a jaguar prowling the primeval forest, swing across a stream on a sinewy jungle vine, and revel in the splashing joy of a cascading waterfall.

We hide away our dreams, but occasionally we do get a chance to release them, to live a little part of them through the creative genius of others. When that happens, as it does for many in Disney World's Adventureland, it's a special joy to be transported to the wonder of our own never-never lands.

To begin your adventure in this part of the Magic Kingdom, stand facing the railroad station and follow the walkway around to your left. Curve around and you will soon see a collection of shops and snacking facilities called Caribbean Plaza.

Here the center of attraction is an adventure called Pirates of the Caribbean, which has spawned a treasure trove of shops offering everything from a skeleton-head flag to a glass ship in a bottle. Stop at the **House of Treasure** to outfit yourself in a pirate's hat, to grab up a shining musket replica, and to find a buried-treasure map.

At **Plaza del Sol Caribe** buy one of the huge straw sombreros you'll see all over the park, and at **Laffite's Portrait Deck** have a photograph taken of yourself in full regalia surrounded by your booty.

Across the way, at the **Golden Galleon,** you can invest in a brass cannon or a spyglass—what respectable pirate would be without one? Or ferret out **La Princesa de Cristal** and get your piratical monicker emblazoned on a goblet or on a ship in a bottle. If you're hungry, stop at nearby **El Pirata y el Perico** for a hot pretzel.

Then, in full gear, stride into **Pirates of the Caribbean,** (37) one of the best and liveliest of the Magic Kingdom's Audio-Animatronic tales. Here you sail on a pirate boat through the darkness as buccaneers lay waste to an unsuspecting village. Fiercesome drunken pirates loll around, a dog barks, chickens cackle, and as you roll by, one of those brigands sits dangerously close above you. It's great fun and an amazing display of imagination at work. A don't-miss at Disney.

Calm yourself (a little) after that adventure with a ride on the **Jungle Cruise** (38), you'll feel like Hepburn and Bogart sailing off on *The African Queen.* You chug right among trumpeting elephants at bath time (and swear you're going to sail right into one) while jungle animals roar and chatter from the shoreline. Watch out for the headhunters (!) and don't get wet in the waterfall that is another remarkable part of this Disney jungle. (In winter when Orlando temperatures drop to chilly levels, a massive heating system keeps things steamy here.) If all that water makes you thirsty, there's an **Oasis** next door.

Remember that Swiss family that ended up shipwrecked and marooned on an island, then learned to like it so well they stayed? You can get a pretty good idea why they found their retreat so tranquil by taking your own fantasy journey to their house, the **Swiss Family Treehouse** (39). Climb up into the house yourself and peek inside to see the amazing results that can occur when people combine necessity with ingenuity. Wait until you see how they get running water.

Across the way is a warbling wonderland formally called **Tropical Serenade** (40), but everyone knows it as Enchanted Tiki Birds. Hundreds of birds and other creatures inhabit this enchanted land, another of those incredible credibles only Disney can create.

Around the bend, the Florida Citrus Growers treat you to the state's number-one product—orange and grapefruit juice—at the **Sunshine Tree Terrace.** Just about everything, including the ice cream, has that refreshing orange flavor in it, so this makes a good spot to stop before you tackle the enclave of tropical shops nearby.

Move from the juices and orange-flavored pastries to **Traders of Timbuktu** where can you can don a shark's tooth pendant or buy a handsome wood carving in an appealing African atmosphere. Next door at **The Magic Carpet** tiny bells jingle and the smell of incense fills the air as you roam among the brass, cotton, and silk treasures of Asia and the Middle East.

The products of China, Hong Kong, and the Orient dazzle you with brilliant color at **Oriental Imports,** and I managed to find a safari hat I'd long sought at **Tropic Toppers.** Need that staple of the tropics, a swimsuit? They've got one or two or a hundred at **Tiki Tropic Shop,** and to go with it, pick up a couple dozen strands of shell necklace at **Colonel Hathi's.**

If you're exhausted after all that browsing and buying, collapse at **Adventureland Veranda,** where you can dine in a Sidney Greenstreet paddlefan atmosphere on crispy salads and sandwiches with tropical fruit touches or full meals featuring the flavors of Polynesia and the Orient. Next door at the **Veranda Juice Bar,** you can sip a cool piña colada punch (without the punch as are all liquid refreshments in this alcohol-spurning kingdom).

So there you have it, all 125 shops and cafés, pockets of hilarity and high spirits in the Magic Kingdom. When it's all over, you'll find yourself humming the tiki birds' songs and breaking out in an occasional chim-chim-cheree right along with the hundreds of others who come here in search of a few hours of Disney's magic, only to find it living forever in their hearts.

Exploring River Country and Discovery Island

It should come as no surprise that here in this kingdom where magic reigns, the wonder of water has not been forgotten. No matter where you go in Disney World, you're not far from its soothing serenity. There is, however, one special place, **River Country,** where you can give yourself over to its restorative powers, revel in the rapturous moments it has to offer. Tarzan enthusiasts can swing out over pools on ropes, and Tom Sawyer fans can experience the abandonment of the ol' swimming hole.

Here creativity has carved from scrubby wilderness a giant water wonderland, piled with boulders, and lined with powder-soft sand. Watery delights challenge you to rocket down a giant slide, splash topsy-turvy and innertube-clad down a surface slick with ripples, to plunge through air to water.

Accomplished swimmer or aquatic amateur, there's something for everyone here at River Country so let's take a look at some of the fun in store for you at this Disney World attraction.

Located on **Bay Lake,** which is also home to Fort Wilderness and Discovery Island and laps at the back door of the Contemporary Hotel, River Country is divided into several sections so everyone from toddlers to teenagers and parents can play here. For openers, there's a huge swimming pool here, the largest in the country.

Better than that is **Bay Cove,** which most people call the ol' swimming hole, and is in fact part of Bay Lake. There's a special version of that swimming hole for youngsters, complete with beach, and around it all are beautifully landscaped grounds with picnic tables, a fountain, and a jungle nature-trail.

In the huge swimming pool you can dive from some of those clever Disney-made rocks, or get yourself into the water by cannonballing down one of the two water slides that streak high above the water. Don't look down, it won't help: So twisty is the slide you can't see the bottom anyway.

In Bay Cove board a rubber innertube at **White Water Rapids** and challenge those swirling drops to do their darndest. Here you board at **Raft Rider Ridge,** set off aboard your spinning wheel, and loop-de-loop down chutes and through whirlpools that spin and splash you downward as you bump and bound off other tubers flying around the bends.

Or trudge to the top of **Whoop 'N Holler Hollow** and leap into one of the two flumes where rushing waters send you spiraling down, faster than a speeding bullet (well, it seems that fast anyway) into the pool below. Sit up to create your own version of low gear or lie down to go into overdrive. To create a watery Indianapolis 500 run, arch your back so the least amount of body is in contact with slide and . . . whoooosh!

On hot summer days Disney World-wise River Country visitors buy their tickets at the Transportation and Ticket Center *before* visiting the Magic Kingdom. They do that because they know so many people want to play here that River Country is often filled to capacity (and the ticket window closed) by noon or earlier. If you've already bought a ticket, however, you can go in anytime during the day. So if you're planning a visit to this wonderland of water fun, buy your ticket early and come back later for an afternoon swim. At any time of year, crowds begin to dwindle about 4 or 5 p.m. so if you're anti-crowd you may find these early evening hours appealing. There's also a $1 discount on admissions after 6 p.m., and the attraction remains open until 10 p.m. most of the year.

Some other things you'll need to know about River Country: since some of the River Country adventures require swimming ability, children under 10 must be accompanied by an adult; you can bring your own towels or rent small ones for 25¢; men's and women's dressing rooms and coin lockers are available; you can bring your own picnic lunch and consume it on the beach or at well-shaded picnic tables; there are two snack stands, **Pop's Place** for burgers, dogs, beer, hot pretzels, and soda, and **The Waterin' Hole** with similar selections but fewer of them.

If you're coming to Orlando in the winter from mid-December through March, you may find River Country a little too cool for comfort, but most other months are warm and wonderful. In summer this is the place to beat the heat.

Admission to River Country is $6.50 adults, $4.25 children. Prices are a little cheaper for guests of Disney World resorts and Lake Buena Vista Hotel Plaza hotels.

Hours are 10 a.m. to 5 p.m., to 10 p.m. in summer months, and you can get there by bus (look for those with a blue flag on the side) from the Transportation and Ticket Center, by boats which leave regularly from the dock near the gates of the Magic Kingdom, or by car (follow the signs as you enter the park). You do not need any identification for the blue-flagged bus, but you do need a ticket or hotel identification for the boat ride.

There's still one more adventure in store for you here in this part of the Magic Kingdom. It's called **Discovery Island.**

If you remember some of those enchanting Disney cartoon movies that brought favorite fairy tales to the celluloid screen, you'll recall that most of the human creatures often walked and talked with the animals. Birds helped Cinderella trim her ballgown with flowers, chipmunks stitched for her, rabbits scampered around Snow White and all the animals of the forest proved friends in time of need.

To visit Discovery Island is to live, like Cinderella or Snow White and their princes, in harmony with the animals, in a rainbow-hued garden where it's always springtime.

Meandering here across nearly 12 acres of island surrounded by the sparkling waters of Bay Lake, you'll find yourself in another world, the sounds of the World you left behind shut out, the chatter of birds and the scent of flowers your companions.

To create this zoological and biological wonderland, Disney creators built up the land, dug out waterways, piled up rocks, and sunk roots. Exotic plants from equally exotic climes were introduced to this wonderland; birds and animals from nations all over the world were transplanted to new homes here, endangered species pampered into procreation.

Nature owns this island, from the barnacles on the wrecked

ship that lies mouldering on the beach and enhances the *Treasure Island* theme of this secluded spot to tall trees where rare bald eagles nest.

You can amble through the paths and boardwalks here in less than an hour but you'll want to take longer. You'll find yourself stopping in **Flamingo Lagoon** to watch the pencil-legged creatures with salmon-pink feathers gangle their way across the water. You'll pause to watch a sassy peacock strut before a potential mate, showing off his royal blue feathers with the pride of a foppish 18th-century suitor.

When something moves just over there, you'll stop to look again as you discover a tortoise eyeing you as curiously as you're eyeing it.

And you'll certainly spend some time at **Cooco Cabana,** where birds with smarts stand on their head for you, roll over, wave, cock an intelligent eye, and struggle to get your attention as demandingly as a small child.

No one could pass the trumpeter swans at **Trumpeter Springs** without stopping for a look at these ballerina-graceful creatures, and you'll want to linger in the great stands of whispering bamboo that create a shady glen known as **Bamboo Hollow.**

You'll pause many times as you roam this huge aviary, claimed to be the largest in the world and home to hundreds of vividly hued birds, ranging from albino peacocks to flaming-pink ibis and cocoa-brown pelicans, all of them squawking, warbling, and singing as sweetly as the tiki birds you met in the Magic Kingdom.

It's quite a sight, especially magnificent in spring when fancies turn to you-know-what and courting dances as elaborate as minuets turn this wilderness into a wonderland of nature.

Admission to Discovery Island, which is open all year long from 10 a.m. to 5 p.m., is $3 adults, $1.50 children 3 to 11.

You can save money by combining a visit to Discovery Island and River Country and buying one ticket to both spots for $8.75 adults, $5.25 children 3 to 11. If you're staying in a WDW resort hotel, you pay a little less.

If you're staying in a Disney resort, you can sail across to the island on water craft that leave from Polynesian Village, the Contemporary, and Fort Wilderness. Boats also leave from River Country, so if you have a Discovery Island ticket, you can take one of those.

There's one other way to get here: Big paddlewheelers ply the waters of the lakes and lagoon and are docked at the entrance to the Magic Kingdom. They offer a narrated **World Cruise** that costs $4 adults, $2 children, including admission to Discovery Island. Cruises leave every hour from 10 a.m. to 4 p.m.

Backstage at Disney World

As you watch singing dolls and tiki birds, ride on electronically controlled cars, watch Mickey Mouse pop up here, then turn up there minutes later, somewhere in the back of your mind little questions begin to appear.

How do they do it? How do all these people dressed in all these elaborate costumes manage to get themselves around their Kingdom? Who makes all those costumes? What's out there in Disney World's thousands of acres of nature preserve?

You'll discover you're perishing to watch an artist draw some of the cartoon characters you know and love and get a look at the electronic wilderness that controls what goes on here.

There is a way you can do that but, alas, adult people, you must be a student in fifth through tenth grade.

If you're lucky enough to fall into that category you can join **WDW's Wonders of Walt Disney World** program which takes youngsters on a six-hour tour focusing on one of four subjects: creative arts, ecology, energy, or entertainment. Each participant can take only one of the programs, however, and there's a $40 fee, which includes books the kids are asked to read before they attend and some materials they can use to follow up on what they've learned when the six-hour course is completed. What's more, many schools give credit for the course, which was created by Florida educators, and/or excuse absences if youngsters plan to attend. For parents that means you can plan a Disney trip during the school year without guilt. It's nice that crowds are smaller then, too, so the trip will be more fun in many ways.

Once youngsters sign up for one of the four programs, which I'll describe in a moment, they get a Polaroid OneStep camera to use during their visit, some film, and lunch, all included in the $40 fee.

If you've got a budding Picasso in your family, send that one off to the **Disney Creative Arts** program. It features a visit with a Disney artist who shows kids how to draw some of the Disney cartoon characters, then offers them helpful hints as they follow those instructions on their own. Later, the course instructor visits the Magic Kingdom with the youngsters and shows them the behind-the-scenes design elements that keep old things looking old and explains some *trompe l'oeil* effects that make things seem to be what they aren't.

The Wonder and Beauty of Our World and the necessity of preserving those wonders of nature is the topic of another course which features a film describing Florida's ecological composition. After the film, youngsters roam with the instructor through WDW's 7500-acre nature preserve, where orchids grow high in the trees, alligators slumber in the marshes, and huge trees drip Spanish moss. Binoculars are added to the cameras for this jaunt, and kids get a nature notebook in which they can write down what they see for show-and-tell time back home. Instructors outline for youngsters the relationship between man, plant, and animal and explain the symbiotic relationship that keeps this World and all the world intact.

Everything from the no-moving-parts motors of the WEDway PeopleMover to a solar-powered office building are discussed in Disney's **The Energy That Runs Our World** course. Youngsters travel from the steam era to solar power as they roam through the Magic Kingdom, focusing on the many ways Disney's creative geniuses have capitalized on the power of energy. There's even a visit to the Walt Disney World Central Energy Plant to see the computers that send energy pulsating throughout the park.

Finally, up-and-coming Julie Andrewses or John Travoltas will love **The Walt Disney World of Entertainment** program. Youngsters actually get to meet a Disney character and learn how to do what that character does. They go backstage and learn some things about what happens there to make the magic out front, and they get to talk with some of the performers in top Disney shows.

To find out more about the educational programs or reserve a place in one, contact Walt Disney World, Box 40, Lake Buena Vista, FL 32830.

Making the Most of One, Two, or Three Days in the Magic Kingdom

As you've no doubt gathered, there's so much to do here in Walt Disney World, you could spend ages peering and poking around the place and still not see it all.

There are, however, highlights, special shows that everyone agrees are wonderful, so I'm going to outline those and give you a few ideas I think might help make the moments you have here as full as possible.

Lucky are those who have a week or so to spend in Orlando, since they can spend some time at Disney World, then head off to see some of the other wonderful attractions in the center of Florida (more on those in Chapter X).

If you can only fit in a **one-day visit** to the Magic Kingdom, get there early—by that I mean actually on Main Street, U.S.A. by 7:30 to 8 a.m. Have breakfast and start moving. Despite the comparative brevity of each of the attractions here, lines do form early and can add up to an hour (or more at very popular stops) to each attraction's actual running time. Only real racers can see more than eight or nine attractions a day, so figure on those numbers as a maximum. If you're not given to a rapid pace, don't expect to cram even that many into your day.

No matter where you go in the world or how much you see, when you get home someone will tell you what you missed. It's the same at Disney World, of course, but most people do agree that the very **best attractions** in the park are: Space Mountain in Tomorrowland; Peter Pan's Flight and It's a Small World in Fantasyland; the Haunted Mansion and Hall of Presidents in Liberty Square; the Country Bear Jamboree and Big Thunder Mountain Railroad in Frontierland; and Pirates of the Caribbean and the Jungle Cruise in Adventureland.

For a one-day visit I'd opt to try and see as many of those as possible (timid types should skip Space Mountain as should anyone if the line is very long, as it often is). I'd do that by working my way around systematically, counterclockwise from Main Street to Tomorrowland, Fantasyland, Liberty Square and Frontierland, and finally to Adventureland. You could, of course, go clockwise covering the same territory or if you have very small children, plan to spend most of your time in their special land, Fantasyland.

For those with limited time, there's a special program few people know about that can get you around quickly and save much wear and tear on both your nerves and tootsies. That timesaver is called a **guided tour** and includes a guide, admissions to four attractions, and a World Pass you can use for the rest of the day. Your guide takes you around the park for 3½ hours, and because you're with a guide, you don't have to wait in lines. That alone is worth the price of the tour: $15 adults, $11.75 children. Guides know a great deal about the park and its operation, so you can learn more than you would on your own. You can sign up for one of the tours at the Ticket and Transportation Center and ask questions about it at Guest Relations or Guest Service (tel. 824-4321).

If you have allotted **two days or more** for your Magic Kingdom visit (and if you possibly can, do, you'll use every minute), get there early both days and work your way through the lands, beginning perhaps at Tomorrowland and working your way around through Fantasyland the first day. Then start where you left off (or at Adventureland) the second day and continue on around and back to Main Street, U. S. A., adding other attractions that have caught your imagination.

If the park's open until 10 p.m. or later, line up on Main Street about 8 p.m. for the 9 p.m. **Main Street Electrical Parade.** Active kids can amuse themselves in the Main Street attractions (Penny Arcade and Main Street Cinema), while someone with patience holds down the curbside space. Usually you can wedge in some time before and after the parade for an attraction stop or two. If you've already seen the parade, visit popular attractions while it's tooting along. Lines are short then, since most people are out on Main Street ooohing and aahhing.

If you think you can manage the time, try to work in **a special dinner** at one of the park's two top restaurants, King Stefan's Banquet Hall (you must make reservations at the restaurant—it's in Cinderella's Castle—first thing in the morning of the day you're hoping to dine) or the Liberty Tree Tavern (same requirements: reservations at the restaurant, in Liberty Square, early in the morning of the day you're dining). Both offer delightful time-warp trips and some pretty good food to boot. If you can't get to either for dinner, try to work in a lunch stop. Lunch is less crowded, too. Frontierland's Diamond Horseshoe Revue also is a good spot for lunch, since you can watch the show while having a light lunch. Same reservation requirements as in the restaurants.

If you have **three days** allotted for Magic Kingdom fun, plan on spending at least one afternoon relaxing on the sands of River Country and uncovering the wonders of Discovery Island. You'll love both spots, and by this time you are likely to need the rest.

Naturally, if you have even longer, say **three or four days** just for the Magic Kingdom, you can go at a much more leisurely pace, perhaps visiting some of the fabulous breakfast, brunch, and lunch buffets in the Polynesian Village or Contemporary

Resort and taking in an evening show at either spot or at Fort Wilderness. Shopping's great at Lake Buena Vista Village too.

If you can, try to spend **one evening** aboard the glittering *Empress Lilly,* dining at one of the three wonderful rooms there or just tuning in on the banjo music and fun that always seems to be going on in the Baton Rouge Lounge. Whatever you do don't miss taking an evening jaunt over to the Village for a look at the *Empress* in her starlit evening glitter.

SPECIAL EVENTS IN THE MAGIC KINGDOM: You think you've heard it all? Not by a long shot. Disney World pours its heart into entertaining you. All year long there are special events, some of them seasonal, some year-round activities, designed to delight, amaze, enthrall, and keep you coming back for more.

Let's take a look now at some of the things you'll see going on around the Kingdom and some of the things you may want to know before you even set a date for your visit to the mouse's house.

DAILY DOINGS: Every day you can tune in on some musical events in the magic Kingdom. One of the first you're likely to see is the **Dapper Dans,** a harmonious quartet of barbershoppers who roam the byways of Main Street, U.S.A. and are at their most picturesque outside the barber shop where you'll often find them. It's located on the first side street on your left as you face the castle. These Dapper Dans are as typically Twenties as they can get, with red-and-white-striped vests, straw hats, and old favorite songs.

Each day at 5:15 p.m., the American flag that flies over Main Street comes down, accompanied by a small band and color guard which perform a ceremony known as **flag retreat.** It's a short but stirring performance, accompanied by the release of a flock of white pigeons symbolizing peace doves.

Steel drums, those island-music mainstays, can be heard on-stage near Adventureland's Pirates of the Caribbean attractions. Those lilting calypso sounds fit this jungle atmosphere to a T.

Mickey Mouse and some of his cohorts plus the **Kids of the Kingdom** sing and dance up a photogenic storm daily in the forecourt area of the castle. Good place for pictures and an entertaining show that includes medleys of popular favorites.

I've already mentioned that popular **Diamond Horseshoe Saloon** production, which despite the "saloon" in its name is more than suitable for even the youngest visitor. Perhaps this is a good time to repeat that no alcoholic beverages are sold in the Magic Kingdom. You must have reservations for these shows, which occur several times a day, so sign up early at the saloon.

Mickey Mouse, Goofy, and a host of Disney's favorites sing and dance several times a day at the **Fantasy Faire** stage just across the way from Cinderella's Golden Carousel.

A Dixieland group called **Pearly Band** takes to that same stage each day and sometimes can be found tooting along Main Street, U.S.A. as well.

You say you haven't heard a washboard lately? Well, don't be deprived of that experience. **Banjo Kings** have one, and they play it and other instruments on Main Street daily.

If you're in Tomorrowland, you're likely to hear the strains of the **Mardi Gras Sound Company,** which entertains at Tomorrowland Terrace and the Plaza Pavilion.

That's also where you'll find comedian-musician **Michael Iceberg** who performs there daily on his electronic musical instruments. You have to see this one to believe it.

Naturally, you'll want to get a good look at those **cartoon characters**—Mickey Mouse, Donald Duck, and the lot—so if you don't just run into them by chance, look for them at City Hall, where they spend quite a bit of time or on one side or the other of the castle. They make an appearance at the castle forecourt at 11 a.m. daily and on the Fantasyland side at other times.

Who's going to be **where and when** is posted each day at City Hall. If you have a special interest in the cartoon characters or one of the musical groups, go to City Hall when you enter the park, and find out when and where your favorites will be appearing.

For the little ones—and even perhaps for the not-so-little ones—a memorable Disney highlight is **Minnie's Menehune Breakfast with the Disney Characters.** You can see Minnie, Goofy, Donald, or one of the gang as you down some basic breakfast goodies at Minnie's bash in the Polynesian Village Hotel. Breakfast seatings are at 8 and 9:30 a.m. daily, and you can reserve a seat by calling Central Reservations at 824-2000. At 9 and 10:30 a.m., those same characters show up for **Breakfast a la Disney** on the *Empress Lilly* riverboat. **Breakfast at the Terrace Café at the Contemporary Resort** is a buffet feast (8 to 11 a.m.), and Disney characters turn up here, too. Price of the breakfasts is $5 adults, $4 children ($4.95 adults and $3.25 children at the Terrace Café.)

NIGHT AND SEASONAL FUN: In summer the **All American College Marching Band** struts its stuff on the Fantasyland Fantasy Faire stage. You can find out when they'll be giving their daily performances there by calling Disney information, 824-4321.

Mickey's Magic Kingdom really turns on at night—literally. Thousands upon thousands of white lights trim Main Street, U.S.A., to form a backdrop for the showiest Disney event of them all, the **Main Street Electrical Parade.** You can read all about that in Chapter V on nightlife in the Magic Kingdom, but let me remind you here that hours are 9 and 11:30 p.m. each night that the park is open until midnight. That occurs, by the way, at holidays like Thanksgiving, Christmas, Washington's Birthday in February, at Easter, and during summer vacation periods from about June to Labor Day. You'll find some tips on good spots to view the parade back there in Chapter V.

When the park is open until midnight, you can also count on a fireworks display known as **Fantasy in the Sky.** Fireworks boom for about five minutes in a kaleidoscope of bursting color that will knock your socks off (figuratively, don't panic). One of the most spectacular sights you can see here in the park, in fact, is the ebony sky above the turrets of Cinderella's Castle ablaze with rainbow-hued stars.

Another evening event is the **Electrical Water Pageant,** which takes place every night on the waters of Bay Lake and features a 1000-foot-long parade of floating creatures, all illuminated with tiny lights. Normal hours for the pageant are from about 9 p.m. to 10 p.m. Parade route begins at the Polynesian Village, moves past Fort Wilderness and to the Contemporary Resort. When the park is open late, the floating pageant goes past River Country just before it gets to Fort Wilderness and then goes on to complete its showy journey at the Magic Kingdom about 10:30 p.m.

More nightly activities are outlined in Chapter V, including information on all kinds of evening fun, from a marshmallow roast to a sophisticated Broadway revue.

HOLIDAY ACTIVITIES: Christmas is the beginning, or the end, of the Disney celebrations, depending on how you look at it, and it is a spectacular season to visit the Kingdom. Just be prepared to join thousands upon thousands of others who want to see this Christmas wonderland too.

Each **Christmas celebration** is a little different, so you never tire of a return trip, but each includes the presence of a huge trimmed tree ablaze with lights and ornaments, special presentations, and carolers who add the soft glow of candlelight and their lovely voices to the Main Street Electrical Parade. There's just enough cool in the air to give you the feeling of a very pleasant Christmas season but usually not so much cold you're shivering. Santa Claus—or Mickey in a Santa suit—is likely to be on hand somewhere, and top-name performers add their famous visages to shows which are nothing short of spectacular.

Naturally Mickey, Minnie, and friends celebrate **New Year's Eve** right along with the rest of us, so there are special festivities in the park that night, too, including a double set of fireworks. Plenty to see and do makes this an interesting place to spend the last hours of the year. Crowds are enormous, however, so be prepared for a Times-Square-South crush.

At **Easter,** Disney's decked out in its Sunday best, complete with those elaborate hats people have come to associate with this holiday, plus antique cars, and special celebrations. Mickey Mouse has a pretty impressive set of ears, but even they pale beside the magnificent appendages sported by the king of this day's activities, none other than the Easter Bunny, of course.

Since much of the Magic Kingdom focuses on the glories of this nation, **Independence Day** is a king-sized holiday here. Throngs turn out on July 4 to spend this special day in the park and to ogle a double display of fireworks over Cinderella's Castle and the Seven Seas Lagoon.

Chapter IX

EPCOT: A VISIT TO TODAY'S WORLD—AND TOMORROW'S

SO QUICKLY DOES THE FUTURE seem to be coming at us these days, that we barely master one method of coping before the revised version appears. Even the simplest details of life change with such lightning speed, we no sooner conquer one change than it's followed by another and, zap, we're back at step one, learning how all over again.

Just when you've deciphered the intricacies of your bank's checking account system, you get a pleasant little note explaining, in steps 1 through 41, how to deal with their wondrous *new* system.

You succeed in setting your digital alarm clock only to be faced with the intricacies of bleeping video games and home computer budgeting. No more watching the needle climb on your speedometer, now you keep your eye on a dashboard of digitals. And restaurant bills? An incomprehensible computerized crazyquilt of PBCD, BR, SBT, SC and ST and BAL tossed in among myriads of numbers.

Things now pop up suddenly in places they've never popped up before, open and close automatically, appear and disappear at some unseen command. And to many, many people you're not only not a *face* anymore, you're not even a *name*, just a string of numbers and letters!

It's head-spinning, this awesomely rapid technological change, and sometimes its even a little terrifying. Still, as unsettling as it may be, there's a thrill about it all, a feeling that you're part of something exciting, a small cog in a huge wheel turning a powerhouse of change that will alter the course of history for generations to come.

Long before the rest of us realized we were living in Flash Gordon's era, Disney imaginations had rocketed into tomorrow and tuned into the technology necessary to turn imagination into image.

You can see those first futuristic efforts in Tomorrowland, in Disney's solar-powered office building, in the park's computer-operated central energy system. Impressive as were those first forays into the future, they weren't nearly enough for Walt Disney and his dreamers.

For the cartoonist had a vision of tomorrow that focused on man's ability to control his environment, to make technology a slave, not a master, and to use it to predict, manipulate, and control the future.

You can get a glimpse into the future at the newest and most ambitious Disney project in the world: a daring enclave dubbed Environmental Prototype Community of Tomorrow and for obvious reasons nicknamed EPCOT.

Polysyllabic mouthful that it is, this "serious" amusement has a simple message, one that Disney held firmly in his heart first spread around the world with the help of a little mouse.

It's a message of universality, of the oneness of this world we inhabit. At EPCOT the message is one of caution, a warning that the world of tomorrow demands a commitment to tolerance and understanding today, a commitment, in fact, to community. EPCOT is Disney's way of alerting the world that one, without all, is impossible.

Orientation

Just as you discovered the immensity of the Magic Kingdom, so will you meet a similar, mind-boggling enormity at the Environmental Prototype Community of Tomorrow.

From the moment you step into the shadow of the huge geosphere that looms over the grounds here, you will know how that mouse must feel in the immensity of man's world. Towering architecture soars into the skies. Massive buildings stand on acre after endless acre of land. Intertwined throughout it all is a network of flower-lined walkways leading you mile after mile through the two new "worlds" Disney-ites have created here.

As in the Magic Kingdom, you will soon discover there are

things you need to know to survive in this civilized wilderness of worlds.

Let's begin then by taking a look at some of the basic survival tactics you will need in EPCOT, and some of the things you'll need to know to get the most from this trip to the world of tomorrow.

WHEN TO GO: Because the Magic Kingdom and EPCOT share this World, they're also expected to share the crowds that will visit here. Disney prognosticators figure those visitors will soon hike the park's 12 million annual visitors to a record 20 million people a year. It's also quite likely many of those will come here especially to see this new World the World has created. All of which means if you expect crowds, you won't be disappointed. On a visit there just a month or so after EPCOT opened, the early-morning line outside Spaceship Earth was one hour long!

It's safe to assume that EPCOT will repeat the Magic Kingdom's busy-day syndrome, with the turnstiles turning fastest during holiday periods—especially Christmas—and in the summer months. For a complete rundown on the crowds and when they're greatest, see the orientation section of Chapter VIII and expect history to repeat itself at EPCOT.

Here at EPCOT, too, crowds increase at attractions as the days go on, receding a bit at mealtimes when they increase greatly in all restaurants and quickie food stops.

If you can motivate yourself to get to EPCOT early in the morning—you'll find plenty of company already there at 8:30 a.m. when the doors open—you stand the best chance of getting restaurant reservations and working your way through the most popular attractions before the real throngs arrive.

Besides, it's pleasant to plunk yourself down at an outdoor table in, say, the Stargate Café and munch away on a simple breakfast ordered, entered, totaled, and sent to the kitchen by computer. What a way to get the day's first glimpse into the future!

One other early-arrival tip: If you do manage to get yourself moving early, don't wander into the first line you see, which willl be the Starship Earth line. Everyone does exactly that, thus making the line at this first futuristic attraction longer in the morning that it is at just about any other time of day.

Instead bear to your left and enter Earth Station, where you will find early-bird gourmets lining up to make reservations for

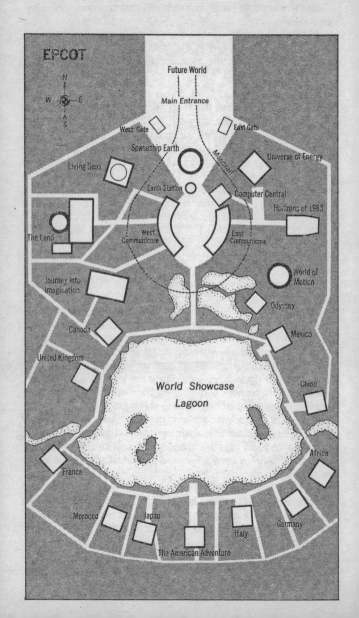

dinner at World Showcase restaurants. More on that later, for now just get in line and get it over with.

WHAT TO WEAR: If you didn't take my advice about shoes for the Magic Kingdom and are crowing about your walking talents, please swallow your pride and take that advice here. That advice, in a few words, is *wear comfortable shoes.* No matter how unfashionable sensible walking shoes may look, your feet will love you for the gesture. Shoes are even more important here in EPCOT than they are in the Magic Kingdom: Distances are enormous, transportation is scanty and always jammed, lines are long, and there aren't that many chances, or places, to sit.

A corollary to that piece of advice is for those who have the slightest, even the tiniest, concern over their ability to walk long distances. If for any reason you think you may tire—you're pregnant, have physical limitations as a result of age or infirmity, or have any kind of health problem affecting energy levels—don't be shy about **renting a wheelchair.** They cost only $1 a day plus a $1.50 refundable deposit. You can rent one at a wheelchair rental kiosk you'll find just to the left of the fountain as you enter EPCOT (that is, directly in front of the geosphere).

That's where you'll find **strollers** for the youngsters, too. Turn a deaf ear to little ones' protests that they are too old, and don't want to sit in a stroller. They may not want to be seen in one during the first few hours they're in this park, but it won't be long before the wailing protests become exhausted whimpers. If it helps you steel yourself to the protestations, picture yourself walking a mile or so in the sun carrying a tuckered-out toddler on your shoulder. See? Wasn't that easy? Strollers rent for $1.50 a day plus $1.50 deposit.

If you'd like to leave the little ones behind on an evening or weekend visit to EPCOT (or the Magic Kingdom), park them at the **Kinder-Care Children's Center** located in Lake Buena Vista (at the employees entrance to the park; tel. 827-5444) where they'll be cuddled and fed for $1.50 an hour (plus $1 for a meal). This service is available to anyone from 6 p.m. to midnight on weekdays, 6 a.m. to midnight on weekends. Children must be at least two years old and toilet-trained.

If you're a Disney resort guest, the kids can stay and play at **Mouseketeers Clubhouses** in the Polynesian Village and the Contemporary Resort Hotels. Here they must be three years old and there's a four-hour maximum on child care. In-room baby-sitting also is available at hotels for $5 an hour.

GETTING THERE: Since the Magic Kingdom and EPCOT are both part of Disney World, you'll use the same roads to get here. Sneak a peek back into Chapter VIII where major highway routes to Disney World are outlined. Once you're on the road, you'll notice that signs directing you to Disney World or the Magic Kingdom now also include EPCOT which is just three miles from the Magic Kingdom. From Hwy. I-4 there's soon to be a new interchange located halfway between the exits for Rte. 535 and U.S. 192.

If you're staying in one of the Lake Buena Vista hotels and driving to Disney World, just follow Preview Boulevard to the Shopping Village entrance and turn left. Follow the road around and you'll find yourself right on the way to EPCOT's entrance.

Once you've found your way to the EPCOT parking lot, follow the same general rules you'll find in Chapter VIII, most important of which is memorizing your parking lot location. Here the lots bear futuristic names, so you'll be leaving your old outdated combustion engine in a lot with a name like Communications.

Here, too, guest courtesy trams will pick you up near your car—just look around, you'll see the trams—and take you to EPCOT's Ticket and Transportation Center.

That same **Car Care Center** that will help you out with dead batteries and the like in the Magic Kingdom parking lot will come to your aid here too. So good are they, in fact, that a friend whose son lost his car keys somewhere in EPCOT called the Car Care Center (tel. 824-4813) not only had the door opened by a friendly Car Care person but he even was presented with a duplicate ignition key so he could get home—and they didn't charge him a penny for that otherwise wallet-emptying service! Now those are knights in shining armor!

There's a special parking lot here for handicapped visitors. Ask one of the parking lot attendants or look for a sign directing you to the lot which is located a little closer to the entrance.

If you're taking a **bus** to EPCOT the bus driver will drop you off in the bus parking area and that's where you reboard the bus at the end of the day. Guests of hotels in Lake Buena Vista's Disney World Village Hotel Plaza can hop on a special EPCOT bus with a red-and-silver flag painted on the side. It's a short walk from the bus parking area to the Ticket and Transportation Center.

If you're in the Magic Kingdom and decide to whiz on over for a look at some future fantasies, just board an EPCOT-bound **monorail** which connects the Magic Kingdom, Contemporary Resort Hotel, and Polynesian Village with EPCOT. Go by monorail to EPCOT from those two Disney-owned hotels by taking the monorail to the Magic Kingdom's Ticket and Transportation Center then hopping the EPCOT monorail from there.

Monorails to EPCOT leave only from the Ticket and Transportation Center at the Magic Kingdom, so you must make your way there first from hotels or from the Magic Kingdom. If you're staying in one of the other Disney-owned resort hotels—the villas or the Golf Resort, take an EPCOT bus to the Ticket and Transportation Center at the Magic Kingdom, then change to the TTC-EPCOT monorail. Same goes for Fort Wilderness guests.

That monorail, by the way, stops only at the entrance to EPCOT, not inside the EPCOT complex, although you'll see it inside EPCOT as it completes its circular journey on the way back to the Magic Kingdom. I mention that so you won't hope to hop the monorail when exhaustion strikes you somewhere in the middle of EPCOT.

BUYING A TICKET: All the scoop on buying a ticket to the Magic Kingdom or EPCOT is outlined in Chapter VIII's Magic Kingdom rundown, but here are the prices again:

A one-day admission to either the Magic Kingdom or EPCOT, but not both, is $15 for adults, $14 for children 12 to 17, and $12 for youngsters 3 to 11. Children under three are free.

There are no two-day World Passes available, but a three-day World Pass permitting admission to both the Magic Kingdom and EPCOT is $35 for adults, $33 for children 12 to 17, and $28 for those 3 to 11.

Finally, a four-day World Pass, again including admission to both the Magic Kingdom and EPCOT—use of all transportation facilities in either—is $45 for adults, $42 for children 12 to 17, and $36 for youngsters 3 to 11.

Real devotees of Walt Disney World who have plenty of time to spend at both the Magic Kingdom and EPCOT can buy a six-day World Pass good for a year for $60 adults, $56 youngsters 12 to 17, and $48 for 3- to 11-year-olds. Those who simply cannot get enough can buy a season pass for $100 adults, $93 teenagers, and $80 for children.

Tickets must be paid for in cash or by traveler's checks, no credit cards.

If you leave EPCOT and want to return the same day, have your hand stamped at the exit, even if you have a multi-day passport.

SPECIAL NEEDS—CHILDREN, HANDICAPPED, FIRST AID, AND MORE: I've already given you the word on renting strollers for children and wheelchairs for *anyone* who might entertain even the slightest doubt about walking capabilities. Both are available at the **Stroller and Wheelchair Rental** kiosk at the base of Spaceship Earth just to your left as you enter EPCOT.

A word for wheelchair guests: You can take the monorail to the Magic Kingdom and Polynesian Village but you must go by bus to other destinations. To find out what bus goes where, stop by the Bus Information counters near the bus parking lots.

Restrooms and telephones accommodating wheelchair guests are marked with the international wheelchair symbol.

All of the exhibits the EPCOT can accommodate wheelchair guests.

If you have a baby with you, those demanding special needs can be met at **Baby Services,** near the Odyssey Restaurant. Here those thoughtful Disneyites have provided facilities for changing diapers, warming bottles, and nursing, and there are even diapers, food, and formula for sale.

Pets must be parked at the EPCOT Center Kennel Club right at the Ticket and Transportation Center where they'll be lots happier and cooler than they'd be parading around the park all day. Charge is $2 a day ($3 overnight, but overnight stays are available only to WDW resort hotel guests).

If you get blisters from sun or pavement or suffer from any of the myriads of other little unexpected first-aid emergencies that can crop up, head for the **First Aid Station** adjacent to the Odyssey Restaurant where a registered nurse is on duty to help you. If you take special medication, however, be sure and have it with you; there are no pharmacies in Disney World.

If you buy a few things the minute you enter EPCOT—not a bad idea, since most shoppers jam the shops on their way *out* of the park, you can stash them in **lockers** in the Entrance Plaza just to the right of the Spaceship Earth entrance. Charge is 25¢ for large-size lockers, 50¢ for even bigger storage space.

Those who lose things can find them at **Lost and Found** at the Entrance Plaza, to the right of the turnstiles as you face the entrance to EPCOT. You can also call Lost and Found at 824-4245.

If it's a **lost child** you're seeking, take your hysteria to Baby Services adjacent to the Odyssey Restaurant. If the **missing person** is an adult, look at Earth Station in Spaceship Earth where you can leave a message. Don't keep this message service to yourself: Tell your group, so you and the losee can simplify regrouping.

There's another convenient EPCOT service that as yet is taken advantage of by only an in-the-know few. That service shares quarters with Lost and Found and is called **Package Pick-up.** It works like this: First, you troop through the dozens of irresistible shops in the World Showcase, spending and buying with the fervor of a sailor on a one-day pass. Do you have to carry all that loot around with you on the long return trip to the entrance? Certainly not. Wherever you buy, just tell the shop to send it over to Package Pick-up. The shop will give you a receipt and deliver your package to this handy pick-up spot at the entrance, thus saving you pounds of parcels. Deliveries are taken from shops to the pick-up center every hour so there's virtually no chance you'll get to Package Pick-up before your package.

As for that little matter of **money,** see to that need at the Entrance Plaza where credit card cash advances, foreign currency exchange, and other credit cardholder services are available. American Express cardholder services are also available at Travelport in CommuniCore East. For details on what requires cash and what can be paid by credit cards and which ones, check the Orientation section of Chapter VIII. Same rules apply at EPCOT.

There are few things more frustrating than knowing what you want to say but being unable to say it in the prevailing language. If you think you or someone in your group might be faced with that difficulty, seek **foreign language assistance** at Guest Relations in Earth Station, adjacent to Spaceship Earth. Information in Spanish is also available on World Key Information Satellites, which are the television monitors set up throughout EPCOT to help you find your way around and discover parts of the place you might have missed. More on that later.

Camera equipment and even rental cameras are available in a

Camera Center at the base of Spaceship Earth and at Journey Into Imagination which is presented by Kodak.

To find out what **entertainment** is scheduled today at EPCOT, ask any of the hosts or hostesses in Earth Station at the Guest Relations desk. They know all about hours for parades, shows, live entertainment, and special events—and quite a lot more besides. Similar information is available on World Key Information Satellites, which I'll explain shortly.

For **general information** on anything at all, call World Center Information, 827-7414.

A Little Geography

Before you plan your EPCOT visit, you'll need to know a little about the geography of this huge "community" that's more than twice the size of the Magic Kingdom.

Here goes. EPCOT is divided into two separate sections: Future World and World Showcase.

As the name suggests, **Future World** offers a peek into the world of tomorrow as seen by some of the nation's largest corporations—Kodak, Sperry, General Motors, Exxon, Kraft, American Express, and the Bell System (AT&T).

You certainly can't miss recognizing Future World, not only because it's the first thing you'll see as you enter EPCOT, but because it's landmark is the landmark of all EPCOT—that giant geosphere lovingly known as the "golf ball." Flanking it on the left and right are two arcing buildings known as CommuniCore East and CommuniCore West, and scattered about the perimeter are the various corporation exhibits, all of which are housed in huge buildings featuring some soaring, innovative architecture.

CommuniCore's long arms enfold a central plaza, crowned by an enchanting fountain that's particularly beautiful at night, when colored lights play across its waters. At the edge of the lake, boats and buses gather in a wide area known as World Showcase Plaza. From here you can see the whole World Showcase spread out around shimmering waters—terrific for photographers.

All that occupies the north bank of a 40-acre lake. Rimming that lake is the section of EPCOT known as **World Showcase,** a complex of international enclaves, each featuring architectural landmarks of the nation represented. As you face the lake and move around it to your right (i.e. west), you pass Canada, the

United Kingdom, France, Japan, U.S.A., Italy, Germany, China, and Mexico.

Overall, EPCOT is entered on the north side so all your normal direction-seeking is backwards. That means the geosphere and Future World are on the north side of the lake, World Showcase on the south side, CommuniCore East on your left as you face the lake and CommuniCore West on your right. A little confusing, but you'll figure it out with the help of plenty of signs you'll see everywhere you look.

If you walk all around that lake, you'll hike 1.2 miles, and the distance from exhibit to exhibit in Future World will keep you pacing about the same distance. Add to that the dozens of shops and restaurants you'll want to explore in both places, not to mention the lines you'll wait in, and you're likely to stride at least three to five miles before the day is over.

Getting Around

You can avoid some of that walking by learning a little about getting around in EPCOT, an activity which can be as much fun as finding your way around the Magic Kingdom—and even more necessary.

You can arrive by monorail, a pretty slick way to turn up anywhere. Once there, you can travel by **antique doubledecker, opensided omnibuses** that toot their way around the World Showcase, or by sleek sailing craft that chug across the waters of the lake in the center of this complex.

To get around here, keep in mind that EPCOT is divided into two sections, Future World which offers you a glimpse into tomorrow, and World Showcase which takes you on an international sojourn, complete with replicas of famous architectural landmarks of the nations represented.

All these wonders are spread over a land area that's more than *twice* as large as the Magic Kingdom. That means that what looks like lots of transportation really isn't much at all, so you'll have to count on walking many a mile in this part of the World.

It is, however, a lovely place to walk, trimmed with flowers in all the colors of the rainbow and filled with nooks and crannies where fountains soar, and dazzling views come suddenly into sight.

As interesting as it may be to walk the miles of land around the lake and through Future World, the transport provided is just as entertaining.

Those doubledecker omnibuses, decked out in shining emerald green, fire-engine red, or buttercup yellow, travel clockwise around the lake. Official starting point is an open area called World Showcase Plaza, just at the end of the long walkway that leads from the geosphere to the lake. Buses stop at marked bus stops located just short of the China pavilion, in front of the German enclave, just beyond the U.S.A. pavilion, in front of France's contribution, and just between the United Kingdom and Canada.

One problem is that not every one of the buses stops at each of the stops, so it may not do you much good to go chasing after a bus. Easiest way to latch onto one is to hike yourself to the nearest bus stop and wait until one comes along that's going where you're going.

Once you're standing in World Showcase Plaza ready to journey off for your tour of the World Showcase, you may be lured by the **boats** you see on the waters. Called *Friendship I, Friendship II,* and *Mariner,* they also make specific stops before returning to the Plaza.

Friendship I, a long, sleek launch, travels to a dock just opposite the German pavilion and its sister ship, *Friendship II,* lifts anchor for France.

Mariner, a replica of an antique sailing craft, heads from the Plaza to France, returns to the Plaza and sails off for Germany, making two runs for each one made by the Friendship launches. Naturally, you can board anywhere the boats dock as well as at the World Showcase Plaza.

A Visit to a Future World

Now you know what's where and how to get there, so let's start right off for a peek at the weird and wonderful days of tomorrow.

First thing you'll see as you pass the ticket booths and step onto the Entrance Plaza is that EPCOT logo and landmark—the geosphere.

SPACESHIP EARTH: Soaring 18 stories high, this massive conglomeration of triangles forms a shining silver globe that stands on giant concrete legs. Visible from miles away, the towering sphere casts its huge shadow over intricately landscaped grounds below and shelters Bell System's **Spaceship Earth** exhibit as well as the information center known as **Earth Station.**

Board a Spaceship Earth car and journey off through history to explore man's age-old questions—who are we, where do we come from? Travel past lifelike cavemen carefully recording their prehistoric hunts on cave walls as they did in the famed ancient caves of Altamira in Spain. Journey on along the Nile where a Cleopatra, seated proudly on her royal throne, gazes deep into your eyes.

Sail with those skilled Phoenician sailors and see scribes working on the first alphabets. As you roll along in time, Greek tragedies take to the boards in the first theater productions. Imperial Rome is born and dies as you glide by, sniffing the smoking ruins of the glory that was Rome.

Islamic monks working in tiny cubicles painstakingly copy the learning left intact, saving it for man's great rebirth, the Renaissance, and bequeathing it finally to that magical invention that changed the world: the printing press. You'll see Michaelangelo lying on his scaffolding putting final brushstrokes on the ceiling of the Sistine Chapel; watch the newspaper, telegraph, telephone, radio, television, and computer spread their message fingers around the world.

Finally, your transport spins you into today and tomorrow, where all of us are linked as passengers on Spaceship Earth, rocketed by technology beyond this planet "into the age of choice, the age of opportunity. . . ."

Back down to Earth whether you like it or not, you exit directly into Earth Station, City Hall of the Future, where Guest Relations hosts and hostesses can help you with questions about EPCOT.

Here you can get your introduction to an amazing creation called **WorldKey Information Service,** which uses touch-sensitive television screens to give you all the latest information about EPCOT attractions, special events, and restaurants. Presented in English and Spanish, the information is retrieved automatically from video discs and computer data banks and carried on lightwave transmission facilities provided by Western Electric. There are 29 terminals throughout EPCOT where you can look at and actually talk to information attendants.

Here, too, representatives of the seven World Showcase restaurants requiring reservations can help you make **dinner reservations.**

A word about those reservations seems apropos here. Be forewarned that France, Italy, and England have the most popular dining spots in EPCOT, and reservations at those restaurants are often gone by 9 *a.m.* If you don't succeed in making a reservation at Earth Station, there is one more chance: Only 60% of the available seats in any of the restaurants are allocated at Earth Station; the individual restaurants retain 40%. That means that if reservations at the restaurant of your choice are not available at Earth Station, you can race over to the restaurant itself and hope luck is with you there. Since World Showcase attractions—including those restaurants—open at 10 a.m., an hour later than Future World, determined diners who go immediately to the restaurant of their choice are often lucky. If you strike out for a dinner reservation at one of those three popular spots, opt for lunch instead. Menus differ some, but quality is uniform at both meals, and atmosphere never changes. Besides, lunch is a way of sampling fare at less expensive prices.

If you can't get either lunch or dinner reservations and you're absolutely determined to try a certain restaurant, there's still one more chance: You can line up at the restaurant at about 11 a.m. and hope for no-shows. Lots of people will join you in line and many are able to get in, despite their lack of reservations.

Come back now from those dreams of homemade pasta or seafood en brioche and rejoin us here at Earth Station.

COMMUNICORE EAST: Let's move along now from the womb of that huge geosphere to **CommuniCore East,** to the left as you face the lake. In this arc-shaped wing you'll find the **Stargate Restaurant,** a popular breakfast and fast-food lunching spot where you can dine indoors or outside on a terrace overlooking the huge fountain that dominates the plaza between the East and West CommuniCore buildings.

Star of the show here is **Astuter Computer Revue,** presented by Sperry Univac and starring a white-suited Cockney dancer, Earlie the Pearlie, who tippy-toes across huge banks of computers that operate much of what moves in EPCOT. This natty, miniaturized, British-ized Gene Kelly hops magically around the computers explaining how MACS (Monitoring and Control System) keeps watch on EPCOT productions to make sure all is going according to plan and how ECS (Entertainment Control System) works the elaborate lighting on all the shows in the park at one time. This one's a stand-up show, so be prepared to stay upright (or you might consider skipping this if you're tired and in search of a seat). It's an amusing production, especially for those who have never seen a massive bank of computers in operation.

In CommuniCore East you'll also find American Express's look at future travel, **TravelPort,** where you step up to a television set, touch a circle in the center, and look over a vast range of vacation possibilities complete with films of skiing sojourns, beach journeys, and off-beat adventure trips of all kinds. If one of the possibilities thrills you, you can sign up right here with an American Express travel counselor whose computers have all the latest information on prices and places.

Sperry's gone all out here, with computerized oddities including an American-flag mobile whose stars and stripes are independently hung and move about forming different patterns. There's a raft of computer games that will intrigue adults and youngsters alike. One is a revolving wood carving with tiny figures that make a complete revolution about every three minutes and then record the number of that revolution, so you computer-brains can figure out how many days and years it's been going around.

There's a robot that talks with youngsters and answers their questions and a huge crystal ball flowing with color and crisscrossed by airplanes.

Exxon has an **Energy Exchange** display that tells you about a lot of energy sources, ranging from solar photovoltaics—don't ask me—to nuclear fusion and home and car conservation projects. There's a display of coal mining buried in the mouth of a huge earth mover and an explanation of oil-retrieval methods. Star of the exhibits is a 30,000-pound piece of shale rock formed in the age of the dinosaurs and containing 500 gallons of oil, enough to keep a car running for a year. You can touch the massive rock and see the oil pockets buried deep within it.

At the **Centorium** gift shop futuristic metal sculptures are the most intriguing items, but there are plenty of the usual T-shirts and toys—and if it's raining, raincoat-ponchos that are terrific for keeping out the damp without tying you up in plastic.

Soon to come is an **Electronic Forum** that will let you send 'em a message by recording your opinion on world events at a special **Future Choice Theater.** An electronic arcade, featuring games based on advanced technology—things like interactive videodiscs, 3-D graphics, lasers and body-sensing devices—is also on the drawing boards here.

UNIVERSE OF ENERGY: As long as we're on the east side of Future World, let's roam over to the **Universe of Energy,** my candidate for EPCOT's most fascinating exhibit.

You enter a large room where you'll see row after row of long pews stretching out in front of you and on both sides. They look as immobile as Winchester Cathedral, but they're actually moving cars, part of a "traveling theater," as you will soon discover. Once seated, you are treated by Exxon, which produces this spectacular show, to an elaborately screened production tracing the cycles of life and death that have created oil deep beneath the surface. On a 220-degree screen you'll see the struggle to build the Alaskan pipeline, the impressive technology involved in seeking and recovering oil and gas then delivering it around the world by tanker.

As the seat you're sitting in turns and begins to move, traveling along a wire only one-eighth of an inch in diameter and powered by solar energy gathered by thousands of solar cells on the roof, you suddenly are thrust into the "dark and mysterious past," the terrifying dawn of history when huge dinosaurs roamed the earth. You see and smell dripping swampwaters as thunder and lightning roars around you and huge dinosaurs tower over you, one chewing rather placidly on a string of seaweed.

Slowly you travel deeper and deeper into the dark, dank swampland where giant tree-ferns soar high above you and a monster-lizard shows its teeth. Overhead pterodactyls, ugly as buzzards, soar menacingly, and from the land sulphurous smoke oozes and steams. As you move slowly through this nightmare land, a water-dwelling monster of prehistory suddenly thrusts a long neck and huge jaw up from the depths of a placid pool and roars in rage. Volcanoes erupt, spilling streams of flaming lava, and the earth hisses and bubbles in internal consternation.

It's terrifying and fascinating, a dramatic and devastatingly effective presentation of the dawn of mankind and the world when the black gold of today's primary energy source was born.

HORIZONS: From oil reserves buried deep beneath the land, let's travel out to the Horizons for a peek into the future. Scheduled for completion in October 1983, Horizons will be presented by General Electric in an unusual multilevel pavilion with strange jutting architectural angles. Here you'll get a look at those now-humorous future-visions of the 1930s and see how right Jules

Verne was in his predictions. From there you move on to Future-Port where you drop in on families of the next century via three-dimensional scenes outlining life in apartments, on farms, out in space, and even underwater. Take your pick!

In something called an Omnisphere you'll visit microworlds and macroworlds in crystal formations and DNA chains, be "part" of a fiery rocket blast-off projected on an eight-story-high screen!

In an undersea habitat, youngsters wearing gills go off on a school field-trip to a seaweed farm, and in a desert, robots harvest the crops—after all, *they* don't suffer from sunburn. When it's all over, you'll choose your ideal future and ride off into your special Horizon production.

WORLD OF MOTION: If you're going to get anywhere, you first have to move. General Motors, perhaps needless to say, has been counting on that for some years now, and in its EPCOT exhibit, dubbed World of Motion, has chosen to focus on man's desire to move by wheel. The giant automobile manufacturer has rounded up hundreds of Disney's finest AudioAnimatronic creations to bring you a rollicking roll back through the ages to man's first experimentation with a form that was to become vital to us all—the circle.

Presented in a circular building that bears an uncanny resemblance to a giant wheel, World of Motion keeps tongue firmly in cheek as it takes you on a ride—what else?—through 24 different scenes, beginning with an early wanderer who just might have discovered the wheel because his feet were sore! From foot power, you move on to animal power as an early mover-and-shaker shoves futilely at a recalcitrant zebra, then you journey on to sail power.

Finally, the wheel really got things rolling, although it took a few unsuccessful attempts with wheels shaped like triangles and squares before round got around. After that, today was in sight in the form of the first car lot where determined dealers—"Hi, I'm Bob the world's wildest trader"—could get you a terrific deal on a barely used . . . chariot (only a few hundred Roman miles on it, *Punica fide,* and owned by a little old lady charioteer)!

When people discovered it was such "fun to be free," the theme of this exhibit, they started moving in anything that would float (riverboats), roll (stagecoaches), chug (Old West "iron horses"), or fly (hot-air balloons). You'll see all those modes of transport up to and including an amusing big-wheeled bicyclist's hapless tumble into a hog pen and the first downtown traffic jam which, come to think of it, hasn't changed all that much.

Through it all, chipmunks flash their tails, roosters flap their wattles, pigs squeal, a ukelele player's fingers move so realistically you'll swear he's real and as for that cop hiding behind the billboard . . . well, hiss right along with the rest of us.

Antique cars, the real thing painstakingly restored, play a big part in the scenery of these mini-dramas, so you'll probably have to drag cars buffs away from this amusing spectacular. Futurists will love it, too, since this historic journey ends with a 3-D-ish, you-are-there ride through a scenic wood, on a thriller of a bobsled ride, and a wild night plane landing.

Just before you come back to earth, you get a glimpse into the future, created by liquid neon and laser beds that form a vision of a futuristic cityscape.

It is, as they say, quite a trip.

When it's over, there are still more things to look at here as you discover, or rediscover, what makes that horseless carriage move and how much more smoothly it's likely to roll in the future.

At the **Aero Test Center,** for instance, you'll see an almost full-size replica of a wind tunnel GM uses in Warren, Michigan, to test a car's wind resistance, a crucial factor in energy conservation. There's a **Bird and the Robot** demonstration of robot-compilation of car parts and a **Water Engine** film outlining a futuristic engine construction.

Aero 2000, GM's experimental four-seat subcompact car sports no steering wheel, only a central control bar, plus orthopedically shaped seats and a video view of the road ahead. Another car on display here, **Concept 2000,** is an 1800-pound silver streak of aerodynamic knowledge. There's a futuristic truck model that's a Smokey-and-the-Bandit dream machine.

My own choice is a cuddly little creature called the **Lean Machine.** It's shaped just like a bullet, so you crawl in, pull the roof over your head, and lean—literally, the whole upper half of the three-wheeled vehicle actually tilts—into curves. They stole the leaning idea from horses that are able to negotiate those quarter-pole racetrack curves by leaning into them. What's more, this little cutie gets *200* miles to a gallon!

Finally, there's a display of some of GM's newest and sexiest models, which prove to be an irresistible lure for look-at-me-in-my-new-car photographers.

Not far from the World of Motion is the outsize **Odyssey Restaurant,** which also includes the Baby Center and First Aid Station. Stop here for lunch or dinner fare like Voyager Hotdogs and Explorer Beef Stew, and enjoy a watery view across the lake to World Showcase.

COMMUNICORE WEST: Moving across to the other side of Future World, (that's to the right, or west, side as you face the lake), you'll find CommuniCore West. Here Bell Systems has surpassed itself with one of the most creative displays you'll see anywhere in the world.

Granted this exhibit is not exciting in the sense of fire-breathing dinosaurs and steamy swamps, but Bell's **Fountain of Information** is a masterpiece of creative thought.

Designed in the rounded curves of the Art Deco style, this "fountain" pours out never-ending streams of the informational material with which we are beseiged every day. Down these "streams" flow stock certificates, newspaper clippings, paperback and record covers, video discs, and advertisements. Neon messages and moving letters join rivers of video monitors and strips of flashing movie film, telephones, video games, playing cards, sheet music, IRS forms, road signs, stop lights—all the endless flood of messages that demand our attention, streaming endlessly, endlessly on. It's a marvelously graphic look at what our brains absorb, discard, and file every day of our lives.

Sharing this enormous room with the Fountain of Information is a giant map, on which an attendant displays the vast Bell network that's in operation even as you watch. On this display, called **The Intelligent Network,** you'll see the constant growth of telephone communication. When the brief lecture's over, you get a chance to try touch-sensitive devices that light up any state across the nation and tell you a little about entertaining events and sights there.

At **Face to Face** you get a look at a new kind of picture phone, called teleconferencing, that will enable you to attend a convention thousands of miles away without ever leaving your desk.

Send the kids off to **The Amazing Microchip,** a large model of an integrated circuit chip magnified 420 times. They can crawl and move around through this maze while adults learn how microchips are designed and manufactured by Bell Labs and Western Electric.

See the best television picture of them all—yourself on the

screen—and get a peek at new telephones that do everything but wash windows. Some help the deaf "hear" through encoded messages, others link to a computer to show you the number dialed, the time, day, and date, and store information in an electronic directory and date book. Pretty slick.

Spread across one wall are dozens of tiny animated figures that form a lighted, musical display outlining modern telecommunications in **The Age of Information.**

Best of all to many people, of course, are the **electronic games** here—all of them free. One, Lost for Words, turns your spoken word into electronic patterns so you can help a mouse find its way through a maze to the cheese. This machine speaks seven languages, including Russian, and provides the basic technology for use of voice commands to control machines, even to dial your phone, no hands.

Another fascinator is a "phraser," which challenges you to type any word into its system and it will pronounce the word back to you. If you can spell supercalifragilisticexpiálidocious, this speech synthesizer, using stored rules of English pronunciation, will say it back to you. Fun.

Think you have a terrific memory? Pit it against Bell's Bit by Bit game, which compares your superstar retention powers with Western Electric's newest memory device, a 256,000-bit chip. This little devil will show you just how hard it is for human minds to remember a piddling 16 bits of information for even a few minutes.

If all that memory-straining has made you hungry, stop off in the Sunrise Terrace Restaurant where you can munch on fried chicken, corn muffins, and clam chowder while you store up energy to tackle the fascinating exhibits on this western side of EPCOT.

THE LIVING SEAS: Scheduled to open in 1984, this exhibit will take you down, down, down into a Disney "sea," a 6-million-gallon coral reef filled with creatures that call places like this home. Poseidon greets you on this sea journey and accompanies you as you sink beneath the waters to a 21st-century seabase.

THE LAND: One of the most popular and certainly one of the most fascinating exhibits in EPCOT is just to the right of CommuniCore as you face the lake. The Land is every gardener's dream world, a place where things grow in sand or in nothing at all, where huge pink squash hang on vines, and a field of corn is likely to share the field with another vegetable as well.

Set in an architecturally impressive building topped by a glittering glass triangle, The Land focuses on man's relationship with the good earth and the products we coax from it. In this 6-acre pavilion Kraft offers you everything from a giant Farmer's Market of restaurants to a look at some of the innovative ways agricultural experts expect to use the land in future generations to provide more and better for all.

In the **Harvest Theater** you can watch an 18-minute motion picture, "Symbiosis," which outlines the interdependence between humans and their environment. "Symbiosis" highlights man's amazing ability to control temperamental environments with creations like Peru's Machu Picchu, France's ancient aqueducts, and the rice terraces of the Philippines. You even get a look at some of the world's successes in reversing its own mistakes: cleaning of the Thames River in England and reclamation of Europe's Lake Constance.

A bi-level building, The Land features the intriguing **Good Turn Restaurant,** a revolving dining room which offers you a glimpse of several sections of the pavilion as you dine on steak with green peppercorns; chicken marinated in lime juice; a cheddar cheese, mushroom and nut-roll appetizer (dinner prices in the $9 to $12 range).

The Harvest Theater and Good Turn Restaurant occupy a balcony overlooking the massive **Farmer's Market** below. In this Americana setting you can dine under colorful umbrellas after collecting delectables from a wide choice of kiosks, including a bakery, an ice cream shop, a beverage house, cheese shoppe (Kraft, naturally), potato store, barbecue, sandwich shop, and soup/salad store.

The **Kitchen Kabaret** is an amusing presentation that will get you cooking, so they say. Hostess Bonny Appetit is accompanied by the Kitchen Krackpots band (a mayonnaise jar playing canned food "drums," singing bananas and eggplants, a barbecue-sauce bottle strumming a whisk). A sexy Ms Cheese, who's "a delightful array of curds," is joined by Ms Ice Cream, the Cereal Sisters singing "Boogey Woogey Bakery Boy, the Toast (literally) of the Town," the comedy team of Hamm 'n Eggz, even a rocking broccoli stalk who's a member of the Colander Combo band and wears a la conga outfit and sunglasses. It's funny, a little crazy, and a hilarious way to learn what you ought to be eating when you're chowing down on junk food.

The stellar production in The Land, however, is the **Listen to the Land Boat Ride.** After boarding a boat, you sail through some of the most innovative agricultural advances you'll ever see. First, you journey through three ecosystems—a rain forest, a desert, and the prairie—then move on to an experimental greenhouse where horticulturists, physicists, metallurgists, chemists, and agricultural experts are experimenting with plants and aquatic creatures in hopes of increasing the world's food production.

On a 40-acre site, you'll find plants growing under artificial gravity, to simulate spacecraft growing conditions, and crops planted alternately in a process called "intercropping," which allows a plant like sugar cane to use nitrogen produced by peas or beans grown alongside it.

You'll see luffa gourds (those nubby creatures used as bath scrubbers) flourishing, pole beans climbing up cornstalks, tomatoes, lettuce, even strawberries growing on conveyer belts that move them to feeding areas where their roots are sprayed with nutrients. Plants grow in giant rotating drums; hormones are used to stimulate pineapples to flower in about one-third the time it normally takes; and lettuce grows on space-saving plastic A-frames.

You'll see cucumbers that grow 12 inches a day, tomatoes whose huge roots dangle in the air, fed and watered through pipes. You'll learn how scientists can use pure seawater to irrigate plants and discover a winged bean with pods that taste like spinach, flowers that substitute for mushrooms, and roots that can be eaten like potatoes!

Aquaculture is part of the activity going on here, too, so some of the chemicals that drip from roof-hung plants fall into ponds where they help fertilize water plants. Even fish get in on the act, as scientists study ways to increase shrimp and fish populations.

If you want to see even more than you'll see on this quickie trip, you can sign up at the end of the journey for a half-hour **Tomorrow's Harvest Tour** that gives you an even closer look at the fascinating things going on here.

JOURNEY INTO IMAGINATION: Imagination is always more fun than reality. No one knows that better than Kodak, which whisks you away into a strange "adult playground" where you can step on a color to create a sound, journey through a rainbow, feel strange feelies, and create a symphony or a computerized art masterpiece with a wave of your talented hand.

Journey Into Imagination rises over Future World in glassy magnificence, its glittering facade towering over a geometric crystal sculpture and a spray of fountains. An eyecatching triangular construction, the building housing this exhibit is a study in geometric forms and contemporary color play.

Inside, Kodak continues to challenge your imagination with an amazing array of hands-on displays you create yourself in a wonderland of electronic effects.

Your hosts are Dreamfinder, an elfin character who pilots a strange Dream-Catching machine, and his sidekick Figment, a purple dragon. Together they roam a universe of the imagination collecting colors, sounds, and shapes, which they convert into new creations of all kinds. When you travel with them, nebulae explode, and you hold lightning in a jar, and play with a bubble machine and colorful rainbows.

You can try a few of Dreamfinder's tricks yourself upstairs in the **Image Works,** a creative playground of the future, where you'll be a child again but not in any childish way. Instead you'll make **Bubble Music** by projecting bubbles on a screen and accompanying them with some very odd electronic sounds.

At **Dreamfinder's School of Drama** you can get right up on stage yourself and follow instructions on video monitors. While you're acting, your talents are appearing on a screen behind you where you become part of the play, enlarged or miniaturized as the script demands.

Walk right over the rainbow in **Sensor Maze** where you're assigned a color by a tunnel of neon rings. Listen to your voice activate a light show and visit **Stepping Tones** where your footsteps set off a blaze of color, light, and sound effects.

At **Light Writer** create patterns with light, and at the **Magic Palette** pick a shape and color, then use a magical pen to create bizarre designs or to color in a sketch.

A **Kaleidoscope** creates changing patterns of color, and odd tables full of blunt-tipped gold dressmaker's pins offer you a weird tactile and visual sensation. Or try **Electronic Philharmonic**—just wave your hands in front of a caseful of musical instruments and out come whatever sounds you command.

Ride a glass elevator to the Magic Eye Theater to see a slide show that uses wonderful photographs to outline the history of photography. Move on then to the star show of this Kodak pavilion, the 3-D production that's won the hearts of the crowds.

Here you don 3-D glasses and fly over field and stream, meet a wicked witch who zaps you right in the eye with her jar of lightning and a kite that persists in sitting right on your eyebrow. It's amazing and amusing and you'll love it—just watch out for those bats!

Outside the building the show goes on with a maniacal fountain that acts like no self-respecting fountain you ever saw. This one persists in leaping right over your head, disappearing down a hole, and leaping right back out again to spring its way around and around you.

A Journey through a World Showcase

Awed with the future and all its possibilities, let's journey now into the present—and perhaps even a bit of the past—for a look at the world we know but never well enough. Let's visit Walt Disney World's World Showcase, an international exposition that will show you around much of the globe almost as fast as the Concorde supersonic jetliner could get you to Europe.

Disney's World Showcase is spread around the edges of a vast lagoon. America's pavilion sits smack in the center, flanked by a variety of other cultures ranging from Japanese to Italian, Mexican to Canadian.

Because the buses and boats which can save you some steps around this showcase move on a clockwise course, in this case from east to west, let's start at Mexico's eerily enchanting pavilion and work our way around the clock to the westernmost entry, Canada.

MEXICO: As you enter World Showcase Plaza, which runs alongside the lake opposite the geosphere, look to your left and you'll see the golden stones of a great, stepped pyramid rising out of the flatlands like a south-of-the-border mirage. Street signs announce the presence of Avenida Esplendida as you stroll to a walk-up window for a taco or a burrito at **Cantina de San Angel.**

Inside, you're greeted by a display of 2500-year-old pre-Columbian art created by artisans who had deciphered the mysteries of astronomy and time measurement long before the U.S. was even a gleam in some revolutionary's eye.

Walk on, and suddenly you're no longer in America but in the middle of **Plaza de los Amigos** surrounded by typical adobe casas where flowers bloom, candles flicker, and romantic wrought-iron balconies are just waiting for a troop of mariachi singers to serenade an ebony-haired señorita. A shell fountain tucked away in a wall burbles merrily, and in the distance mysterious, deep-blue light illuminates a pyramid.

In the center of it all, a busy marketplace is jammed with sturdy baskets, colorful pottery, pastel paper piñatas, delicate lace dresses, and rainbow-hued paper flowers big as hats. At **Artesanias Mexicanas** pick up a soft woven serape, an onyx carving, a delicately crafted ceramic cathedral or tree of life, intricately carved wooden candlesticks, ornate birdcages, leather huarachis, guayaberas, and colorful Mexican glass.

You can dine in the eerie glow of that towering pyramid as jungle birds chatter around you, silenced occasionally by the distant snarl of the jaguar. In the **San Angel Inn** you'll be greeted by a pretty señoritas in a long white dress and you're entertained by that mariachi band as you dine on mole poblano, carne asada, huevos rancheros, tacos, tamarind water, margaritas, tamales, chili rellenos, and the like, for prices in the $10 to $15 range for dinner, about half that for lunch.

Step into a flower-trimmed boat and whiz off on a cruise through Mexican history brought to life with AudioAnimatronics, beautiful three-dimensional settings, and film. Back you'll fade into ancient Mexico when the Mayan civilization flourished. A stone priest comes to life to greet you as you wander through time, accompanied by singers and dancers, even an occasional determined vendor or two, working hard to strike a bargain. Finally you sail into the excitement of Mexico in this century and then bid adios in a burst of fireworks.

CHINA: Now the music changes as you wander into the strange sounds of the Orient through the huge **Gate of the Golden Sun** and stroll across a tiny stone bridge over a serene lotus-laden pool. Above you soars the curving roofline of the **Temple of Heaven,** its royal blue tiles glittering in the sun.

Wander among art treasures in the **House of the Whispering Willows,** then go into the ornate **Hall of Prayer for Good Harvest** where you'll step back more than 1200 years as eighth-century poet-storyteller Li Po, Shakespeare's Chinese equivalent, appears on a 360-degree screen to introduce you to the wonders of this rarely seen country. You enter the Forbidden City, visit the Dalai Lama's priceless palace, sail along the Yangtze and Yellow Rivers, roam the Great Wall of China, visit the Harbin Ice Festival in Manchuria, and see a performance of the Peking Opera and a demonstration of shadow boxing at Hangzhou's West Lake. This 20-minute classic took seven months to film and contains footage of parts of China never before filmed by westerners.

As you leave, a diminutive hostess garbed in emerald-green silk trimmed in gold threads bids you goodbye with a tiny bow.

AFRICA: Between China and Germany you'll soon find Africa, which will feature a film narrated by *Roots* author Alex Haley. That production will be supplemented by a tree-house overlooking a jungle watering hole in a simulated setting that will include trees, rushing water, sounds and scents of the forest, and a rear-projection motion picture of African animals. You'll be able to see a reenactment of village life and a museum of African arts as well as a **Heartbeat of Africa** show depicting the histories and cultures of those equatorial regions.

GERMANY: In the land of oom-pah-pah and dirndls, sausage and singers, beer and bratwurst, you're greeted by the painted walls and timbered architecture of the Alpine region, medieval spires, and a picturesque *Platz* (town square) where scarlet geraniums spill from flowerboxes and the German zest for life spills over. There's even the inevitable town clock chiming away as a fountain bubbles over gray stones.

In a huge **Biergarten** you can guzzle mugs of suds or down a glass of tangy German wine presented in etched, green-stemmed glasses. Amid massive stone walls hung with tapestries, begin lunch or dinner with the traditional white radishes carved and twisted into a spiraling stream. In this village rathskeller atmosphere handsome herren in liederhosen and damen in dirndls yodel their hearts out, toot away on the long, long Alpine horns, and dance up a storm of clap-slapping traditional dances. Your hunger will be well satisfied here on sauerbraten and sauerkraut, huge platters of sausage and pork chops, and German chocolate cake, for prices in the $10 range for dinner and show.

Crafts in Germany are handsome, so expect to be lured into enchanting shops like **der Bucherwurm**, which sells attractive original oil paintings and etchings. **Volkskunst** is stocked with candles in intricate designs; $75 foot-tall ceramic mugs; angels dressed in elaborate gold-trimmed brocades; and large wood carvings, include one $1500 masterpiece featuring a lamplighter carved in a thick slab of wood, his copper lantern lighted. Look up at the ceiling here and you'll see an entire mini-oom-pah-pah band in full swing.

Young ones will love the offerings of **der Teddybar,** and wine-lovers will find treasures in the **Weinkeller.** Chocoholics should avoid the **Suissigkeiten** where products of the cocoa bean are joined by delicate cookies and confections. To put your goodies in a worthy setting, stop by the **Glas und Porzellanhaus,** purveyors of Germany's famed porcelainware which here includes a $12,000 Hummel figurine!

ITALY: Just a few steps away from Germany rises a tall column crowned by the Lion of St. Mark, talisman of Venice's most famous piazza, St. Mark's Square. Here a gondola is moored at dockside and the Doge's Palace beckons you into an arcade filled with handcrafted leathers, delicate Venetian glass, and hefty clay pottery filled with plastic fruit and vegetables so realistic you'd be wise not to mix them with the real thing.

Star of Italy's pavilion is **L'Originale Alfredo de Roma Ristorante,** a place created by the *original* Alfredo, who's certainly been flattered by plagiarism over the years. Naturally those delicate pastas are the lure here, and you'll see them created right before your eyes in the shadow of dozens of photographs of Alfredo stuffing his famous pasta into the willing mouths of the famous. One of the three most popular restaurants in EPCOT, Alfredo's is booked for dinner very early but often has more lunch spaces than you'd expect.

It's no wonder it's so popular, since you dine in a beautiful rust-colored room with sunshine streaming through tall windows curtained with heavy drapes. Chandeliers glitter and murals of Roman scenes beguile you as white-coated waiters deliver antipasto misto, spaghetti carbonara, linguine al pesto, cannelloni filled with spinach, veal in a cream sauce, bocconcini featuring veal and mushrooms in wine sauce, zabaglione, zuppa Inglese, and cassata di ricotta. Entrees are in the $10 range or less, and there's a children's menu, here as in other restaurants, for $3 to $5.

Out in the piazza at **Il Teatro di Bologna,** Commedia dell'Arte actors present amusing skits, and Carnival in Venice dancers perform in the shadow of the Triton fountain. When the show's over, stroll by the shops to see the glittering gold jewels, delicate Venetian glass, and fragile Capodimonte flowers. **Il Bel Cristallo,** for instance, features beautiful Italian pottery, wood carvings, intricate coral cameos, and a flashing $29 glass paperweight that's a beauty. Don't miss the music boxes, particularly the miniature grand piano with an inlaid wood mandolin, music and pipes entwined in flowers. It plays Offenbach's "Barcarolle," and it can be yours for $890.

Terracotta pottery is a specialty at **Arcata d'Artigiani** while 14-carat gold's the lure at **La Gemma Elegante,** where Venetian beads are a temptation. Finally, there's **i santi** where glove-soft Italian leathers are downright irresistible.

THE AMERICAN ADVENTURE: Occupying stage center at EP-COT's World Showcase is America, complete with Liberty Inn, hot dogs, and a brick replica of Independence Hall.

On your way to the fascinating AudioAnimatronics history lesson, you pass under the flags of America's first two centuries and walk a long formal hall carpeted in scarlet and lighted by candle lamps in wall niches.

America's animated production takes place in an impressive theater lined with white columns and arches showcasing marble-like statues of various "spirits"—the spirit of freedom, adventure, tomorrow, self-reliance, pioneering, and knowledge, set against a backdrop of burgundy velvet.

The crystal chandeliers glitter then dim, as 35 full-size animated figures, the most lifelike ever developed by Disney's imagineers, tell the story of America's early days and the nation's struggles for liberty and justice.

The hosts are Benjamin Franklin, who has the distinction of being the first AudioAnimatronic creation to walk up stairs, and Mark Twain, as irascible and witty as ever.

Pride, Twain tells us, is our national heritage, and even those Americans who have overcome it manage, nevertheless, to be proud of their humility! It goes on like that: a look at the nation's struggle over slavery features a stirring speech on the subject by Frederick Douglass; a call for an end to Indian suffering is delivered by Chief Joseph; and an impassioned plea for women's rights comes from Susan B. Anthony.

You'll see soldiers fighting and dying in the Revolutionary War and watch brave men, women, and children fight the wilderness to survive and to expand the nation westward. It's a moving presentation and one that may bring a tear to the eye of many a proud American.

If you're suffering an attack of the munchies before or after the

29 minute show, stop by the **Liberty Inn** next door for hot dogs, hamburgers, and other oh-so-American fare, served in a covered outdoor café or beneath umbrellas in a patio overlooking the lagoon and the great stage on which various international stars perform.

JAPAN: High above you, a massive red Torii gateway welcomes you to the Japan pavilion, where you'll spot the flash of a golden fin in a koi pond and hear the wind whistling through a stand of bamboo. That tranquillity for which the Japanese are so justly famous pervades this serene enclave where everything, from pebbles to trees, seems made to measure.

Its front entrance guarded by a five-roofed, blue-tiled Shinto temple trimmed on each corner with bells, the Japan pavilion features the **Katsura Imperial Villa,** "best viewed in the romantic light of an autumn moon," they tell you. Here a palatial villa has become an intimate restaurant serving yakatori, skewered meats, and colorful, simmered vegetables inside or outside under a parasol, on a tiny serene patio where musical entertainment is provided by a tinkling waterfall.

Japan's **Mitsukoshi department store** stocks fragile mobiles of inch-high kimono-clad maidens, plus silks, fans, wall hangings, Japanese lanterns, elaborate enamelware, and rubber gourmet hors d'oeuvres so realistic even the $22 shrimp or the $5.40 lemon slice seem worth their weight in realism. The department store is housed in a grand Sishinden Hall, and at its back door loom the towers of a forbidding feudal castle with huge brass-trimmed double doors and a heavy wooden bridge spanning a moat.

A priceless suit of Samurai armor is displayed here and proves most intriguing: It's made of small scales of lacquered iron laced together with silk cords. It weighs only 25 pounds yet was far more impervious to the forces of war than heavy European chain mail. An accompanying sword was made of steel so strong it could cut through a pile of copper coins without a nick!

You can see a movie outlining some of the wonder of this lovely country, then climb the steep staircase up to a collection of restaurants and a pleasant cocktail lounge, the **Matsunoma Lounge,** that boasts the best view in EPCOT. Here you'll find the **Teppanyaki Dining Rooms** where master chefs prepare grilled steaks, lobster, huge shrimp, and chicken right before your eyes as you sip Japanese beer, saki, or plum wine (dinner prices in the

$10 to $14 range, lunch $6 to $9). Or try the **Tempura Kiku's** batter-fried delicacies, brought sizzling to your lacquered tray at the tempura bar ($10 to $20 for dinner, $7 to $10 for lunch).

MOROCCO: Morocco's carved out a spot for itself between Japan and France, so by 1984 you'll be able to wander around delivering lines like "take me to the Casbah" with reasonable equanimity. Brasses and magic carpets, souks and things both bazaar and bizarre will be featured in this re-creation of that veiled land. In the meantime you can see French Foreign Legionnaires striding about the grounds in full-dress whites up to and including flowing scarves dangling from white hats: World Showcase's clean-up helpers are dressed as Legionnaires and there are legions of them in this spiffy-clean showcase.

FRANCE: In the shadow of the Eiffel Tower stands the line everyone wants to be part of: the line for reservations at France's **Les Chefs de France** restaurant, created and cuisined by three superstar chefs—Roger Vergé, Paul Bocuse, and Gaston Lenôtre. It is well worth the wait, every delectable morsel of it.

Definitely the star of this charming enclave, the restaurant features what may very well be the best food in Central Florida, not to mention the best vittles in Disney World. Dream along these lines: salade de homard (lobster), snapper topped with salmon mousse and baked in a puff pastry, braised beef with scalloped potatoes, filet de boeuf au poivre et aux raisins in Armagnac sauce. For starters: French onion soup, aspic de foie gras, pâté de veau en croûte, oysters topped with spinach and a champagne sauce.

In one pretty glass-enclosed dining room there's a tranquil garden atmosphere, in another dining area attractive booths, masses of silk flowers, gleaming brass and crystal, even an outdoor patio. You can feast on complete appetizer-to-dessert (chocolate cake layered with chocolate mousse) dinners for $16 to $19 and less ambitious feasts in the $12 to $15 range. Lunches are likely to run up to the $10 range when you see the tempting array of crisp salads and gorgeous desserts available.

While it's more than a little difficult to pull yourself out of this entrancing restaurant, you may be lured by the delectable scents emanating from the **Boulangerie Pâtisserie.** Delectable pastries draw a crowd of the hungry, many of whom can't wait: They sit right outside in a tiny patio **Au Petit Café** and consume the goodies from within this typical French bakery.

If you figure you can create delectables just as irresistible right in your own kitchen, give your talents a little boost at **La Casserole,** which sells all the accoutrements of a gourmet kitchen from escargot dishes to huge whisks and special spices. At **Barton & Guestier** pick up a bottle of *vin* to carry under your arm along with your loaf of crusty bread, a little cheese, and all you'll need for a lakeside picnic is a thou beside you singing in the wilderness.

Art buffs will want to peek into **Plume et Palette** and perfume fans will find **La Signature** offerings hard to resist. Love silk flowers and baskets to put them in? Stop at **Les Halles** and fulfill your fantasies with their floral creations.

France also wants to show you its wonders—and they are many—so it's produced a beautiful film, **"Impressions of France,"** that takes you across the green French countryside and shows you why Paris is called the City of Lights. You'll go on an airborne trip across this picturesque land via a spectacular 200-degree screen presentation that takes place inside the **Palais du Cinema,** a replica of a famous Paris theater.

UNITED KINGDOM: From Gallic shrugs to veddy, veddy British accents is only a hop, skip, jump, and a bridge here in EPCOT's World Showcase. As the last strains of the "Marseillaise" fade in the background, you'll stride into the land of tea and ale, transparent china and cuddly woolens.

It is, of course, the incomparable kingdom, interpreted here at EPCOT with gabled rooftops, cobblestone streets, timbered architecture, and a pub so British they'd have difficulty duplicating that much atmosphere in the Mother Country.

Third of the triumvirate of most-popular restaurants in the Showcase, the **Rose & Crown Pub & Dining Room** is, old chap, British beyond British. Rest your weary foot on a brass rail as you quaff a pint, warmed at a special beer-warmer to a very British 53 degrees or cooled to a Floridian 45. Shafts of sunlight sneak through the etched glass and café curtains to bounce off polished woods, and there's a lovely view across the lake from the tiled dining room out back or the small patio dining area.

As for the fare, . . . well, talk about typical: bangers and mash (that's sausage and mashed potatoes), fish and chips, ploughman's lunch (bread and cheese), Scotch eggs (hard boiled eggs and sausage with a mustard sauce), and raspberry fool. Lunches for $5 or less, dinner a dollar or two more, and at dinner a chance for beefeaters to try some roast beef and Yorkshire pudding. Ales, stouts, and the like are $1.25 a half-pint, $2.25 a pint—try an ebony Guinness Stout for something different.

Outside in the cobblestoned courtyard you'll find **The Tea Caddy** occupying a white cottage with a thatched roof and purveying Twining's fancy teas and yummy jams. Complete the tea part with some biscuits from **The Biscuit Barrel** and wander over to **The Queen's Table** to select some elegant Royal Doulton china on which to present this masterpiece high tea you're creating.

Plaid kilts and wool sweaters in soft heathery colors, not to mention your clan's traditional tartan, are spread wall to rafter in **Pringle of Scotland** while at **His Lordship** you can treat his lordship to a fancy pipe, a glass ship in a bottle, or a most unusual chess set.

Don't miss **The Toy Soldier** where the "King" is a chubby bear complete with crown and royal robes. The highlight of this enchanting shop is a glass-cased display of a royal dinner, featuring tiny minstrels on the balcony, jesters spinning hoops and tottering on a teeter-totter, a winking maid, knights with bejeweled shields, and waiters delivering heaping trays of fancy viands to some of the dourest royal visages this side of Alice in Wonderland. Perhaps Alka-Seltzer hadn't been invented yet.

CANADA: The star of our northern neighbor's exhibit is a stunning 360-degree motion picture **"O Canada!"** Surrounded by film you'll travel through this largest country in the Western Hemisphere as freely as the 50,000 wild geese that take to the skies in a flurry of feathers. Ride in the Calgary Stampede, then fly downhill on skies, and climb Toronto's C. N. Tower for a goose-eye view of that sophisticated city.

Back down on terra firma, wander through this Canadian village, which includes everything from a Northwest Indian village to a 19th-century French chateau. As you near the abandoned gold-mine tunnel, you may get splashed by drops from a waterfall that cascades over huge rocks nestled beneath tall pines.

Some of the World Showcase's most interesting—at least to Floridians—treasures are to be found at **Northwest Mercantile** where you can buy soft rabbit skins, raccoon caps, plaid wool jackets, leather mittens, sheepskins, and figures carved from coal. Fur-collar-trimmed jackets, moccasins, Indian dolls and totem poles, maple syrup, and wild rice, they're all here in a most unusual Showcase shop.

If you're hungry, drop in at the buffeteria-style **Le Cellier** restaurant, a study in stone and wine-cellary atmosphere gleaming with candles, copper and pewter accessories, brocaded chairs, and a vaulted ceiling. You'll find some unusual treats, each representing a province or major city: Manitoba beef short ribs, baked salmon, Toronto sausages and Canadian bacon, sauerkraut baked in cider, and a special Quebec *tortière* (pork pie).

Entertainment at EPCOT

Just as there's never a dull moment in the Magic Kingdom, there's always something to watch at EPCOT.

If you arrive here early in the morning, you'll get a musical greeting from the **Future World Brass,** a 12-piece contemporary group that begins its day's work near Spaceship Earth and makes appearances in other parts of the park in the afternoons.

A favorite Disney entertainer, **Michael Iceberg,** the electronic musician-wizard, turns up here in EPCOT with synthesizers and weird sounds.

You'll find **costumed robots** scampering about the CommuniCore area, chatting up the youngsters who can talk back to them by remote control.

Most of EPCOT's entertainment focuses on World Showcase, where an international festival is scheduled to keep going strong all year long.

An outdoor stage in front of The American Adventure hosts changing shows featuring **national dance and folk singers.** Shows include music and dance traditions of 40 different nations by performers in handmade costumes of their countries.

Huge **costumed "dolls"** representing more than 60 nationalities will be on hand to greet you at each World Showcase pavilion and to participate in parades through the grounds.

World Showcase Dancers, an international folk company featuring 16 dancers and seven musicians, appears along the lakefront promenade and even gets you dancing and singing with them. Good way to learn the mazurka.

What's more, each World Showcase pavilion features entertainment representative of its culture.

Mexico has a five-piece marimba band on stage at the pavilion's Plaza de los Amigos and a strolling nine-piece mariachi group playing in the courtyard, cantina, and dining areas.

Chinese artisans create woodcarvings, clay seals, stamps, woven baskets, and the inimitable Chinese calligraphy in the China pavilion. There are even some of those huge papier-mâché lions, peopled by dancers, slinking around the pavilion.

In Germany you'll see a **Bavarian Oktoberfest** complete with dancers and a seven-piece **baskapelle** band, plus a one-man oompah band, a **yodeler,** and alpenhorn player. Join in—they'll love it.

A **street actors group,** Teatro de Bologna, performs in the centuries-old Commedia dell'Arte improvisational style in the piazza at the Italy pavilion. Some of their improvisations are a scream. In Alfredo's restaurant **singing waiters** warble opera classics, and here and there three **puppeteers** pull strings.

Voices of Liberty sing in the American pavilion, and their drummer-piper counterparts, the **Sons of Liberty** fife-and-drum corps pound the pavement much the same as they must have done in the Revolutionary War.

A **traveling candyman,** who magically turns rice toffee into dragons and birds, wins top marks from the small fry at the Japanese pavilion. Here, too, **musicians** stroke traditional string instruments called kotos and samisens and a five-piece group performs **authentic Japanese songs.** There's even an adorable **dragon** who performs on the porch of the pagoda.

In France's enclave three **white-faced mimes** perform classic French mime routines, and a **strolling musical group** plays favorite Parisian songs. There's a **strolling accordionist** too.

Pearly Kings and Queens, a comical group of Cockney London street musicians, dressed in velvet and satin costumes covered with pearl buttons, perform in the United Kingdom. A **bagpipe band** creates those wailing piper sounds, and a **wandering troubador** serenades on ancient instruments.

Those **Scots bagpipes** turn up again in Canada's pavilion, where they're aided and abetted by a zany musical group called the **Maple Leaf Brass.**

Finally, as a finale each day, EPCOT presents an elaborate **Carnaval de Lumiere,** an elaborate festival of lighted floats that stream across the lake.

It's all quite a show.

Chapter X

MORE THINGS TO SEE AND DO IN CENTRAL FLORIDA

ONCE UPON A TIME —say all of five years ago—Orlando's Chamber of Commerce suggested visitors plan a three- or four-day visit to see all the area's attractions. Now, they say, you should plan three or four days for Disney World alone!

So fast has the circus followed the whale that followed the Mouse, here in Central Florida, that there are now enough attractions to keep you busy for two weeks—moving fast.

There's simply no doubt about it anymore—Central Florida is the state's playground, a place filled with so many amusements you can go on day after sunny day touring and traipsing, ogling and ooohing, getting a look at everything from a re-creation of the dry Serengeti Plain (complete with elephants) to wet ocean depths (complete with a performing killer whale).

It's fun, and it can provide a wonderful place to spend part, if not all, of a memorable Florida vacation. Let's take a look now at some of the other places to play, here in the land a Mouse built.

Orientation

Defining where exactly you'll find Central Florida is not as easy as it seems. Certainly Orlando forms the center of the center, but how far you can go in all the other directions and still remain central is a matter interpreted differently by every Chamber of Commerce within a 300-mile radius.

We'll have to be arbitrary about our definition, though, and say we're talking about an area that goes as far west as Tampa and St. Petersburg (which, come to think of it, is about as far west as you can go in Florida) and east to Cape Canaveral and Daytona Beach. For northern reaches let's count St. Augustine, it's such an intriguing place to visit, and Ocala. On the south Sarasota's about as far as the attraction belt goes, although if soft, sunny beaches are your forte, you'll want to get down farther south where the sun *really* shines, and the ocean is the state's number one year-round attraction.

Okay, all defined and determined, off we go.

Other Adventures in the Orlando Area

After you see the crazy ducks and looney tunes at Disney World, it's time to start exploring some of the other weird and wonderful attractions in and around this Central Florida city. Give yourself two days at least, three or four if you can manage it just to visit some of the varied amusements you'll find hereabouts.

SEA WORLD: Right in there chasing Mickey's tail in popularity is Sea World (at the Hwy. I-4 Sea World exit; tel. 351-3600), largest marine-life theme park in the world. You can spend a whole day here without any difficulty since they keep the entertainment going at a rapid pace practically from dawn to dusk.

Fifteen different shows are crowned by a performance of none other than **Shamu,** the gigantic 8000-pound killer whale who's so sweet it's hard to believe he'd kill a shrimp. Shamu lets his trainer ride on his huge back, loves to kiss pretty girls and children, and seems to get the world's biggest kick out of performing a delicate ballet—no toe shoes.

Joining this pulchritudinous pile of blubber are dolphins, otters, seals, sea lions, and waterskiiers (the human kind) who cavort about to your amazement and amusement.

There's even a new attraction here, **Cap'n Kid's Fun Ship,** a splashy playground built around a 60-foot pirate ship. Kids can play here on everything from ropes that reach out over the water and often drop you splashing and giggling into it, to splashy slides and tunnels.

A real spine-chiller at Sea World is the **Shark Exhibit,** a veritable *Jaws* come to life all around you. You enter a huge tank made of enormously thick, transparent acrylic and ride on a moving conveyer belt through a tunnel while those toothy denizens of the deep swim all around you.

At Sea World you can see what a coral reef looks like, watch Antarctic penguins play in the coolest home in Florida, examine the mysteries of a tidal pool, watch waltzing fountains, pet tame deer, rise to the heights in a 400-foot skytower, and even buy an oyster—with a pearl inside, guaranteed.

You'll never starve here either. There are seven theme restaurants in the park, and they're all open when the park is, from 9 a.m. to 7 p.m., later in summer and on holidays. Most evenings there's a Polynesian luau, too, with swivel-hipped dancers, fire-bearing terpsichoreans, and a Polynesian buffet dinner (see Chapter V on nightlife). Sea World admission is $11.50 adults, $10.50 children 3 to 11, younger ones free. You can take a special behind-the-scenes tour for $2.50 adults, $1.75 children. Parking and kennels for Fido are free, too.

While you're here, be sure and explore Sea World's newest major project, **Florida Festival,** where there's lots to eat, more than enough to buy, and plenty of entertainment to keep you amused. There's no admission charge either and it's open later than the park, usually to about 1 a.m. Read more about the fun and frolic at Florida Festival in Chapters IV and V on restaurants and nightlife.

CIRCUS WORLD: You say Rodney Dangerfield isn't the only one who doesn't get any respect? People think you're just a clown? Well, why not enjoy it, and get on over here with your soul brothers and sisters who clown around every day of the week at Circus World. They'll be happy to turn you into a real clown-for-a-day at this huge Big Top, and they'll complete the image (or lack of it) with makeup and a photograph.

Still another adventure here, a new one, is the **Aqua Circus,** featuring the antics of six world-champion divers who splash into the water in a series of clowning events before the finale, a daring torch dive. There's a new **Circus of Spins and Grins,** dubbed the largest bumper-car ride in the nation, and a **Flying Tigers** show, featuring some very daring cats and an even more daring trainer.

You can't miss the candystick-striped canvas that covers this Big Top at Hwy I-4 and U.S. 27, about ten minutes west of Disney World (tel. 422-0643), and you won't want to either. Clowns, puppets, high-wire artists, enormous trained polar bears 12 feet tall commanded by a tiny blonde, and performing elephants are all here to entertain you.

A special heart-stopper, the **Hurricane**, is billed as the fastest rollercoaster in the East, and who's got courage enough to challenge that assessment? Circus World is open from 10 a.m. to 6 p.m. daily, later in summer. Admission, which includes all the rides and all those shows, is $11.50 adults, $10.50 children 4 to 12.

WET 'N' WILD: Orlando doesn't have much beach, so it dreamed up Wet 'n' Wild (6200 International Dr.; tel. 351-3200), a water wonderland where you can splash and splutter to your heart's content. A surf pool produces constant four-foot waves, a whitewater slideway and a Kamikaze slide send you whizzing down into a pool from a platform six stories up in the air, and a Corkscrew Flume spirals you through a figure-eight and a tunnel before depositing you in the blue.

Real adventurers should try the Bonzai Boggan, a water rollercoaster that races you at speeds up to 30 m.p.h. into a very large splash. Picnic by the lake or stop in at a snack bar when all that exercise turns to hunger. Admission is $7.95 adults, $5.95 children 3 to 12, free to others, and there's a $1 to $2 discount after 3 p.m.

STARS HALL OF FAME: Bogart and Bacall, Taylor and Burton, John Wayne and horse, they're all here at Stars Hall of Fame (6825 Starway Dr. at Hwy. I-4 and Rte. 528; tel. 351-1120), immortalized in more than 100 wax sets re-creating memorable moments of their careers. Streisand is here and so are Superman, Valentino, and Al Jolson.

You can take a screen test to see how you'd do in, say, an episode of "M*A*S*H", and if you're really good, you might win a Hollywood screen test!

Movie buffs will freak out over this attraction, which also features a multimedia presentation called "The Hollywood Experience" that highlight some of the major moments in celluloid history. More than 200 of the famous are presented here at Stars Hall of Fame, which is open daily from 10 a.m. to 10 p.m. and charges $7.35 adults, $4.30 for children 4 to 11.

MYSTERY FUN HOUSE: Nothing's what it seems here, as magic takes over to trick you and treat you to a look at all the world turned inside out. You can lose yourself in a mirror maze, try to fathom the topsy-turvy room, walk a magic floor, and have a million laughs and an equal number of surprises. You'll find the Fun House on Major Boulevard just off Hwy. I-4 at Rte. 435 North in the Florida Center area (tel. 351-3356). Admission is $4.11 adults, $3.07 children.

REPTILE WORLD: I'd rather even write for a living than do what those people do at Reptile World Serpentarium. They milk cobras here and cozy up to all kinds of friendly vipers, 60 varieties of the crawly creatures, in fact, including everything from crocodiles to lizards. If you'd like to scare yourself silly, this is the place. It's open from Tuesday through Sunday from 9 a.m. to 5:30 p.m. Admission is $2 adults, $1 for children 6 to 17.

GATORLAND ZOO: I know one or two human morsels I'd like to throw to the alligators that slither around this attraction, perhaps you do too. It's *fun to think about,* anyway, as you watch these oddities of nature attack a hunk of meat at feeding time. Besides who doesn't want to get a close-up—without confrontation—of one of these marshland critters? You'll find the zoo on Rtes. 17/92 and 441 just north of Kissimmee (tel. 855-5496). It may be worth the trip just for a picture of yourself fearlessly petting a boa constrictor. Hours here are 8 a.m. to 6 p.m., later in summer, and admission is $3.60 adults, $2.60 children 3 to 11.

CENTRAL FLORIDA ZOO: You can stroll a half mile of elevated nature trail here and get a look at some creatures in their natural settings. There's a picnic area and pony rides, too. The zoo's at U.S. 17/92 North in Sanford (tel. 323-6471) and is open daily from 9 a.m. to 5 p.m. Admission: $3 adults, $1 chiidren 3 to 11.

SOME OFFBEAT ATTRACTIONS: If you're one of those city slickers who think steaks are created in the back room of a supermarket, it may be time for you to see the real thing on the hoof. Do that at Kissimmee's weekly **cattle auction,** where real honest-to-goodness cowboys cajole and caterwaul with tonight's prime rib. In the audience cattle barons, looking more like punchers than princes, set the prices at this boots-and-jeans event that goes on every Wednesday early (8 a.m.) at the city's Livestock Market, just north of U.S. 17/92 and U.S. 441 on Donegan Ave. (tel. 847-3521). When the bidding and the roping's over, you can lunch at the Auction House while cow punchers shove those big bruisers around outside. There's no admission charge.

Now here's something you'll have to go far to top: a museum of food containers. By that I mean **Tupperware's International Headquarters,** where the plastic containers are lauded. You can learn how those plastic boxes and bowls are created and discover what you can create with them at this museum located on U.S. 441 and 17/92, just south of Orlando (tel. 841-3711). It's open from 9 a.m. to 4 p.m. Monday through Friday, and it's free.

Citrus trees laden with fruit are among the most beautiful sights you'll see in Central Florida, and there's no better place to get a look at them than the **Florida Citrus Tower** on North U.S. 441, Clermont (tel. 904/394-2145), the highest observation point in the state. Here you can gaze out across 2000 square miles of emerald citrus trees laden with orange and gold fruit— quite a sight. Later, visit a glassblower's workshop, a citrus packing plant and a citrus candy kitchen; send some oranges home to less fortunate frozen friends and buy some yourself (and see if you can resist eating all of them before you get home). Citrus Tower is open from 7:30 a.m. to 6 p.m. daily and charges $1.75 adults, $1 for students 10 to 15, others free, for the ride to the top.

Mormons own a huge ranch in the center of Florida and they call it **Deseret Ranch.** They're kind enough to invite you in to take a look at a working Central Florida ranch, but you need to call first so they can meet you for a tour. It's free. You'll find the ranch on Rte. 192 about 25 miles east of St. Cloud (tel. 892-3672).

It's uniforms, uniforms, everywhere and every one of them with razor-edge creases when the gobs graduate each Friday at the **Orlando Naval Training Center** off Corrine Drive, north of Rte. 50 (tel. 646-4474). A fifty-state salute, Navy band, bluejacket chorus, and drill team all turn out for this 1:45 p.m. event that's free to all, as is a war museum on the grounds here.

Watch oranges go in one side of a machine while gum drops and other delights roll out the other at the **Citrus Candy Factory** (U.S. 27 in Dundee; tel. 813/439-1698). This factory located between Cypress Gardens and Circus World makes a toothsome visit and it's free. Open 8 a.m. to 6 p.m. daily, later in summer.

Other Attractions in the Central Florida Area

Moving a little further afield to Tampa on the west, Cape

Canaveral on the east, Ocala on the north, and Winter Haven on the south, you'll find still more places to play.

CYPRESS GARDENS: Once dubbed "a photographer's paradise" by *Life* magazine, Cypress Gardens is one of Florida's most elegant attractions. No gardener should miss this devastatingly beautiful acreage overflowing with exotic flowers and trees. Women dressed in antebellum hooped skirts pose in glamorous, green-lawned surroundings and are so perfectly turned out they look like human floral creations.

Once a huge cypress swamp, Cypress Gardens has retained much of that exotic marshy mystery but turned part of its acreage into gardens where the scent of rare roses joins the perfumes of jasmine, gardenias, orchids, hibiscus, and flowers in every color of the rainbow and quite a few hues even a rainbow would envy.

Visit a **Living Forest** filled with tame animals who want nothing more from you than a pat; take photographs of the lacy domed gazebo that's been the setting for television films and weddings, and don't miss the frequent waterskiing shows. The stars of these performances are world famous for their performances and their precision on skis. There are trick skiiers who ski barefoot, skiers who take their skis airborne aboard a kite, and precision skiiers who do carefully choreographed dances on skis while traveling 60 or 70 m.p.h. or more. How they manage to hit the beach so gracefully and so perfectly every time is a mystery. The grand finale of this magnificent—and very photographic—show is a three-tiered pyramid of skiers balanced on each other's shoulders!

There's plenty to do and see, but perhaps the most satisfying of all is just a quiet walk through these magnificent grounds, wandering down deep jungle paths that wind through ginger plants and coffee trees, ancient cypresses centuries old standing near inky, haunting lagoons. There's a hushed air about this place that makes it a welcome relief from the noise and crowds that go with so many area attractions.

You'll never lack for something to eat here or something to do. There are plenty of restaurants and dozens of boutiques full of treasures. You may have to drag devoted photographers out of here since there's something photogenic around every tree, even a special section where shutter settings are marked and the skiers ski right into your photograph.

Open daily from 8 a.m. to 6 p.m., Cypress Gardens has shows at 10 a.m., 1 and 4 p.m., and admission is $7.95 adults, $4.50 children 6 to 11. To get there head south from Orlando on U.S. 17 (or branch off Hwy. I-4 onto U.S. 27, picking up U.S. 17 in Haines City). Signs all over the Haines City area will help you find your way to the Gardens on S.R. 540.

BOK TOWER: One of the most majestic sights in Florida is Bok Tower, which rises in ghostly magnificence high on a hill above the shores of glittering Lake Wales, just south of Orlando on U.S. 27 (tel. 813/676-1408). Few places are as tranquil as the grounds around stately Bok Tower, where you'll be tempted to find a shady spot to just stare up at the magnificence of this Georgian Gothic Tower. It's set in the stillness of Mountain Lake Sanctuary atop Iron Mountain, once a sacred Indian site and the highest point in peninsular Florida. Donated to the nation by Dutch immigrant publisher Edward Bok, the 225-foot, pink-and-gray marble octagonal tower houses a 53-bell carillon whose gentle notes ring out each half hour, and there's a 45-minute recital presented at 3 p.m. daily by resident carillonneur Milford Myhre. Admission to the sanctuary is free, but there's a $2 parking charge used to maintain the road to it.

SPOOK HILL: While you're here in Lake Wales, it's fun to stop by Spook Hill, a wacky sight that's absolutely free. Spook Hill's just off U.S. 17 at North Avenue and 5th Street, and here's what you do when you get there: Just drive your car up to the designated spot, put it in neutral, remove your foot from the brake and watch the car move slowly backward . . . *uphill*! No one's telling why or how it works, but there are some local yarns about an Indian chief protecting his people, a pirate curse, and an alligator. Hmmmm.

BLACK HILLS PASSION PLAY: Another Lake Wales attraction, open from mid-February to mid-April, is this dramatic re-creation of the final weeks of Christ's life. Performances are each Tuesday, Thursday, and Saturday at 6 p.m. and on Good Friday evening. Tickets are $5 to $8; the natural outdoor amphitheater in which the play's performed is nestled in a citrus grove. It's a sight worth seeing, whether or not you make the play.

JOHN F. KENNEDY SPACE CENTER: It's an easy day trip from Orlando to Cape Canaveral (quickest road is Rte. 528, the Beeline) and a pretty drive to this east coast area on the Indian River. From Orlando follow the signs to the John F. Kennedy Space Center (not Cape Canaveral).

At the Kennedy Space Center and NASA launch complex, begin your visit with a stop at the **Visitor Information Center** (tel. 451-2121) on Merritt Island, between the mainland and the cape, about six miles east of Titusville. Huge rockets and spacecraft fill the yard here, and inside you can see a piece of moon rock and get a closeup look at Apollo capsules, rocket engines, and a lunar module.

In the Hall of History a film traces the development of the space program. It's open daily (except December 25) from 8 a.m. to sunset and is free.

To get around this massive complex, line up for one of the two-hour NASA escorted bus tours which leave every few minutes from the Visitor Center. The tour costs $3 adults, $1.75 for children 13 to 18, and $1 for others. You can take either the **Blue or the Red Tour:** The Red Tour includes the fascinating astronaut training building where simulators reproduce conditions of an actual space flight, and lights illuminate the craft as its components are explained by a narrator. The Blue Tour covers the Cape Air Force Station and Museum.

As you cruise around this enormous acreage, which happens also to be a wildlife refuge that harbors many an endangered species, you'll pass the 52-story **Vehicle Assembly Building** and the huge transporters that carry spacecraft to the launching pads. You'll get a look at a lunar launch pad and visit the mission control from which the moon flights were organized and directed.

As you probably well know, flights continue to be launched from these pads, and if you'd like to be there for one, call NASA toll free at 800/432-2153 for information on dates of launches and best vantage points.

BUSCH GARDENS: Over on the state's west coast in Tampa is one of Florida's top 10 attractions, Busch Gardens, an otherworld place where Tarzan and Jane stroll blithely by and an elephant gives you a high-eye stare.

Second most popular attraction in the state, Busch Gardens earns its top spot with a massive African jungle re-creation built by the famous brewery. To get here, take Hwy. I-75 to the Busch Boulevard exit, then just follow the signs to the park (tel. 971-8282).

It will take you every bit of a long day to see all there is to see here, and you won't go astray if you allot a couple of days to add Busch's **Adventure Island** to your adventure list.

You can get around this vast complex on foot, on a monorail, or on a Skyride cable car that crosses the Dark Continent's Serengeti Plain for a giraffe's-eye view of even a giraffe!

If you love trains, you can see everything from ground level aboard a little train that chugs around the park, passing by animals that roam free, separated only by moats or natural barriers.

Out on the dusty Serengeti are 500 head of big game chasing their tails around a 160-acre veldt. Gazelles streak across the sands here, and elephants amble slowly about spouting water over their warm backs as water buffalos and rhinos get their water the easy way—by sloshing in it.

Turn-of-the-century Africa, shades of that famous "Dr. Livingstone, I presume" era, is the theme here, and Busch creators do plenty with that theme. They've created a make-believe **Marrakesh** where snake charmers hypnotize those slithery creatures and belly dancers hypnotize everyone; a **Congo** where huge Bengal tigers prowl about their domain looking ever so much like sassy pussycats, until they leap into their river; a **Timbuktu** where the Dolphins of the Deep perform; a **Nairobi** where night creatures prowl Nocturnal Mountain; and a **Stanleyville** where Tanzanian tribesmen practice their ancient woodcarving art.

Roam here among the largest collection of mammals, reptiles, and birds in North America—3000 in all—then play on some of the amusements like the state's largest log flume ride. You can tour a tantalizing array of craft shops and when you tire, head straight for the **Hospitality House,** possibly the most popular stop in the park, where Busch gives you free samples of its famous product. Guzzle away at the edge of a pretty lagoon or under the trees of a bi-level patio where a piano player entertains.

While you're here, try not to lose your head on an *African Queen* boat ride up the river to a headhunters' village, or your tummy on the Python rollercoaster which does a terrifying 360-degree loop.

Busch Gardens is open daily from 9:30 a.m. to dusk (about 6 p.m. in winter, 8 p.m. in summer), and one admission of $11.75 per person (children under 3 are free) includes everything in the park except parking ($1 a car). One learned-the-hard-way piece of advice here: Remember your parking lot number. This is a huge lot, and it's sickeningly easy to forget where you left Ole Hoss. Here, too, wear comfortable shoes and clothes—you'll do a lot of walking in the sunshine.

Next door to the gardens, you'll find **Adventure Island** (tel. 813/971-7978), a 26-acre water park complete with waterslides and endless surf, lots of kids games that are fun for I'm-a-kid-again sojourns. One-day admission is $6.75 a person, with children under 3 free; the park is cheaper after 5 p.m. It gets a little chilly for this kind of fun in winter, so the park is open from March to October only from 10 a.m. to 6 p.m. You can camp here, too, for $10, and a tentsite is $5.50.

UNIVERSITY OF TAMPA/TAMPA BAY HOTEL: This is not a honky-tonk sight, but it's a wonderful way to get a look at the posh early days of Florida when people traveled in considerable style. Once one of the most elegant hotels in the state, this antique hostelry is now a university, but you're still welcome to tour it free each Tuesday and Thursday at 1:30 p.m. It's bright silver onion-domed minarets are a city landmark, and it's long hallways, once transversed by rickshaws, no less, are worth a look.

When these elegant quarters were opened in 1891, the price tag on this hotel was a whopping $3 million—an enormous sum of money in those days! In the basement rathskeller here Teddy Roosevelt's Spanish-American War troops are said to have invented the drink that came to be known as Cuba Libre. There are priceless works of art here, too, collected by builder Henry Plant, whose treasures are in a free museum. You'll find the university by taking the Ashley Street exit from Hwy. I-275 and following Ashley toward downtown to U.S. 60 (West Kennedy Boulevard). Turn right across the bridge and you'll see the campus guardhouse on your left. It's free.

ST. PETERSBURG'S MUNICIPAL PIER AND MGM'S BOUNTY: You can see two attractions in one by taking a trip over to St. Petersburg, where MGM has created a replica of the ship it used to film *Mutiny on the Bounty*. Its flags flapping brightly in the sun and its massive decks shining, the *Bounty* is docked in the Vinoy Basin (tel. 813/896-3117). You won't have any trouble visualizing the epic contest between Captain Bligh and Mr.

Christian when you hear the narration by Charles Laughton and Clark Gable! Admission is $3.50 adults, $1.75 children 4 to 12. The ship is open daily from 9 a.m. to 10 p.m.

You'll find the *Bounty* docked right next door to the **Municipal Pier,** which may not sound like an attraction, but it is. At the end of this long streak of concrete is a building you'll swear is upsidedown, but that's not all: This city landmark has been here in one form or another since 1889, when horse-drawn flatcars carried passengers from the boat docks, two miles away, to land. It's still a mile long and there's still a jitney to take you from one end to the other of this huge pier, which now features a gift shop, restaurant, lounge, observation deck, and a tiny strip of bathing beach where they'll charge you a whole dime to stick your toe in the water.

RINGLING MUSEUM/CA' D'ZAN/ASOLO THEATER: South of
Tampa/St. Petersburg, you'll find the serene city of Sarasota, home to writers, artists, and other creative types now, but once home to a creator of a far different kind: circus king John Ringling. Ringling may be famous for his gaudy sequined performers and the Day-glo colors of the Big Top, but in his own life he knew how to find lasting beauty of a far different nature.

He did that by collecting priceless works of art from all over the world and hanging them in a museum that is itself a work of art. **Ringling Museum** (5401 Bayshore Dr., Sarasota; tel. 813/355-5101) is a columned Italian Renaissance building of tranquil symmetry. It's a delight to the eye both outside, where a copy of Michaelangelo's famous "David" casts a tranquil eye over the patio, and inside, where the art masterpieces grace the walls. Admission is $4.50 adults, $1.75 children 6 to 12, which covers both house and museum.

As if that weren't enough, Ringling went on to create **Ca' d'Zan,** a palatial bayside home where he lived with his wife, Mabel, whose extravagant tastes are said to have been the inspiration for this palace. One of the ten richest men in the nation when he died in 1936, Ringling gave the beautiful peach-colored art gallery and his rosy-cream stucco palazzo (the name means John's house in Italian), plus a 68-acre estate and his art collection, and his entire fortune to the state of Florida which gave it to everyone by opening it to the public.

More than half a million people come here every year to look at the 30-room mansion capped by a 60-foot tower and filled with carved and gilded furniture from the estates of the Astors and Goulds. Roam the 30 rooms here and you'll see priceless tapestries, a $50,000 Aeolian organ with 4000 pipes, Venetian glass in every color of the rainbow, a bathtub hewn from a solid block of yellow Siena marble, and bathroom fixtures made of gold!

There's still more: the **Asolo Theater,** a jewelbox of a playhouse that looks like something you'd dream. This froth of gold-and-white baroque architecture was once part of the castle of deposed Cypriot Queen Catherine Coranor who lived near Venice. Her tiny theater, filled with gold-leafed, festooned boxes, twinkling sconces, arcing tiers of white columns, and once visited by Robert Browning, was lost for some years after it was replaced in the palace by, predictably enough, a movie theater. An antique dealer found it, and it eventually ended up here, where it's one of the most glamorous theaters in the nation, presenting repertory theater from mid-February through Labor Day. It's worth the price of admission to plays here (about $8) just to see this gem.

SILVER SPRINGS/SIX GUN TERRITORY: North of Orlando up toward Ocala you'll find one of the state's many crystal-clear mineral springs. **Silver Springs** is one of the state's most famous springs. Located five miles west of Ocala on Rte. 40 (tel. 904/236-2043), Silver Springs features a glass-bottomed boat that ferries you around as you look at the fish in their habitat and the lovely "mermaids" who go below to feed them by hand. More than 2 million visitors turn up here to gaze at these crystal waters every year, and you'll enjoy joining them for a look at both the springs and the exotic wildlife that roam alongside them. It's open daily from 9 a.m. to 6:30 p.m.; admission is $7.75 adults, $5.75 children.

There's a water-theme park here too, **Wild Waters,** open from 10 a.m. to 9 p.m. from late spring to late fall.

Yet another attraction is **Six Gun Territory,** where you can relive the days of the Old West with gunslinging antics, high-kicking can-can girls, and honky-tonk music. But watch out: Don't get caught in the jail break, the gunfight in the OK Corral, or the bank robbery at Courthouse Square. Six guns blaze daily from 9:30 a.m. to 5:30 p.m., and admission is $4.95 adults, $3.95 children 4 to 15.

Side Trips from Central Florida

Florida's a fascinating place wherever you go, but it can be especially so if you get off the main tourist treks and out into some of the places native or honorary-native Floridians go.

These range from a tiny village packed end to end with spiritualists and séance experts to a lovely country town where spirited horses are the most important residents. Let's take a look at some of the interesting side trips you can take in the Central Florida area.

DAYTONA: Daytona's fame and fortune was born a couple of generations ago with the birth of the motorcar. Every famous automotive name from Olds to Ford came here in the early days to drive on the hardpacked sands of this oceanside city. You can still drive on the sands, although racing's out. After you've driven just inches from the briny deep, park the flivver and sit on that sand with the hundreds of other sand lovers who come here to do just that. Daytona's packed during its annual tribute to speed, known as Speed Weeks, in early February and July, so if you're planning to stay over, make sure you reserve hotel rooms far, far in advance for that busy time. **Marineland** is a popular attraction here and features performing dolphins of renown. Adults pay $5, children under 12 $1.50. Open 8 a.m. to 5:30 p.m.

CASSADEGA: This is the spiritualists' village, founded in 1874 by spiritualist George Colby, guided by three other worldly guides. He founded a town and psychic center and donated 35 acres to the Spiritualist church. Today you'll see small signs outside many homes announcing the services within of a medium. These mediums claim not to permit charlatans among them, and all are registered by a national spiritualists' association.

SEBRING: Sebring's another town made famous by speed—it's the home of the annual Sebring International Grand Prix of Endurance for sports cars in March—but it's also a pleasant citrus country village with sapphire-blue lakes and lovely old homes. A tranquil spot to visit.

GAINESVILLE/MARJORIE KINNAN RAWLINGS HISTORIC SITE: Gainesville's fame is its university, the University of Florida, which has a pretty campus that has bred many a governor and legislator. Just south of town lived Florida's Pulitzer Prize-winning author, Marjorie Kinnan Rawlings who wrote *The Yearling, Cross Creek,* and *The Big Scrub,* based on her experiences in Florida. Her home, completely furnished just as she left it, is on Rte. 325, which you can reach from Rte. 20 East (tel. 466-3672). Its isolated location beside Lake Lochloosa gives you an idea how she got the setting for those touching Florida stories. At the **Yearling Cross Creek Restaurant** in Micanopy (tel. 466-3033), you will be served dinners made with recipes suggested by the author in her *Cross Creek Cookbook.* Prices are in the $10 range and the restaurant's open daily.

OCALA: Ocala's the home of many a Florida champion thoroughbred, winners like Needles and Carry Back. About an hour's drive from Orlando, this small town has green lawns, and mile after mile of pristine white fences. These rolling hills, like Kentucky's famed blue-grass country, helped shape the champions that bred on 150 farms in the area.

If you speak horse, you'll fit right into this environment where the impending birth of a white-blazed foal is likely to outrank a human baby's arrival. If equine talk isn't part of your vocabulary, stop by and learn something at places like **Castleton Farms** about five miles west on Rte. 307, just off Rte. 26. Second-largest breeding farm in the world, Castleton raises trotters and pacers for harness racing. Give them a call (tel. 904/463-2686) before you drop in. Other farms are outlined on a map distributed by the Ocala Chamber of Commerce (110 E. Silver Springs Blvd.; tel. 904/629-8051). They can even tell you where to find greyhound breeding farms in the area.

ST. AUGUSTINE: In few other cities in the nation can you travel from century to century as easily as you can in this old community that was 55 years old when the Pilgrims landed on Plymouth Rock. In the quiet lanes of this seaside city, past and present merge into an amalgam of centuries.

There are, of course, the neon intrusions of the 20th century, but look beyond them and you will hear the echoes of a 16th-century cannon and the melodies of a ballroom where crystal sparkled in the glow of hundreds of candles as swashbuckling cavaliers and ebony-haired señoritas twirled across polished wood floors.

You'll find those haunting echoes of the past in a tiny two-room soldier's cottage shaded by the huge branches of a live oak and the polished magnificence of a reconstructed home filled with shining silver and trimmed in jewel-colored velvets. You'll find them in the foot-thick walls of towering Castillo de San Marco and in the simplicity of the tiny red-cypress schoolhouse.

As the nation's oldest city, St. Augustine has many sights that will delight you, ranging from what some claim is the site of early governor Ponce de Leon's search—the Fountain of Youth—to more certain historic sites like the huge Castillo that protected this city from a variety of invaders.

First visited in 1493 by Columbus and Ponce de Leon, the city was not settled until 20 years later, in 1513, when Ponce de Leon came searching for the fountain of youth reputed to be found here. He never found it—or perhaps he did, who knows?—but other Spaniards settled in and fought first the French and later the British for sovereignty.

Seminole uprisings were fought here, and the British and Spanish exchanged control over the city for several generations until finally ceding it to the U.S. In the late 1800s kingmaker and railroad builder Henry Flagler extended his railroad to the city, and life in St. Augustine began to focus on sun seekers who journeyed here by steamer and train. They spent the winter here in lavish style, dancing under the stars atop the old fort and parading in carriages down Avenida Menendez.

St. Augustine is about an hour's drive north of Daytona along sweeping strips of snow white hard-packed sand trimmed with sea oats. If you decide to stay over here, I'd recommend the **Kenwood Inn,** an old hostelry built just after the Civil War and revamped in 1981 by two very talented restorers who have brought the magic back into these ancient boards. A perfect place to begin your return to another century, Kenwood Inn charges just $25 to $35 year round.

Top sights here are the fortress, the Oldest House, all the restored homes and shops along St. George St., called San Agustino Antigua. There is quite a lot more to see, too, and **Sightseeing Trains** (3 Cordova St.; tel. 829-6545) are a good way to see and understand much in a short time. For complete information on everything there is to do and see here, visit the **Visitor Information Center** (10 Castillo Dr., it's right on the main road through town; tel. 829-5681).